PRIESTS in LOVE

Roman Catholic Clergy
and Their Intimate Friendships

JANE ANDERSON

continuum

NEW YORK • LONDON

2006

The Continuum International Publishing Group Inc
80 Maiden Lane, New York, NY 10038

The Continuum International Publishing Group Ltd
The Tower Building, 11 York Road, London SE1 7NX

www.continuumbooks.com

Printed in the United States of America

Library of Congress Cataloging-in-Publication Data
Anderson, Jane (Jane Estelle)
  Priests in love : Roman Catholic clergy and their intimate
friendships / Jane Anderson.
     p. cm.
  Includes bibliographical references.
  ISBN 0-8264-1702-7 (hardcover : alk. paper)
  ISBN 978-0-8264-1830-9 / 0-8264-1830-9 (paperback : alk.
paper)
    1. Catholic Church—Australia—Clergy—Sexual behavior—Case
studies. 2. Priests—Australia—Sexual behavior—Case studies. I.
Title.
BX1912..9.A54 2005
  253`.252—dc22
                                                  2004019400

bought 7/11/08

Contents

Preface

Clerical sexual abuse, gays in the priesthood, priests having affairs: this litany of complaints and criticisms is commonly heard in the global media and gossip of local parishes. For many the priesthood seems to be plagued with so many ills that it is hard to imagine a way out of the sexual morass.

But there is a story that moves beyond negativity and mere titillation. That story belongs to priests who love their friends and treasure the priesthood. In caring for both, they are attempting to find a pathway towards a happier future, not just for themselves but also for the church and the world.

This book records some elements of this venture. At different points in their journey, these men discover that celibacy—no matter how hard they might try to honour the practice—is destructive of their lives and ministry. In finding a remedy in sexually intimate friendships, these priests are then forced to make their way through a jumbled mass of complexities. That struggle is made more arduous because the papacy rejects such a journey.

In their venture, these priests must renegotiate their promises made to celibacy and participation in the Eucharist, tasks that are difficult because they feel considerable pressures to restore their celibacy. They are also torn by their need for intimate companionship. Some priests don't make it. But those who do must continue on the less-travelled road of social change, constantly threatened by the expectations of a powerful church hierarchy and of concerned confreres and loyal parishioners.

Along the way, these priests encounter major moral dilemmas, undergo struggles about their priestly identity, and seek to create strategies that will resist a defensive and controlling patriarchy. In wrestling with these problems, they reexamine tradition and scripture. Their contemporary interpretations and experience subsequently lead many to the belief that their friendships are both moral and divinely blessed.

Finally, they arrive at a place of understanding in which they know that the future of the priesthood depends upon priests being allowed to have sexually intimate friendships. They therefore urge the church to move beyond compulsory celibacy.

Over the past ten years, I have listened to approximately fifty priests who have had the faith and courage to share their experiences of celibacy and sexually intimate friendships, despite the fear and hostility they expect to endure.

These interviews took place in Australia. Nevertheless, their stories represent that of many priests the world over. They include both heterosexual and homosexual priests. The latter group made it known that they not only cope with the imposition of celibacy; they also endure homophobia. Such priests are double heroic, for not only do they attempt to express their God-given sexuality, they also challenge the prevailing ethos of the church. The priests interviewed are both secular and religious. While there are differences in related claims on celibacy—secular priests make a promise of celibacy, and religious priests take a vow of chastity—they make it obvious that the issue affects all Catholic priests.

Yet, ironically, those priests who have sexually intimate friendships, hereafter referred to as "priests with friends," frequently express their respect for celibacy. They are certain that celibacy is a valuable way of life for some priests, and they nuance their comments in this regard. Consequently, in this book, the term *celibacy* is used in reference to the canonical obligation unless otherwise stated. It is not meant to be read as minimising celibacy as a valid and valued state for priestly service.

The stories of priests are presented on a background of work that attempts to further tease out the dynamic forces that are at play in their lives. One key force is the papacy, and consideration is given to how it puts forward its vision of celibacy. This approach aims to promote a greater understanding as to why the papacy is experiencing problems with celibacy, why priests are finding it difficult to practise celibacy, and why dissension is likely to continue in the priesthood and church while this practice remains compulsory.

A considerable amount of original material is presented in this book. Apart from minor editing, the texts that have been put into italics are the direct words of priests. In addition, every effort has been made to protect the identities of priests who contributed their stories. Where I thought that an identity could be exposed, I have combined one priest's contribution with another, thereby creating a composite story. As well, I have given these priests and their friends pseudonyms, names that I have randomly drawn from the Bible, and at times have contemporised. For these people are not distant, anonymous characters but men and women who participate in the everyday life of our church. Therefore, any name that appears to correlate with a particular priest or a priest's friend is purely coincidental. Furthermore, in honouring the courage of these people, I request that readers respect the anonymity of priests and their friends.

The Challenge of Fr. Abe

The church grew chilly and dark as the evening ended. Light that streamed down through the windows had long faded, leaving the walls cloaked in grey shadows, dulling the graphic detail of the Stations of the Cross. At the altar, lilies that had earlier bloomed with beauty drooped with tiredness, while a faint smell of burnt-out incense hung in the air. To the right, where a large statue of Mary stood, a few lights still burnt on the candelabra, the leftover prayers of pious old women. In the other wing, an electric light flickered a red flame, a constant reminder of the sacrifice that Jesus had made for life. Under these vaulted ceilings a still quietness reigned while thick stonewalls muffled the sounds of distant traffic speeding home.

In the pews a priest knelt at prayer, oblivious to the elements and surroundings that showed no compassion for his pain. Alone, Fr. Abe poured out his heart to God about the predicament in which he found himself. In this divine communion, he saturated his petitions with a mixture of anger at the injustice of it all and fear that held hostage his priesthood and his friendship with Sarah.

One of his parishioners, a thin and highly strung man hell-bent on restoring the Catholic Church to former glories, had observed Fr. Abe and Sarah too frequently in each other's company. Fr. Abe once worked with Sarah in a previous parish. She had long since divorced her husband, and while she was in no rush to have an intimate relationship with anyone, she and Fr. Abe found that their friendship blossomed. Together they enjoyed pleasant meals and other entertainments, helped each other in their respective ministries, and shared their thoughts and feelings about a whole range of issues. This was a stroke of good fortune as far as David was concerned. David had already spoken scathingly of Fr. Abe's pastoral approach that attempted to put people before canon law. These doctrinal detours led him to believe that the parish was riding a slippery slide into damnation. Now he had the means to prevent that from happening. With this news, he could force the bishop to get rid of Fr. Abe. The local bishop was duly told about the affair and given curt instructions to "move Fr. Abe on." The bishop contacted his priest later that afternoon, seeking an explanation for this accusation. His concerns about how much damage was being done to the church over sexual abuse allegations and the shortage of priests made his investigation awkward. This bishop wanted neither scandal nor the prospect of losing yet another good priest to a woman. He only wished to be assured that the matter was no threat to orthodoxy or an embarrassment to his position as bishop in an already shrinking and demoralised diocese.

When Fr. Abe had picked up the phone that sunny afternoon, he was feeling cheerful. Life and love, and ministry and devotion, were all in harmony. The winter blues of ill-health and tiredness had passed away as had the bleakness of the damp season. And he was grateful to Sarah for helping him get back to his usual self. Her laughter and determination to maintain their relationship in spite of their difficult situation also left him with a sense of hope. As well, parishioners had recently decided to accept more responsibility in their Christian lives. In a greater effort to reach out to the sick, the poor, and the marginalized, he hoped the parish would become a vibrant and compassionate community.

Fr. Abe had also finally resolved the difficulties of his commitment to both Sarah and the ministry. The commitment and loyalty that he showed to each seemed to him to be simply two sides of the same coin. One without the other cancelled out the sum of the total wealth, leaving an impoverished deficit that he could no longer envision as God's will.

The bishop first enquired of Fr. Abe's well-being, to which he responded with cheer and optimism. Then after courtesies were exchanged, the bishop carefully brought to his priest's attention the nature of the accusation made against him, tentatively enquiring as to whether there were any grounds for such a complaint.

An uncomfortable silence wedged itself between the two callers. Fr. Abe was completely taken aback by the news; then a torrent of questions flooded his mind about who his accuser might be, how this person might have come to know about Sarah, and how much did he or she know. Eventually, after some struggle, he regained his composure and told the bishop that he was shocked by the news. He also added with sincerity that all his relationships were honourable.

The bishop was relieved to hear what his priest had to say. No longer would he have to be concerned about unwanted consequences. But he thought that perhaps he should speak further with Fr. Abe about the matter. There was, after all, a need to respond to the parishioner so that his priest's reputation and that of the church would not be damaged. He then arranged to meet with Fr. Abe later in the week.

For a while Fr. Abe wandered aimlessly through the presbytery, not quite knowing what he should do next. A cacophony of competing thoughts struggled for attention, but numbness deadened the urgency of the demands. The only thing that made sense was to go and visit the hospital. Mrs. Dawkins, a very ill parishioner, was expecting him at 2:00 PM. Then a dozen or so other patients must be looked in on.

A mixture of pastoral care and pragmatism saw Fr. Abe through the rest of the afternoon, but at the day's end the content of the bishop's call caught up with him.

It was Fr. Abe's habit to say Evening Prayer in the church and so he started with the usual petitions, appeals that quickly focused on his plight. Questions then tumbled about in his mind. What was he to say to the bishop? How was this going to affect his priesthood? What was he to do about his friendship? Why was this happening to him? Fr. Abe struggled to quieten his mind, but it was useless. Overwhelming anxiety and the need to find answers that might extricate him from this unfortunate situation hijacked his prayerful intentions.

Then scruples set in. Fr. Abe entertained the idea that the accusation was objectively true, that he was in an illicit relationship. But he hated that word "illicit," and while he acknowledged that he had stretched the rules in terms of celibacy, it seemed as though it was a small sacrifice to make compared with what he had gained by having such a friendship.

⟞⟝

Looking back, Fr. Abe remembered his earlier years of priesthood. He had poured his heart and soul into exciting and stimulating pastoral work. *Those were the days of hope where I put my all into trying to implement a Vatican II vision of church, ministry, and community.* Moreover, celibacy appeared to be well within his reach. A decade passed. Fr. Abe realized that he was tired and exhausted. *I began to feel the first twinges of dissatisfaction with my life, which excluded any real closeness with friends, especially female friends. I felt disappointed that I had not deliberately fostered some of the friendships that were important to me, especially as I looked back to see a lot of my endless work leading to nothing in particular.*

Fr. Abe was then moved to another parish where he had more time and energy. *Suddenly I found myself in the midst of pastorally caring for one of the women, being invited into a deep and close physical relationship. I had not intentionally sought out this friendship but when I was with her, I experienced an overwhelming sense of closeness, warmth, and joy. It was like coming alive again.*

Even though she was married, Fr. Abe quickly found justification for accepting the love she offered him. When that relationship ended, he knew things would never be the same again. *In many ways, what I had done was morally wrong, and yet it had brought a new vitality into my life and reminded me of a dimension without which my life would be always very incomplete.*

Some years later, he renewed his acquaintance with Sarah. Fr. Abe and Sarah eventually admitted their love and made a deep commitment to each other. *I have come to value her as a very, very close friend, and am willing to be committed to that friendship with all its consequences. Our commitment to each other can be measured by the way we share with one another. I tell Sarah things I never tell anyone else, as she does with me. That's an indication of the depth of our friendship and the trust I have in her.*

They also started to have moments of intimacy but their affections were very disciplined. During this time, Fr. Abe experienced some concerns about whether he should venture down that path: *Are these actions selfish or loving? Do I want to take that risk? What might this mean for Sarah?*

After much thought and prayer, he concluded: *I believe that our intimacy is a valid, genuine, and valued expression of our friendship. And because it is a genuine expression of real love, God has to be in that.* Gradually, Fr. Abe and Sarah became more and more open to each other. In these times of tenderness, they found a happiness and pleasure that graced their friendship and invigorated their lives.

Fr. Abe also felt that because of his love for Sarah, he could now talk with parishioners about love with an enriched understanding and sympathise with their struggles. His relationship with Sarah brought with it a whole new understanding of the complex meaning of love. *Love is the essence of the life of God, and of God's community. It's something you can read about, but if you haven't experienced love then it's not real. You have to have an experience of love in order to make it a lived reality.*

Then there was the joy of knowing at the end of a hard day that there was someone with whom he could spend a short time sharing conversation and a cuppa, and enjoying some affection before returning to an empty presbytery. But he hastened to add: *I would never use her as a crutch to my ministry just because at times ministry gets rough. But Sarah is the one person I can talk to, not necessarily to gain sympathy or affirmation, but because she keeps me real. Sarah helps me keep things in perspective.* Fr. Abe's parish had once been a three-priest parish, but because of the shortages, a replacement for his now-retired confrere cannot be found. Fr. Abe has had to find a balance in his life, despite all the demands he is now faced with.

⌒

Fr. Abe finally found the answers in his own heart: *If truly the command of God is to love, then I feel our love is where God can be found. As for celibacy, it's an injustice in so far as it is mandatory, and God can't be found in that kind of contradiction.* He felt certain that the imposition of celibacy is an opposition to love and therefore has no future for the priesthood. He also concluded that leaving the priesthood or Sarah didn't necessarily help bring about change. So Fr. Abe decided to invest his faith, courage, and imagination in continuing down the path that love had opened to him.

Now with his fears calmed and his thoughts organized, Fr. Abe considered what he might say to the bishop. He knew he had been discreet about his friendship and realised that the accuser more than likely did not know the extent of their relationship. He also felt that with good judgement and being more careful he could avoid upsetting or embarrassing the bishop. Fr. Abe knew things would never be the same. The journey forward would be much more arduous than it had been, but he was sure that both his friendship and priesthood were life-giving, and worth the risks he was about to take.

It was dark now and he felt cold. Fr. Abe closed his prayers with thanksgiving and genuflected. He went over to the candelabra, blew out the last of the candles, and then with a confident step and peaceful heart, he walked down the aisle with one thought at the forefront of his mind. After he locked the church, Fr. Abe drove to Sarah's home where he knew he would find a warm fire and a hot meal awaiting him. He also must remember to tell her that Mrs. Dawkins was looking much brighter.

1

Changing Confessions

Fr. Abe found celibacy no longer relevant to his life and ministry. He, like many other priests, wanted to realise a loving and companionable relationship. These men, however, serve in a church that is unsympathetic to their predicament. Moreover, the papacy of John Paul II has been quite adamant that it is not about to change the rule of celibacy.

The Politics of Penance

One of the difficulties for priests with friends is the fact that the priesthood is not a level playing field. Priests have a relatively low status in the hierarchy of the church, are not allowed to organize a union to promote their cause, and have few means with which to finance reform. This is in stark contrast to the pope and the curia that have at their disposal abundant resources and a powerful network to communicate their message.

Church governance is further enhanced by the centralised power of the Vatican. The pope and cardinals who head pontifical congregations and councils have great influence over church policy. These Roman clerics also dominate the synod of bishops, a body of bishops that are supposed to represent the international interests of local churches. Yet the pope appoints these bishops and chooses topics for the various national synods. As well, heads of curial offices serve as ex officio members of these synods, thereby determining the discussion and the documents that result.

By concentrating leadership and decision-making powers in a church bureaucracy distant from the life and ministry of priests, the pope and the curia are well placed to promote their belief that God desires priests to observe celibacy. Convinced that celibacy has graced importance in the service of the church, they are able to bolster this belief by fixing the practise in doctrine and canon law.

Nevertheless, this dominating influence can only be sustained if the Vatican is able to convince priests that they should live celibate lives, that is, permanently forgo a wife (or partner) and children. But the task of maintaining this ideal is difficult because priests have to work out how this practise might be played out in their everyday life and ministry. Some priests find such an ideal far too abstract. No matter how hard they try, their attempts to adapt celibacy to their local circumstances result in a lack of wholeness and well-being. Priests, such as Fr. Abe, consequently resolve the problem of celibacy in ways that are at odds with church policy.

But for the moment, let us examine why the papacy considers celibacy congruent with the priesthood. By taking this route, we can more fully appreciate the background and context in which priests are expected to practise celibacy.

The pope and curia believe that for a priest, the shared loving of human beings competes with the loving of God. A priest must therefore prioritise his dedication and service to God alone. Confident in this presumption, they are able to assert that celibacy is possible for all priests. Moreover, they maintain, if the church prays for this gift of celibacy, it will never be denied to those who ask.[1]

By assuming that celibacy is absolute and bound up with eternity, the papacy puts the onus on each and every cleric to remain faithful to celibacy. Garnered with the assurance that God wills this practise for priests, that priests are praying for the grace to live celibacy, and that those prayers will be answered, the pope, the curia, and those bishops who support this practise remain confident in the validity of compulsory celibacy.

The papacy does acknowledge that priests can have problems with celibacy, although the nature of these difficulties is not spelled out.

However, it remains convinced that whatever these problems are, they can be overcome if priests adopt the prescribed safeguards to protect their practise. These protective measures include sufficient prayer, regular participation in the sacraments, and the practise of asceticism.[2] The belief in the effectiveness of these safeguards assumes that a priest is not only willing and able to live a life of perpetual self-denial, but that these measures will bring about the desired result. The papacy is basically saying that there are no contradictions or anomalies in the practise of celibacy, and that if a priest obeys directions, then all will be well. This approach enables the pope and the curia to avoid addressing historical circumstances, social and cultural complexities, and the personal character of a priest, all of which affect his ability to practise celibacy.

In being certain that celibacy is the one and only true way for a priest to serve God, the papacy is able to ensure a uniform priesthood. Moreover, by insisting that all priests observe celibacy, it is able to position them above and apart from the rest of the Catholic community. Indeed, priests are considered the *alter Christus* (another Christ) able to live and minister beyond human capability. Some priests, nonetheless, believe this to be an unrealistic expectation and are convinced that celibacy can cause considerable harm to their own and other priests' lives.

⁓

Some priests have great difficulty in accepting the ideal of celibacy. They believe it is a complex calling, and no matter how austere they are in their lives, or how many prayers they offer and sacraments they attend, they are still not able to resolve the complications they encounter in the sometimes stormy and often unpredictable sea of life. Moreover, when they do row against the current, they find that celibacy can manifest many difficulties, ranging from personal and social problems to different sorts of illness, including sexual disorders. One such priest added: *I've seen so many friends suffer needlessly and so many vocations stuffed-up or never even started because of this bloody crazy law.* He then went on to recount the story of Fr. Joe.

Fr. Joe as a young boy had often helped in the stables, mucking out pens, grooming and feeding the horses, and at times doing some track work. He also enjoyed the camaraderie of those in the racing fraternity. Their easy good-humoured friendliness and kindliness helped him to overcome his shyness and gave him something to look forward to after school.

After Fr. Joe was ordained to the priesthood, he reacquainted himself with these friendly folk down at the racetrack. He also developed an eye for a winning horse, but his social betting soon developed into a habit of gambling. The bishop eventually got wind of the news of his problem. The small irregularities in the parish accounts and his debts had begun to create a scandal. So the bishop reappointed him as a chaplain to a remote parish, far away from any racetrack.

Fr. Joe again had to confront his loneliness, but this time he could not resort to the panacea of gambling. Opposite the presbytery lived a woman with four teenage daughters. Her husband was a salesperson who was often away on business. She too was lonely, and soon Fr. Joe began visiting her home. At first, these visits were sporadic but later they became an almost everyday occurrence. In the evening he would call in, and Mary and he would sit in front of the fire with a cuppa and biscuits, sharing their daily news. He sometimes helped the girls with their homework. Eventually Fr. Joe told Mary that he loved her. Nothing changed, but everything changed. Their fondness for each other was almost palpable, but Fr. Joe always respected the fact that Mary was married.

A year later, Mary moved with her husband and daughters to a distant town. The bishop, meanwhile, hearing that Fr. Joe had apparently recovered, transferred him to a city parish. But without the love and companionship of Mary, Fr. Joe soon returned to his habit of gambling.

Several priests report how their intimate friendships help them to control or overcome various problems. Fr. Jude, a middle-aged priest in charge of a large parish, explains: *Having another person around often prevents temptation to other forms of sensuality that I can be prone to.*

Before his friendship with Anna, Fr. Jude had problems with drinking and womanising. Drinking helped him to find the courage to flirt with women, and several times he ended up in bed with his newfound companions. But when Anna came and stayed in his life, he was able to maintain emotional stability: *I know for sure that I'd be the most crazy, mixed-up priest that you could ever imagine if it weren't for her. I believe her being in my life has not only affected positively my ministry, but also my sense of well-being, and I am far more at peace with God because I am not "searching" around restlessly for new experiences of relationships.*

For Fr. Mark, the situation was much more dire. As he grew older, his loneliness grew deeper and his obsession with sex increased. At first, he tried sleeping tablets to help him stop tossing and turning in bed at night. Then he turned to alcohol to numb out his longings. *After ten years of drinking, I went to Alcoholics Anonymous for a while. Then one day I called into a brothel to see a prostitute.*

But loveless sex turned out to be demoralising. *It might be all right for a very short time, but its not fulfilling at all.* It also added to Fr. Mark's desperation: *I knew I was heading for a breakdown.* His drinking increased. Then an angel came to his door. For years now, Fr. Mark has had a housekeeper. Through her patient and caring love, she helped him to overcome his addictions. *And I think without her, I would go under.*

⌐

The personal benefits of engaging in sexually intimate friendship are backed up by research. According to Richard Sipe, most people only access their spirituality and the reality of transcendence with the aid of direct sexual encounter: love within a sexual relationship.[3] Being intimately loved is a powerful antidote for some priests who suffer from the lack of wholeness and well-being they associate with having to practise an enforced celibacy.

Fr. Jude confirms this with his own experience: *My personal well-being has always been boosted when I have been in love; knowing somebody out there is waiting for you to be with them is very uplifting. When you touch love, it touches you, and you are changed.* Fr. Mark adds: *You suffer for love, but it is better that you suffer than never love.*

Alarming Consequences of Celibacy

Some priests maintain that celibacy plays havoc with their sexuality. The obligation to practise celibacy becomes so preoccupying that a priest can lose sight of who he is as a sexual being and the goodness that sexuality can bring to life.

Fr. Luke doggedly avoided questions about sexual intimacy and sexual orientation. For twenty-three years, he stoically endured celibacy. Nevertheless, Fr. Luke enjoyed being in the company of good-looking men in his parish and was quick to help one young man, Matthew, who found himself homeless and unemployed. Fr. Luke put him up in a converted garage, adjacent to the presbytery, and he worked for his keep by doing the gardening around the church and carrying out some basic maintenance in the parish.

Fr. Luke and Matthew thoroughly enjoyed each other's company, and it was evident to many that the parish priest had a fondness for this young man, which they interpreted as a fatherly concern. But it was more than that. Deep down in his heart, Fr. Luke felt the type of warmth and closeness that only love can bring. He longed to share moments of intimacy with Matthew. But the obligation of celibacy stopped him from telling this young man of his affection and desire. It also prevented him from facing the many questions that his thoughts and feelings for Matthew provoked.

Some months later, Matthew became friendly with another man. Fr. Luke was quite jealous of Tom and sought to reinstate himself as the preferred company. He started to increase Matthew's workload and, at the same time, often helped him with these chores. One consequence was that Tom could no longer hang about so much. This arrangement eventually produced considerable tension between Fr. Luke and Matthew. Matthew left the area, while Fr. Luke was left grieving his loss. He felt that heartbreak keenly, but as the sorrow diminished, he began to admit his homosexuality and need for intimate friendship.

Fr. Luke now believes that enforced celibacy maintains a destructive body-spirit dualism that undermines wholeness and well-being. *It creates a deep mistrust of the body and of ecstasy, which results in the alienation from one's very own body.* Fr. Luke, speaking from experience, feels that *this is the most horrible fragmentation that can happen. The papacy doesn't talk about the mistrust of the body; it talks about spirit as if it were something else, and we priests chose the higher calling in celibacy and go away from the body. In effect, that puts a wedge between parts of our selves, and it becomes very hard then to grow together and become a full human being.*

Fr. Luke contends that estrangement in the fabric of a priest's very own being occurs when the spirit is divorced from the body, as is reflected in the elevation of celibacy and the denial of sexual intimacy. This split results in an opposition within the individual, where the antagonistic forces of spiritual/celibate-as-good and body/sexuality-as-evil are so hostile to each other that *it's very hard to achieve poise, equilibrium, and balance of mind and body, and be able to operate as a whole, really well-functioning unit.*

⸺

Fr. Jethro, an inner-city priest known for his ardent views, elaborates upon Fr. Luke's view: *Priests who deny their sexuality go sour; they become very strict on others and become very rigid when it comes to doctrine. We priests don't see ourselves as good or beautiful, or as whole. We have a sense of being broken and dis-eased.*

Fr. Jethro went on to tell of a young priest known to him. Fr. Seamus upheld everything that was orthodox: he always dressed in clericals, ensured that the rubrics of the liturgy were strictly followed, and in his pastoral ministry would apply the letter of the law, particularly with regard to sexuality.

One day, Fr. Seamus attended a parish event in which he and his parishioners went swimming. He somehow lost his swimsuit and had to leave the water naked. A parishioner offered him a towel, but he refused. He then walked to his car, put on his cassock, and drove off.

The next thing Fr. Jethro heard was that Fr. Seamus had left the priesthood and was living with his gay lover. Fr. Seamus lived in an environment that both demonised his homosexuality and demanded that he practise celibacy; this he did scrupulously. Furthermore, he insisted that his parishioners also maintain sexual rigour in their lives. The parish event, however, revealed not only his physical nakedness, but forced him to consider his person and role as priest from the additional perspectives of sexual and moral nakedness. Stripped of the exterior façade of priesthood, symbolised in clerical clothes, Fr. Seamus finally acknowledged his sexual orientation and loneliness. A similar report was given of a heterosexual priest. At a priest's seminar, the keynote speaker who was also a priest frequently made insulting remarks about women. One priest in the gathering was quite disgusted by this behaviour. He slammed down the lid of his desk, got up, and walked out. An embarrassing silence interrupted the seminar for a few minutes and then the speaker continued, though somewhat subdued. Several years later, the priest-speaker left the priesthood and married. Attacking and ridiculing women appeared to be his way of coping with celibacy, but eventually this strategy became unstuck.

꙳

Some commentators believe that compulsory celibacy is a contributing factor in certain priests who become sexually dysfunctional in their relationships with minors. Fr. James, a priest who specialises in counselling, argues *that the level of sexual maturation amongst Catholic clergy in general could well be compared to that found amongst adolescent boys. If, for example, you were to listen to some of the conversations amongst the clergy gathered for drinks in the privacy of their own company, you could be forgiven for thinking that the average age of the gathering was between fifteen and eighteen years. Not surprisingly—since sexual/relational maturation of many clergy was in fact frozen at this stage. They joined the seminary system in their teens; their contact with women was severed, and so they went into their adult lives stunted, emasculated. It is not merely co-incidental that many of the clergy sexual abuse cases have been perpetrated against minors.*

Various researchers support the anecdotal evidence of Fr. James. Eugene Kennedy and Victor Heckler state that a large proportion of the priests look like adults but on the inside they still struggle with the challenges of a previous level of development. These underdeveloped men have not successfully passed through adolescence.[4] Sipe elaborates on how this immaturity might lead to sexually abusive behaviour. He asserts that some priests who abuse minors do not fit standard psychiatric categories. These priests are a product of a social system that is specifically clerical. These men sacrifice their psycho-sexual development in order to fit within the clerical culture, which demands intellectual conformity and asserts a male-dominant theology of God as Father, Son, and masculine Spirit. In this culture, emotional affirmation is given to men who are revered and powerful (pope, bishop, and priests), and boys are treasured as the future of the church. Women, on the other hand, are shunned except for those female tokens that are venerated as mothers and/or virgins. These are the forbidden objects of sexual fantasy. Consequently, some dysfunctional priests are impelled to act out with individuals who are essentially at the same level of sexual immaturity.[5]

This evidence is further supported by an in-house study commissioned by the Australian Catholic Bishops Conference and the Australian Conference of Leaders of Religious Institutes. Accordingly, most child sexual offences by priests and religious involve ephebophilic[6] rather than pedophilic behaviour and are frequently associated with situational factors relating to lifestyle and ministry.[7]

Meanwhile, the pope and the curia contend that celibacy is not linked to any lack of wholeness or well-being of particular priests. Indeed, they regularly reaffirm the value of priestly celibacy as a gift of God to the church. Nevertheless, anecdotal and clinical evidence suggest that in some instances they are mistaken.

Some priests also raise questions about their own sexual immaturity. Because celibacy imposes a condition of sexual abstinence on all relationships, these priests find it difficult to arrive at an integrated and positive understanding of their sexuality. Indeed, one priest joked *that it is a bit of a dirty trick on God's part that we are given strong sexual desires and yet required to remain celibate.* That paradox is also spelt out in Fr. Ben's tortuous tale.

In the first decade or so of his priesthood, Fr. Ben taught in a boy's school. Then he took up ministry in a parish where there were many young couples and families: *That I was a late developer in the emotional stages that most human beings follow soon became evident. I was thirty-four, presumably entering that adult development state which is sometimes labelled "questioning." This phase deals with the search for personal values, the reappraisal of relationships, career progress, the putting-down of permanent roots, reassessment of one's life commitment, adjusting to the single life, etc.*

In truth, this was not where I was up to. I was still back in an earlier stage, something like the late adolescent/early adult. There the agenda was things like settling into work, beginning a career, learning social interaction, achieving autonomy, and entering significant relationships. At the psychosexual level, I seemed to be even younger—the genital phase was just beginning.

Here I was now surrounded by so much life that was very married, very fertile and productive, with young couples establishing and seeking to deepen their married relationships. Even though the women were married, it didn't make them less attractive to this celibate male.

My fantasy-life worked overtime. Because I had no practised way of getting into contact with my deepest feelings, and now they were very sexual ones, I was in a vulnerable situation. I employed my usual response of avoiding and ignoring these strong feelings and intense desires. I threw myself into my work even more earnestly. Now I was really running on the inside! I didn't want to admit to myself the distress, broken sleep, mood shifts this was all causing.

Trouble loomed in this way. I was counselling Jean, whose husband had left her, and he was living with his de facto partner. Jean was devastated, as well as being left to look after three young children. As she shared her pain, loss, and anger, this all set off similar feelings of loss and emptiness within myself. I was transferring my personal needs on to hers. Our relationship began honestly, but soon we grew very close, and too often sought each other's company. Our physical contact proceeded no further than embracing.

My mind was in confusion, and mild panic. I felt so secretive, morally guilty, ashamed, and a failure to my religious commitments, and to the people I looked after. We tried to break it off and create some space. But deep inside me, I didn't want to call it off. Through these recent years of frustration, I now grew reckless to the point where I didn't care any more what happened. We did break off for some quite miserable months. Then it all flared again, mainly at my instigation. This time, it reached intercourse, just the once. Now I was completely lost, very confused, and even frightened. Full of shame, I just wanted to escape. The pain, sense of failure, and scandal we both had caused weighed most heavily. I was even con-fused as to why it really happened! This was certainly one of the worst and darkest times in my life.

Fr. Ben admitted his failure to his provincial superior, and he was promptly transferred. He undertook a directed retreat, went to con-fession, and attended a group therapy session over a number of weeks, conducted by a nun who ran a clinic for religious in crisis.

For the first twelve and painfully slow months, Fr. Ben was very depressed: *life hung heavily on my shoulders. To survive I had to choose to persevere one day at a time.* Later, he undertook a renewal course for priests, which he found helpful. A number of years passed, and he seemed reasonably satisfied with ministering to those in an older, settled, and very conservative parish. His parishioners found him af-fable and approachable, and they liked being around their parish priest.

Then both of Fr. Ben's parents died. This again triggered his need for love and affection. *On the inside of my person, I was running fast and fearfully. Emotionally, I seemed to be working overtime. I made the mistake of not being still before this painful, personal need, of avoiding my sexuality by transferring it into over-energetic pastoral activity. I was on something of a roller-coaster ride of ministry activities, work, administra-tion and people! More and more, I was losing contact with my own inner self and becoming over-active. I never truly relaxed, even on days off, and any breaks and holidays I took tended to be ineffectual. My health was be-ginning to deteriorate. I was steadily going down the burnout trail.*

Fr. Ben had serious difficulties dealing with his public commitment to celibacy and the interior demands of his sexuality. In an attempt to cope with this contradiction, he endeavoured to perfect his priestly identity by being constantly available to his parishioners and attendant to institutional demands. Yet, in attaining this perceived excellence, Fr. Ben denied other dimensions of the self, resulting in psychological and spiritual exhaustion. This diminished further his ability to carry out his pastoral duties.

A few years later, Fr. Ben formed a friendship with Susannah: *This was a very healing and healthy association for me; as a result, I have since grown very much in my own person, in confidence and self-possession.* After ten long years, Fr. Ben left the priesthood to marry Susannah.

Later, Fr. Ben attended a reunion for his ordination classmates. This anniversary was held within the religious order's main house, where he joined fellow priests who were still in active ministry. *Many of my former confreres remarked on how well I looked. And I do; I feel great. But I honestly couldn't say the same for most of them. These men look so, so tired and haggard, over-worked and under-loved captains of embattled ships.*

Some researchers also raise issues about the difficulties priests have with achieving maturity. The U.S. National Conference of Bishops, for example, commissioned Eugene Kennedy and Victor Heckler in the early 1970s to conduct research on the psychological development of priests. The results of this study indicated that 66.05 percent of the priests in the United States were psychologically underdeveloped and 8.48 percent maldeveloped.[8] According to these researchers, underdeveloped priests are genuinely uneasy about intimacy, and those priests who have not solved the problem of intimacy have not reached maturity.[9]

Kennedy and Heckler also feel that immature priests may not need medical or psychological treatment as much as they need a broader and richer experience of life itself.[10] This brings into question the papacy's requirement of celibacy. Nonetheless, when this report was subsequently delivered to the Conference of Bishops, it was politely received but no follow-up action was initiated.[11]

The problem of immaturity is not confined to the United States. An Australian profile of the priesthood conducted in 1990 reports that priests often have unrewarding relationships and uneasiness about intimacy with resulting difficulties with one's personal identity, non-integrated psychosexual identity, and lack of self-confidence.[12] The study reports that only about one in ten (9 percent) of the priests in the sample have comfortably and consistently reached a high level of maturity where they each think for themselves and take note of their feelings.[13]

Significant numbers of priests, it seems, have difficulty in valuing and establishing a personal identity. That difficulty is not made easier by their obligation to celibacy. This restraint disallows the necessary freedom for exploring the breadth and depth of a relationship; its consequence is stunted development. These priests may be reasonably adequate in their ministerial functions, but they could be far more effective personally and professionally if they were able to achieve greater human and religious maturity.[14]

The Commitment to Celibacy:
Absolute or Conditional?

In the past, many priests received sufficient affirmation, adulation, and care from their parishioners in order to protect and bolster their practise of celibacy. In return, these priests ensured that their parishioners received the expected leadership, moral guidance, and pastoral care to support them in their faith journey.

Times, though, have changed. This mutually beneficial relationship no longer remains for a number of reasons. The leadership that priests enjoy is often challenged, the advocacy for a rigid moral code is increasingly being contested, and welfare is frequently available through secular institutions. These developments have ensured that the returns needed to balance the cost of celibacy have decreased. Consequently, priests look in all sorts of directions to restore the social equilibrium so that they might achieve an acceptable quality of existence.

Those priests who wish to uphold celibacy, for example, often encourage a coterie of sometimes ingratiating parishioners to support them in their practise. Some other priests compensate their loss of affection by enjoying various luxuries such as going on expensive holidays, occasionally rationalised as taking a sabbatical. Other priests may purchase expensive cars or clothes that attract a safe social return in attention and admiration.

Priests may also take on specialised ministries in which they establish a network of companionable relationships that provide them with a sense of intimate belonging. Other priests, however, endeavour to restore the social equilibrium by developing close friendships, some of which are sexually intimate. These latter priests place a value on love and intimacy because they believe that such relationships sustain and energize their lives and ministries.

Yet, from an official perspective, such priests simply break the vow or promise that they once gave to celibacy. For the papacy, it is a non-negotiable law that brooks no questioning or challenge. Once a priest makes a vow or promise of celibacy to priesthood, he is bound to honour that pledge in perpetuity.

Nonetheless, from the viewpoint of priests with friends, they feel shortchanged by Vatican officials and by others who exploit celibacy for their powerful and controlling purposes. They also feel that the papacy's belief in celibacy is fallible and certainly fails to take into consideration their plight.

Priests with friends dream and imagine a future and more compassionate church in which they can again be trusted to take responsibility for their lives. They knew that celibacy was right for them back then, but in the current circumstances they know that sexual intimacy is right for them now. Yet unfortunately for these men, only the centralised bureaucracy of the church has the means to make changes. This leaves them unable to formally or publicly negotiate alternatives to the rule of celibacy.

Since only the papacy can determine the parameters of Catholic priesthood, it is also in a position to ensure that priests comply with celibacy. At least publicly. But this demand for obedience creates the conditions for priests to become skilled in deception. These priests, without any officially recognized sources of empowerment, take advantage of questionable or illicit avenues to restore social equilibrium. Moreover, their choice to go down this avenue is taken not just for themselves. In their commitment to the priesthood, priests with friends use their creativity to restore a balance in the church.

When a priest becomes sexually involved with his friend, he finds himself negotiating dangerous and unchartered waters. Each aspect of his life and ministry has to be reexamined in order to understand how his friendship stands before God, and how such a relationship is to be integrated with his priesthood. Often that means reflecting on the times prior to ordination when he made his original commitment to celibacy.

As seminarians, these priests genuinely felt drawn to the priesthood. In choosing the priesthood they subsequently "offered up" their sexuality, foregoing wife and children, so that they could pursue their call to ministry. Fr. Thomas, though, emphasises the order of commitment:

I cannot remember anyone arriving at the Seminary saying they felt called to celibacy before priesthood. Most of them felt the call to ministry, and this led us to accept the duty of celibacy.[15]

At the initial stage of priesthood, taking on celibacy was not a great difficulty for some priests such as Fr. Nathaniel, whom we meet again in chapter 3. *Celibacy was not a big issue in those early days because I was totally taken up with my idealism. And there is no one more faithful and chaste than an enthusiastic, idealistic seminarian. In those days, I would have confidently resisted a "come on" from Elle McPherson or Meg Ryan!*

Making a promise to celibacy was not so easy for Fr. Jack, a priest who had gone through the seminary during the late seventies/early eighties.

After we became deacons, we spent sometime in our home parish. Here I was introduced to an ex-nun. She was very active in the parish. We found much to talk about, and it was all very open. She was quite apprehensive about her future as far as relationships went. She had started at the convent at an early age. Now in her midthirties, she told me that she felt incompetent in the sexual sense. She very nervously asked if I could show her how to kiss.

It sounds so naive now, but at the time it was a real need. Upon reflection, what was naive was to think it could stop at a kiss. My ordination to the priesthood was deferred six months. As the time approached for my ordination, my spiritual director, who knew about the ex-nun, was surprised to hear that I was still seeing her. He said that he expected "all that to be tied up by now."

So I was sent to an independent psychologist because the order's psychologist was too busy. I opened up to the lady psychologist all my darkest memories but to no avail—she found me to be quite normal. She was incensed to learn that her job was to say I was okay for ordination.

Part of the deal with the spiritual director was that I would stop seeing the lady in question. The news of this sudden end was painful for her. We promised to see each other twelve months later. After a long and lonely year, I dropped around at the usual time of evening. She was entertaining the local curate. She was polite but had no wish to resume any sort of relationship.

Older priests such as Fr. Joel initially understood their commitment to celibacy as part of God's command over their lives.

When I made that commitment to celibacy, I made it before God, and I suppose, ultimately, I saw that as binding. Not just in the sense that it is a heavy burden, although it is at times. Like most others, I would have taken celibacy as part of the package deal. I wanted to be a priest, but I didn't necessarily want to be celibate. I unquestionably, at that stage of my life, saw that it was the only way to be a priest, that you gave up the opportunity to be married.

Yet over time, priests, especially those with friends, began to question the practice. This was the case for Fr. Thomas, a professor in a seminary.

Some seminary staff are more energetic than others in defending celibacy, though they often blur the distinction between promoting celibacy as a personal choice and advocating that it be mandatory.

On the issue of personal celibacy, I feel I have little to offer students outside of the consideration that it might be a valid choice for some people for life and for others for a period of time. As for the imposed rule, it is something neither I nor anyone else ever defends directly. It is just there and does not look like being changed in the short term. So, in my formal capacity, I try to respect the policies of the institution, though privately I think it a pity that the students and I are not allowed to recognize relationships which could make the formation and spiritual discussions more fruitful.[16]

Fr. Thomas then went on to make the case for why a priest can recant his vow or promise to celibacy: *Promises are conditioned by their contexts and are not absolutes in themselves. If the context loses its validity so then does the promise. The promise to separate priesthood from women and families was such a promise. I made it originally in good faith, with the understanding of the situation I had at the time. But, eventually, the context changed and my faith in the purpose, place, and even probity of the promise dissolved.*

The circumstances in which Fr. Thomas made his original promise have changed so dramatically that it has undermined the moral integrity of the promise itself. For Fr. Thomas, celibacy is no longer sustainable or defensible, and his only moral option is to abandon such a promise. Subsequently, he chose to live in a state that accommodated the love of Lydia.

After some years, Fr. Thomas left the priesthood and married. *What inched me over the line was primarily my relationship with Lydia, but that relationship only brought to a head the recognition that the better side of priesthood was being impeded more and more by bad philosophy, inherited bias, frustrated and disguised sexuality, plus unjust and uncourageous leadership.*[17]

The returns for living a celibate life are so negatively geared for some priests that they have no other choice than to abandon celibacy.

Fr. Tobit, an older priest who has served in many rural parishes, also suggests that God is not as absolute about celibacy as the papacy maintains.

I think the Spirit is saying that this kind of commitment is not meant to be permanent because it has almost become a sign of the times. What is happening with so many priests is that they are suddenly forming a friendship. The Holy Spirit is very definitely saying something, and the fact that it is happening to a number of priests is kind of saying that the present church's idea of celibacy may not be God's way of doing things.

Definitely, the church fixes celibacy in law. Yet there's also a lot of humanness in celibacy. So perhaps the signs of the times are saying there could be a change. After all, where there is real love, the Spirit is there.

Sex and the Confessional

Each time a priest goes to the sacrament of penance, he is under external pressure to renew his commitment since the pope frequently issues formal reminders to priests to go to confession to increase grace, to strengthen virtue, and to prevent temptation.[18] But some priests learn, often after much heartache, how to subtly change the terms of the sacrament to take advantage of their understanding of a priesthood that includes sexual friendship.

There is, however, a more important principle at stake when priests go to the sacrament. This sacrament is one of the key ways in which the members of the church can be pressured to conform to the religious and social expectations of the Catholic community. By submitting himself to this religious rite, a priest calls on God for the grace to lead a life that befits his position. In doing so, priests seek to safeguard the public reputation and collective image of the priesthood and the church.

From the papacy's perspective, the reputation and image of the priesthood can be maintained if priests confess their sexual sins so that they might reconcile themselves to celibacy. The church bureaucracy simply concludes that the moral boundary has been transgressed and that this wrong must be made right.

Priests with friends realize a different understanding that prioritises intimacy in their relationships over sexual actions. Most priests see a value in their friendships that they could not locate in their solitary lives. To them, sexual intimacy is primarily a sign of loving union, not an act that indicates a straying from celibacy. And in becoming aware of this intimate signal, these priests have come to understand celibacy as merely an institutional requirement rather than a command from God. They therefore feel that the papacy is acting unjustly in its demands for them to live a life of celibacy. This recognition of injustice bolsters their belief in the appropriateness of their friendships for priesthood. Moreover, it provides the grounds upon which to subtly renegotiate the sacrament of penance. In doing so, such priests uphold the value of the priesthood, which they argue is essential to the ongoing life of the church, unlike celibacy, which is not.

One way in which priests with friends are able to renegotiate this sacrament to advantage the link between priesthood and sexually intimate friendship is by emphasising a particular reading of this ritual.

Two aspects, namely penance and reconciliation, constitute the sacrament of penance. Firstly, penance stresses the importance of practising asceticism to conquer sin in one's life, and so to overcome in oneself what is of the flesh in order that what is spiritual may prevail.[19] This emphasis implies that there is a duality between the body and the spiritual. Such a dichotomy has a parallel in celibacy and sexual intimacy. In subordinating sexual intimacy to celibacy, Vatican officials create an opposition between what they regard as the "pure" priest and a defiled priest, that is, those priests who have friendships.

Priests with friends, on the other hand, prefer to emphasise the second aspect, reconciliation; indeed, these men commonly refer to this sacrament as the sacrament of reconciliation. Reconciliation emphasises the necessity of reconciling relationships that have been damaged by sinful behaviour. By seeking reconciliation through a dialogue of healing and forgiveness, a penitent aims to restore a relationship. This requires such a person to harmonise both spirit and body in oneself and in those who have been injured or hurt. This approach to the sacrament implies that there should be no war between spirit and body, either with self or others. Spirit and body should be on intimate terms with each other, a bond that can be achieved in intimate friendship and in priesthood.

~~

Some priests, as Fr. Peter discovered, exercise a good deal of leverage in the penitential system. As a senior priest known to many, he reports that significant numbers of priests claim and use the right to be confessed and directed by priests who overlook or accept their friendships. *In the big cities there are priests who are known to be expert at kindness. So often you would choose one of these priests.* These priests select confessors who exercise a considerable amount of compassion and latitude with regards to sexuality. Such confessors feel that penitent priests need to be given some scope for freedom of choice and reflection about their adult relationships. Sometimes these confessors are also known to have similar relationships, or have had them in the past. In these confessions it essentially becomes a matter of *you tell me yours, I'll tell you mine.*

Alternatively, *in confession nobody says much at all. It's sort of like, well, that's their business, and you know that they will do it again. It's a hidden secret you don't talk about. Non-verbally, there is an acceptance of sexual activity amongst priests.*

Yet, for other priests there are more immediate concerns that have to be overcome, especially feelings of guilt. This awareness of wrongdoing is principally built upon a belief about what God regards as shameful and what merits penance. Thus, if a priest is not fully decided as to whether celibacy is an institutional requirement or a command of God, it can be very difficult for him, as was the case for Fr. Jerry who had to choose between guilt and friendship.

Fr. Jerry, a religious priest who lived in community, fell in love several times. Each relationship *was passionate, lasting for a long time.*

The context in which this happened becomes the important factor in all this—religion—because it is here that the environment brings me in total contact with males. Not all of them are an attraction, though it is obvious that in such a male-dominated atmosphere most become attractive almost by default. Only by chance would an attraction develop into a mutual sexual affair. But then I would try to "give it up," to spiritualise it all. Today I call this stupidity.

Once I mentioned to my spiritual director that I thought I might be homosexual, although I don't know if I put it like that, but that was the concern. I was told to examine my dreams to see if when I have a "wet-dream" it is with a woman or a man. I'm not sure of the answer now, but knowing me then, I probably said with a woman. "Well, there's your answer, of course you're not homosexual." So all through my religious life, I fought with my homosexual tendencies and attractions to males. But this battle really came to the fore when, after a relationship that went sexual, guilt settled in.

Guilt, the scourge of everything good, is something that I never had before my involvement with religion. Twenty-one years lived without religion in my life should have been good preparation for coping with these guilt feelings. But no, guilt is such an ingrained part of religion. Yes, I acknowledge that guilt can be an early-warning system to pull you up to think about your actions. But it can also pervade and pervert the thinking processes and the character of what a person is.

Guilt is also deadly as it pulls apart anyone who moves outside the accepted norms of that society. There is almost a corporate guilt essence, captured in a container and released on unsuspecting citizens who dare to move outside the norms—it keeps them in control, fearing the outcome of dissent.

Over time, the gravity of sexual sin can become significantly reduced for some priests. These priests shift to a moral ground that includes sexually intimate friendship. They then begin to consciously renegotiate morality in the sacrament in light of their own experiences. On the face of it, the confessions of these priests seem to be contradictory, but, from their viewpoint, they try to maintain a mutual loyalty to both the priesthood and their friends.

Fr. Philip explains his effort at reconciling this apparent contradiction: *I wouldn't class sexual intimacy with my particular friend as a serious sin. It's kind of tradition to go to confession, the way we were brought up. There's always that tension of years and years of training. So there's just a bit of guilt, but not major guilt. I wouldn't lose any sleep over it.*

Being intimate with a woman is not a negative guilt; confession is something mechanical—even though you don't think it's a sin, the church does. Going to confession is a kind of insurance. It's a part of the Catholic habit. But confession would never stop me being with her again. What I did was deliberate and conscious.

Fr. Philip's habitual participation in the sacrament signifies his loyalty to the church, but he also defends the intimacy he shares with his friend. As a result, he insures his continued place in the priesthood, whilst giving equal priority to his friendship.

Some priests with friends, however, are not willing to juggle the papacy's demands with their own experiences, as is the case with Fr. Jacob.

I have stopped going to confession because I do not believe the present relationship is against God's wishes. It challenges me to fidelity the way no church ruling could. Sex will be part of our relationship. Not being genitally intimate with others is also part of my relationship with her. To be forgiven for breaking my vows, I have to call the sex we have a sin, and I have to say that I do not want to be with her again. If I broke my commitment to her, I could go to confession every three months, but God is calling me to commitment, not away from it.

For Fr. Jacob, the confessional acts as a spiritual courtroom where his case is to be heard according to a strict interpretation of canon law. With no court of appeal available to him, Fr. Jacob argues that his only option is to forgo the use of the sacrament. In adopting this stance he refuses to be controlled by the papacy.

⌐◡

Fr. Aaron, a gentle and very giving pastor, is also torn between the rules and his love for Marianne. Marianne once challenged him by saying that if he ever felt that their lovemaking was a sin before God, *we should end this.*

This proved to be a watershed for Fr. Aaron: *You know, I would have held quite an orthodox approach to that area of sexuality: sex outside marriage was illicit, sinful. Not only did I accept this, I also taught it, although we would have offered the possibility that it was acceptable for engaged couples to become sexually intimate.* Then Fr. Aaron was faced with his own situation in which he asked himself: *What would lead me to think differently?* After careful consideration, he came to an understanding *that in a truly committed relationship that isn't taken lightly, and where there is a real mutual relationship, there is room and a place for that expression of love.*

While this understanding provided some resolution to his difficulties, Fr. Aaron still feels uneasy *in front of God, because I have a whole mind-set that was there for years. It took a while to become comfortable with the idea of not confessing the sexual nature of our friendship, and I still have qualms on occasion.*

These qualms seem to revolve more around notions of selfishness rather than guilt. Fr. Aaron feels that looking after one's own wants, needs, and desires while ignoring those of others is the epitome of sinfulness. His preference is in giving, so it is difficult for him to sustain the idea that it is reasonable to have his needs and desires met in this intimate way. He also believes that his friendship with Marianne *would have been just as deep without that expression.* A degree of body-spirit dualism is still apparent in Fr. Aaron's thinking. Spirit and body have yet to fully reconcile with each other in the soul of this priest.

Some priests like Fr. James are well on the way to resolving the conflict and contradictions that present themselves in the dilemma of a priest being in love.

My friendships with Evelyn and other women have impacted on my relationship with God. I suppose one aspect of my understanding of God as I grew up might be described as a "quid pro quo" approach to God: the type of relationship that a child might have with its parents. If it behaves itself, then its parents will love it more and reward it. If it doesn't, then it will be punished and loved less. I had strong taboos within me with regards to sex, and much of my relating to God in those days was spent either on guilt trips for "impure" thoughts or actions (sexual fantasies and masturbation) or experiencing "relief" after having been to Confession.

Once I crossed the boundaries with Evelyn, I had to redefine my understanding of God. My feelings of guilt began to wane, and I found myself relating to a God who was with me—in the very midst of my struggle. For I figured out that, after all, it was God who created me, the whole of me, with my sexuality—and therefore it must be good.

It was about this time that I went on sabbatical and began to read widely, almost voraciously, about human relating. A revolution began to occur within me. I was able to so clearly see the narrow dualistic upbringing that I had been given and the liberation that was being offered by the Gospels. "Good old plastic Jesus" —those depictions of Jesus known in many a Catholic home—was now being replaced by the total all-human, blood-and-guts Jesus, who identified with me in every way.

Within this context, I recall seeing a show around this time which was set within a girls' boarding school. It satirised the old Catholic religion. At the very end of the show, the frustrated and angry teenager—locked in this Catholic institution—sneaked into the college chapel one night. She made a huge penis out of plasticine and stuck it to the image of the crucified Christ figure. Though she was sixteen, I could strongly identify with the "point" being made. That for me was a moment of liberation. Jesus did after all have a penis and it would have become erect.

Priests such as Fr. James have undergone a conversion in their understanding of the sacrament of reconciliation. They engage in this ritual in order to reconcile themselves to God and others in ways that emphasise the importance and value of loving and mutual relationships. Nevertheless, some of these priests still hold residual understandings of a punishing God in which God is likened to a distant Father who judges and chastises the sinful child. But gradually they appear to be replacing this likeness with a new image of God who is friend and lover. Such a God desires that each person ends conflict, including sexual conflict within one's self. God aims to restore friendly and loving relationships that are whole and therefore inherently holy.

In effect, these priests have set aside an ethic of perfection, which emphasises the riddance of sin through the practise of penance, and have replaced this with an ethic of holism through the practice of reconciliation. In their subtle acknowledgement of this moral principle, these priests recognize the integrity and goodness of God's creation.

Priests Seeking Dialogue

In their pursuit of wholeness and holiness, priests with friends hope for a future in which their relationships will be publicly supported and blessed by the church. With such encouragement, these priests believe that they will be much healthier and happier in their own selves and be more able to minister in ways that are relevant to the contemporary era.

These priests don't just simply dream about such a future; they have also worked out ways in which they can realise this outcome. They feel that dialogue is the key for unlocking their vision and making it a reality. Opportunities to publicly discuss and formally negotiate celibacy and related sexual issues are regarded as essential for progressing towards more acceptable and suitable forms of priesthood. Indeed, Fr. Jethro is quite adamant that *we, as a church, should openly debate this very relevant topic of celibacy, among others, with its effects and defects and its impact on the priests and people. The challenges offered by such discussions would bring to the Catholic Church a new and vibrant people, committed to their church and openly working for its betterment. What could be wrong with that?*

Priests with friends are not only convinced that dialogue will result in changes to the celibacy rule; they also predict what is likely to happen. These priests often express the opinion that celibacy as an option in the priesthood will remain. Fr. James suggests that *celibacy should be put as a counsel of perfection rather than law*. Priests who realize that they do have the charism for celibacy, a gift that enables them to achieve wholeness and holiness, should continue with that practise. Indeed one priest said: *I am definitely in favour of celibacy—for those who **freely opt** for it as a way of loving God. The vow of celibacy is only **for a few**. Theirs is a noble choice and a clear sign that they are men/women of deeply sensitive love. But celibacy should **never be required** of persons, for example, as part of a package deal for priestly ordination.*

Fr. Jude is convinced that married priests are inevitable, but he added a note of warning: *I don't know what is going to happen in the future because marriage is going to create all sorts of problems, but certainly compulsory celibacy has created lots of problems.* Marriage, in this priest's view, is not a magic pill to cure the current difficulties that are being experienced in the church. Different problems will be presented when priests are allowed to marry. Yet these priests recognize that there are ways to resolve these potential difficulties. In a more open church in which dialogue promotes negotiation and reconciliation, there is a real possibility that priests and laypeople alike can realize an inclusive and more harmonious community.

Fr. Luke also raises the issue of homosexual priests. He asserts that *it is clear that homosexuality is a phenomenon that is part and parcel of the human condition. So the questions about this have to be faced. They're not going to go away. It will be messy at first, but after a while the church will come to a reasonable and peaceful resolution.* Fr. Luke is convinced that homosexual priests will have a place in the future church, in which they will be accepted for who they are. No longer will the priesthood be a refuge for closeted and repressed men but a place in which these people can openly serve the church. But as with Fr. Jude, he acknowledges that the church will have to undergo a tumultuous period before resolving these issues.

Fr. David, a kindly and knowledgeable pastor who is in a long-term relationship with Ruth, has a more overarching view. *Without the law of celibacy, the church will be enriched with more freedom for, and greater commitment from, all who have then to decide responsibly as to how they will express their sexuality in their full-time ministry.* Such responsibility implies a greater degree of maturity and self-awareness. It's not a matter of choosing whether one should be celibate or married or committed to a homosexual partnership. Rather, it is a matter of integrity. Each Catholic, whether priest or layperson, must try to arrive at a sense of completeness that allows both the individual and community to benefit.

Nevertheless, Fr. Stephen, a religious priest with a high profile in the church, suggests that *the big change will be in the model of priesthood. I think the full-time, lifetime commitment will be only one option for service. I think there will be men who are ordained for a certain period, and I think priesthood has got to be extended to women. You'll be looking at different models of priesthood altogether. Celibate or married clergy will be rather minor in the overall development of the church. One solution could be part-time priests and priests who work on weekends while holding secular employment. This would undermine the myth of the priest as the man apart, which is not necessarily a bad thing, but it would also introduce priests more into the workplace and into the ordinary experiences that most people have access to.*

Collectively, these priests underscore the need for a variety of people to fulfil the role of priest, people who will make responsible decisions as to how they express their sexuality. They also believe that the priesthood of the future will be shaped by a diversity of people who will be variously situated in the heart of the Catholic community.

Priests with friends indicate the conditions under which these changes might occur. Celibacy, according to Fr. Peter, will be done away with *simply because the celibate male clergy are dying out. So, when they reach that stage when they are really low, the church will change. But as with most things, the church changes only when it's forced to.*

Fr. Reuben adds to the idea that expediency will eventually resolve the issue. He asserts that the current model of priesthood is at fault. In this model, *the priest in charge acts like the little god with all the gifts.* By being represented as supernatural beings, priests are practically worshipped, for they control the church's wealth, both economic and spiritual. Yet such power is rarely relinquished; indeed, power actively inhibits the journey of conversion.

Nevertheless, while the current model holds in check any development, *it actually accelerates change.* When people experience oppressive conditions over time, it forces them to cope with their situation through invention. Fr. Reuben believes that is exactly what the current model of priesthood is provoking. Catholics, priest and lay alike, are clarifying their criticism of the present system with the view to toppling the existing regime and replacing it with a relevant and meaningful priesthood.

Fr. Ben supports his confrere's view. *The bottom line in all of this is the urgent need of reform within the official church. This will not happen* *until the groundswell grows bigger, more vocal, and efficient among lay people. The whole issue is **not** about celibacy, ordination of women, married priests, etc., etc. It **is** about authority, leadership, and power. As it has been from day one. Such reforms require the present form of authority and power to be examined and challenged by the grassroots church.*

⌒

Despite their forecasts, such priests are aware of the objections to change and the consequences for its advocacy. Fr. Stephen has already experienced such repercussions when he publicly aired his views on national television.

One viewer contacted him to tell him he was a *Judas*. Fr. Stephen recognizes that *when somebody with some degree of authority in the church speaks out in this way and questions the discipline of celibacy, then one is seen to be letting the side down.* He went on to say: *Most of them aren't aware that celibacy is a matter of church discipline rather than a command of Jesus; it is one of those things that can be changed. There is a failure to distinguish between what is central Christian doctrine and what is, in a sense, peripheral church discipline.*

Fr. Stephen explained why some people object to the reform of celibacy. *People are fearful of change. They are also fearful of those who have any authority to make change. Because, as a result, many of the certainties and securities they are afraid to question might inevitably have to be questioned.*

He also identifies who these people might be: *Eminent people in right-wing church organizations; those who come from European countries; those educated prior to Vatican II who have not received any updated information.* First, people in right-wing organisations generally favour the preservation of the existing order and are averse to, and distrustful of, change. Secondly, conservative Europeans tend to have a Eurocentric view of the church that discounts other expressions of Catholicism. Thirdly, the Second Vatican Council required Catholics to update their knowledge of the church; however, many Catholics have not done so. Politics, culture, and education therefore seem to be the key areas that have to be addressed if changes are to occur.

Fr. Stephen closed our interview by saying that *with all due respect, although the Vatican can make adverse comments, you can never close down the debate on clerical celibacy. But in the present pontificate, with the present consensus, we will not reopen discussion.*

The State of Play

The papacy of John Paul II confines a priest to a celibate existence, limiting not only the way in which he can relate to others, but constraining other ways in which the priesthood can be understood and exercised. The papacy argues that celibacy is the only proper way in which a priest can identify himself, and, if he follows the prescribed spiritual directives, God will look after his priesthood in ways that are good and proper for him.

Meanwhile, priests with friends, and certain theologians and researchers, contend that the papacy's claims are false, and they do so by highlighting problems within the priesthood. These people are convinced that a priest's lack of wholeness and well-being can be aggravated by compulsory celibacy. They insist that there are too many contradictions and anomalies between the institutional view of celibacy and their private experiences. So these priests resolve their difficulties by enjoying a sexually intimate friendship, a relationship that provides them with the mature disposition they require for their lives and ministries.

In order to be at peace with these intimate but illicit contracts, these priests have had to renegotiate their original commitment to celibacy, which they now understand as being historical and contingent, rather than absolute and eternal. In doing so, they endeavour to find a bridge between institutional unity and individual will. Loving friendships are believed to be mutually beneficial, in contradistinction to the one-sided focus that they previously experienced in celibacy. These priests define their moral integrity not in opposition to the papacy and others in the church but in reevaluating and contemporising the priesthood's values. What they try to do is to make the priesthood more relevant and accommodating of their own and others' needs.

As a part of the process of contemporising the priesthood, priests with friends are reassessing how they understand reconciliation. These priests have been able to do this because they exist in a shared and contested universe of theological and pastoral discourse. Through the sacrament, priests with friends seek to reconcile their relationships with God and others, emphasising the importance of context, wholeness, and well-being, rather than abstract religious perfection. Consequently, these priests are able to challenge the ecclesiastical monopoly of celibacy by reframing their experiences. The pragmatic corollary of this is that priests can limit the impact of others' judgements on their sexually intimate friendships.

The current situation is, however, extremely unequal in its effects, and this recognition is likely to be realised by more and more Catholics. This is because the practise of officially disguising such inequalities with doctrine and canon law is becoming steadily less convincing. Furthermore, as the direct interests of the Vatican are revealed through various avenues, compulsory celibacy is undermined.

His total control of the church leaves the pope looking less and less like the selfless soul whose mantle he has for so long claimed for himself. As a result, the pope, the curia, and the synod of bishops have begun to occupy a different space in the church. Complaints about the suppression of dialogue, the frustrations of secrecy, and progressive corruption increasingly challenge the autocratic claim of the papacy that it is answerable only to God.

There is a further irony. While the papacy of John Paul II does not publicly accept priests with friends, it has risen to power and maintains it partly through the practise and patronage of such priests. Nevertheless, Vatican officials have disguised this embarrassing situation behind constant denunciations of precisely the practises that those with clerical ambitions have perpetuated so effectively. Meanwhile, priests with friends insist that these growing tensions can only be resolved with dialogue; and without that, the façade of the priesthood, indeed of the church, is increasingly in danger of collapsing.

2

From Celibate Sacrifice
to Intimate Communion

Two decades ago, Fr. Jon had fallen in love, and for this his bishop moved him to a distant parish far away from his friend. Time passed and Fr. Jon continued to struggle with celibacy. Sometimes he experienced moments of sexual intimacy in passing friendships, and whilst he could not sustain a relationship for fear of disclosure, neither could he bear the loneliness that left him feeling wretched.

Often he contemplated ending it all. He once recounted to me how he would stand on the curb of a busy street thinking how easy it would be to step in front of an oncoming bus. Fr. Jon then fell in love again and he felt the rapture of intimate companionship. In his euphoria he remembered how good it felt to be alive. He was happy in himself, and his ministry took on an even more compassionate tone. But after two years his lover moved on, leaving him to endure the pangs of yet another ended friendship. During that time of intense grief, I attended the Sunday Eucharist he was presiding over. I was acutely aware of how his agonies made a cross of priesthood, especially as he began to say the Eucharistic Prayer.

Fr. Jon stood at the altar alone, overshadowed by a large corpus hanging on the cross, an eternal reminder of the price of human faithlessness. Yet his loyalty attempted to transcend this betrayal. Troubled though he was, Fr. Jon took up the cosmic host and, by rote, uttered the words of institution.

On the night he was betrayed,
he took bread and gave you thanks and praise.
He broke the bread, gave it to his disciples, and said:
Take this, all of you, and eat it:
this is my body which will be given up for you.[1]

As Fr. Jon broke the bread, loneliness appeared to break his body, for at that moment he slumped as if his carriage had buckled under an unbearable burden. The "heavens and earth" seemed suspended, and he wept. In that brief uncontrolled moment, Fr. Jon seemed to challenge us to know life as he did, for the sacrifice of his sexuality was the price of his priesthood. He struggled to regain composure and then continued.

Later, after the Eucharist had ended, some of the congregation left quickly, as usual, while others gathered in the porch. Casual parishioners and the priest, now with a jovial mask, greeted each other, the fleeting revelation hidden behind a façade of comfortable humanity.

In that brief event, Fr. Jon's wretched experience of celibacy threatened to sully the Eucharist. Yet, by regaining emotional control, Fr. Jon returned the Eucharist, and the church, to its domesticated form that demanded he surrender loving companionship. By emphasising the sacrificial nature of the Eucharist, the papacy continues to deny this priest intimate friendship regardless of the heartbreak that plagues his life.

Another priest, reflecting on his own fate, cynically responded, *even if it means sacrificing his own heart, a woman (or man) must not come between a priest and God*. This view is confirmed by Vatican officials. They challenge new priests to a life of sacrificial service.[2]

Sacrificing Priests

The papacy is able to sustain the rule of celibacy by inculcating the practice into the core of Eucharist. Like Fr. Jon, priests are required to stand alone at the altar, set apart from the congregation as an *alter Christus* (another Christ). Priests act not as ordinary men but as supernatural mediators between God and the faithful. In offering petitions and prayers over the gifts of bread and wine, the transubstantiated body and blood of Christ is offered to God to wash away the sins of the people. Communion then restores social order in which human-ity is subordinated to God, layperson to priest and woman to man.

Eucharistic sacrifice maintains hierarchical order. At the apex of this hierarchy is celibacy. As the offerer of the sacrifice who stands in divine company, a priest is required to be pure. Celibacy is used by the papacy to represent that purity, implying that sexually active men and women are impure and therefore have an incompatibility with the sacred.

Such a notion of purity has its historical foundation in the Jewish priesthood where bodily discharges, including semen, prevented priests from participating in cultic service. Christianity later adopted that idea, requiring even married priests to forego sexual relations so that they might be fit for altar service.

While Rome asserts that ritual purity is no longer demanded for priests, it continues to use phrases such as "perfect chastity in priestly celibacy" and "the grace of purity and fidelity in the obliga-tion of celibacy," phrases that are used to support its legislation for celibacy.[3]

The pope also maintains that "[i]n virginity and celibacy, chastity retains its original meaning."[4] In the Garden of Eden, according to St. Augustine, Adam and Eve were unable to control their sexual urges, thereby disobeying God. From that point on, humankind has main-tained its sinful state. Thus, the papacy feels that priests who repre-sent Christ are required by God to restore the original perfection of humankind.

As well, doctrines that are used to support celibacy rely on texts originally constructed by the church fathers in the fourth century to support ritual purity. In the Second Vatican Council's Decree on the Life and Ministry of Priests, for example, it is asserted that the "Church from apostolic times has wished to conserve the *gift of perpet-ual continence of the clergy.*" This claim is supported with a lengthy footnote citing conciliar and patristic texts as evidence.[5]

Related to the concept of the pure priest is the idea that celibacy resembles the divine. The papacy argues that celibate priests are a living sign of the world to come in which the children of the resur-rection will have no part in marriage.[6] By giving absolute meaning to these biblical metaphors, celibacy is promoted as an exclusive eschatological witness, thereby making celibacy the sole state worthy of altar service.

⌐⌐⌐

Prior to the Second Vatican Council (1962-1965), the liturgical pattern reflected the firm belief in the Mass as a sacrifice in which the priest and his actions were held distinctly separate from the people. Everything was centred on the priest at the altar: Latin as the language of the elite was used, the back of the priest was turned to the people during consecration, and only the priest communicated from the cup.

The sacrificial emphasis, along with its associated hierarchical order, however, could not be fully sustained in the postwar era. The church was living and functioning largely within more or less liberal, democratic societies. This fortress mentality, which set the church against the world, was no longer able to insulate Catholic society from the world. Nor did Catholics for the most part want to be insulated. Outside the church change was being marked by the beginnings of space-travel, the spread of communism, sounds of rock and roll, and Western affluence that led to extended education, resulting in fewer people giving uncritical acceptance to the directions of paternalistic clerical leaders.

Internally, there was growth in the liturgical movement, the lay apostolate, biblical scholarship, and the need for Catholics to participate in democratic politics.[7] All of these social developments pressured John XXIII (1958-1963) to convoke an ecumenical council to facilitate updating of the church.

The Second Vatican Council was a concerted effort to reform and renew the church in relation to the modern world, but it was not unequivocal. The Council, for example, adopted democratic notions such as collegiality, freedom of conscience, synodal structures, and emphasised human rights, although the organisational order remained hierarchical and the prominence of the priest was still emphasised.[8] It also reevaluated marriage and stressed the relationship between Christian love, sexuality, and friendship. This gave some priests the rationale for replacing the traditional claim that celibacy is the better, if not the only, road to perfection, with the understanding that marriage and celibacy are different but equal paths of Christian perfection.[9] Sexuality could now no longer be considered impure, and this eroded ritual purity as a necessity for sacrifice. Furthermore, the Council's attitude of openness, engagement, and even an embrace of the world undermined the meaning of ritual purity as a symbol of the church's separation from the world.[10]

Despite these changes, deliberations about celibacy were exempted from the overarching reappraisal of the Council. At the request of Paul VI (1963-1978), the matter of celibacy was not formally discussed. This was a concession to the conservative bishops who insisted that the Council had done enough damage to the church already by introducing so many new ideas and changes.[11] Consequently, the practise was reaffirmed, and priests were still set apart as "witnesses and dispensers of a life other than this earthly one."[12]

Concessions to modernity affected the eucharistic liturgy. The Eucharist was to be said in the vernacular. The laity were encouraged to actively participate and were permitted to communicate with the cup, and the priest was to now face the people. This in effect diminished priest-lay distinctions. This blurring of the essential difference between the priesthood and the laity subsequently created substantial difficulties in maintaining the sacrificial emphasis of the Eucharist and the practise of celibacy.[13]

Nevertheless, under the pontificate of John Paul II, emphasis has been given to the difference between the ordained priesthood and the laity. This difference has also been signified by the constant promotion of celibacy that serves to strengthen priest-lay distinctions.

The difficulty in sustaining celibacy as a worthwhile sacrifice is being felt by many a local church, a problem that is aggravated by the shortage of priests and its consequences. These can suffocate the life out of some communities, as is the case for Fr. Matthias and his parish. This came into sharp focus when I attended one Sunday Mass.

The congregation was sparse and predominantly grey-haired. A few parishioners sat in familiar pews, chatting softly to each other. Some were on their knees praying. Others quietly read the local Catholic newspaper or greeted friends seated afar with a restrained wave.

Mass started a few minutes late. The priest, perhaps in his early seventies, was small of stature, slightly hunched over, and with a small rounded belly. A few wispy hairs covered his head, while his face was bland, emotionless, and tired. It looked as though he was fading away. The acolyte was not much younger, but a little taller and broader, with a mop of thick white hair. They processed slowly down the central aisle to the dirge-like music that the old organist cranked out.

A litany of formulaic prayers followed, the priest leading in monotone with the opening line, the parishioners dutifully coming in on cue. The readings followed, and eventually the priest got up to proclaim the Gospel, followed by the acolyte who took his place at the side of the pulpit with candle in hand. It was a tired, faltering reading made worse when he lost his place. Then he delivered his homily, a dull, dismal affair. He read slowly from a book of prepared sermons for what seemed like an eternity. The muffled, detached rendition also made it difficult to understand what was being said.

For the first five minutes, most parishioners respectfully listened with faces seemingly attendant. But as the minutes ticked by, a subdued restlessness set in, a discreet shuffle here, some eyes venturing elsewhere.

While the priest lethargically rattled through the ritual prayers, the standing and kneeling of the Eucharistic Rite, along with receiving Communion, provided some welcome relief. The closing hymn was then sung, the blessing given, and the congregation dispersed with a sprightliness that contrasted acutely with the passing of the last hour.

This was a study not only of the aged, but also of impotency. Here was a man who presumably had made the sacrifices necessary for priesthood, a celibate priest to be sure, and asexual to boot. For there was not even a spark of energy, no glimmer of passion, a complete absence of virility. Just a worn-out, impotent old priest. He served as a feeble channel, an automated function that echoed no enthusiasm or intimate warmth. Here was the church's gatekeeper going through the motions: a bland old sexless priest in a bland old sexless church.

Everyday Costs of Celibacy

The ritual sacrifice of sexuality is also reflected in the everyday lives of priests, some of whom are well aware of the personal costs involved.

These priests feel that they have surrendered their sexuality to the system. *For most of my life, I have had a sense of nagging loss, all for the sake of some idiotic idea. It's not a sacrifice for what's valuable,* opined one priest who had given decades of service.

Fr. Caleb spelt out that sacrifice more specifically, blaming the papacy for denying him opportunities for intimate human companionship: *They slam the door of human warmth and ecstasy in priests' faces—not entering themselves, and filling the hearts of those who would with fear and dread. They bind heavy burdens on priests' backs, and don't lift a finger to help.* For Fr. Caleb, the demand of celibacy has warped his sexuality with terror and emptied his relationships of intimacy. In his grief over the loss of sexually intimate friendship, he remains disgusted at the lack of awareness and compassion for priests who suffer from bureaucratic legalism.

Other priests recount the price they continue to pay for their priesthood. They express the sorrow of foregoing a wife or partner. *What a shame I wasn't free to enjoy a friendship twenty or thirty years ago. My best years are behind me,* said one priest, *I regret not having the experience of sexual love.* Fr. Toby, an older priest who has lived in many rural parishes, also laments over giving up the chance to marry: *Such love would have produced a rich harvest for the kingdom.*

These priests also give vent to grief over their sacrifice of fatherhood, as did Fr. Ben. *At about age twenty-six, I became friendly with a young married couple who were "busy" having a family. Occasionally, when with them, I recall feeling some regret that I would never "be able" to father a son. This sorrow stayed with me over the years, and is still with me: I would have loved to have had a son.*

Fr. Aaron, a well-loved and compassionate priest, echoes this sadness. In his mind, *a good priest would make a good father.* Such was the depth of his longing that he even named the son and daughter he would never have after his two favourite bible characters.

Other priests went on to nominate when these feelings of loss become acute: *There are the good and bad times—it gets bad when you baptise a child or when you marry others.* Fr. Zachary quietly states: *At one stage it even became painful for me to visit parents in hospital when they had a new baby—the sight of which made me grieve for the loss of natural fatherhood.* Fr. Luke contends: *The sad thing about celibacy is that it has made me like a tree with neither root nor fruit.*

These priests are not always alone in their grief; their friends are also sometimes implicated in their loss. *We have shared [feelings] about the sacrifice of not being able to immortalise ourselves in our children,* said Fr. James and Sr. Evelyn. The sadness of not having one's lineage perpetuated is again reflected in the sorrow of another priest: *In three generations, maybe even in two, I will be totally forgotten.*

⚊

An awareness of the sacrifices that are entailed in celibacy extends to confreres. Some priests with friends are now concerned for their brother priests who are still without love and companionship. *I see priests who do their job, but they are so un-giving,* said Fr. Joe, a middle-aged priest who has lived in presbyteries with older confreres. *They cut off communication as soon as it becomes "You and I." Life is kept so functional; everybody is kept in his or her box, and the priest keeps himself locked away in the celibacy box.*

Fr. Joe adds: *Many older clergy have not been able to liberate themselves and appear to live out their final years in a vacuum. They had their beliefs that set them apart from others. It even made them feel better than the "common herd of humanity." But most of that has been undermined, and these folk have been left dangling. Some hold onto the old form, but I know that many harbour a deep anger against the church for misleading them and foreclosing opportunities.*

One such older priest reiterates this quandary from a personal perspective: *I look on and see my brothers and sisters in their retirement having companionship and care that is denied me. I am unsure if I resent all that or have the bravado of erstwhile years to suppress those feelings and to say that I am enjoying the way it is for me.* In a lonely clerical environment, these priests experience the burnt-out feelings of loss in a life that has dutifully forsaken intimacy.

Killing Priests

Church leadership is prepared to risk much in order to maintain its particular belief system. Indeed, in recent years, there have been a number of claims that suggest that the central authority of the church is sacrificing priests. Francis Dorff maintains that "we are killing priests because we equate the present exclusive, male, celibate, clerical paradigm with the essence of priesthood. This colours everything we do. It leads us to forbid discussion of possible alternative forms of priesthood and to maintain a priori that they would be unthinkable. By defining the priesthood in terms of the status quo, we make the increasingly dismal priest present our only imaginable future."[14]

This lethal paradigm is further expressed in the everyday lives of priests. While priests experience the high levels of stress found among other professional groups, some of the causes are unique to the priesthood. Priests running a parish are on call twenty-four hours per day, seven days a week, and assume a lifelong commitment. They maintain high levels of responsibility for the lives of others, and are often intensely involved in the life crises of people. The sacralisation of the priesthood also evokes an idealisation of clergy by the laity, placing huge expectations on priests. In addition, the limits of ministry are not clearly defined; hence, the priest is expected to be (or can insist on being) a veritable "jack-of-all-trades." Such role-ambiguity is also compounded by a general lack of recognition of hard work and commitment; this contributes to burnout.[15]

The burden of stress is compounded by particular situational characteristics. Significant numbers of priests live and work within the walls of the presbytery, leaving no personal space to escape from the pressures of ministry. Being always on call does not enable a priest to escape from a constant sense of responsibility for others and prevents him from living a balanced life. In addition, a priest has contact with a large cross section of people and is inevitably recognised wherever he goes. This gives him very little opportunity to debrief, as conversations inevitably return to parish matters or to personal problems and concerns. Priests may also count many acquaintances, but few, if any, close friends. Priests are therefore subject to pronounced levels of occupational stress from the degree of personal investment in the work role, and from the lack of stress-mediating effects of social support because of their commitment to celibacy.[16]

Such an admixture has concrete consequences, as was the case for one priest: stress led him to hang himself. The statement that was issued after his death indicated that this priest had been *deeply committed to his vocation, to the priesthood, to his diocese, and to his parish.*

He had made himself available to all who asked, but this giving had been at his own expense, leaving him exhausted, burnt-out, and in need of rest.[17] His confrere went on to say that many priests find themselves under pressure: *Often in the same day you have to move from sharing someone's sorrow to sharing someone's joy. That might mean going straight from a funeral—perhaps even a child's funeral—to a wedding, where you owe it to people to be upbeat and bright. This could put priests under stress and leave them emotionally tired: It's very unfortunate that my confrere felt this was his only way out.*

Priests generally recognize that their friendships mediate stress. One highly motivated priest who is often in great demand indicates just how important his relationship is in maintaining his everyday well-being. *Just having a cup of tea or ringing her gives me a chance to restore my flagging energy. I don't know how I could survive without Elizabeth.* Another priest, whose pastoral responsibility extends to two parishes, also expresses gratitude for his friend: *at times, she is my sanity.*

Yet, these imaginative solutions threaten the papacy's understanding of the church. Consequently, it promotes its own methods for overcoming the social pressures that can jeopardise the celibate commitment of a priest.

> We know well that in the world of today particular difficulties threaten celibacy from all sides. . . . But they can overcome these difficulties if suitable conditions are fostered, namely: growth of the interior life through prayer, renunciation and fervent love for God and one's neighbour and by other aids to the spiritual life; human balance through well-ordered integration into the fabric of social relationships; fraternal association and companionship with other priests and with the Bishop, through pastoral structures better suited to this purpose and with the assistance also of the community of the faithful.[18]

However, the problem is that when this advice is translated into the local realities in which a priest finds himself, such generalised solutions frequently fail to address the substantial complexities he encounters in his everyday life, as is the case for Fr. Jim.

Fr. Jim pastors to a large and remote rural community. Alone on the endless highways that traverse his parish, he travels long distances to make visitations to isolated farms and to celebrate Mass in outlying parish centres. He loves his ministry, although in this parish he is expected to be a bit of a universal "fix it." He also enjoys the down-to-earth friendship and acceptance of these country people and has a sense of being close to them in both sorrows and joys. But sometimes the isolation and the aloneness of his task weigh heavily on his soul, especially in the evening. After returning from a long day of travelling, he comes back to the presbytery and collapses in his well-worn chair. Too tired to prepare supper, he snacks on apples and stale biscuits that he softens in microwaved milky tea.

Sometimes he would like to call on his own family or a confrere, but the latter lives a three-hours drive away; the former requires a flight back home. Ringing is expensive too, as is every other form of communication out in the country. Except for prayer. Fr. Jim prays a lot; the quietness lends itself to his spiritual pursuits. But sometimes prayer is not enough. Sometimes, he finds that God's love needs to be enfleshed.

That's when Fr. Jim visits Maria, the local publican. During the summer, when tourists are swarming about the town, she doesn't get much time to chat. But when it's winter, only a few old regulars prop up the bar and that's the time she gives him sweet attention. Yet, there's a problem. Fr. Jim and Maria have fallen in love. Maria wants more, but Fr. Jim is troubled, and so he wrote to his friend:

I still want us to be good friends. Not lovers. I say that, or rather, write that, in all sincerity. Because our friendship is still developing. But, of course, I'm as subject to temptation as the next person, and, as last week, at times I give into temptation. I do what I don't want to do, or shouldn't do. The body language I used was inappropriate. It was wrong. It was in conflict with my commitment. I asked your forgiveness at the time. I ask it again now.

Fr. Jim's story isn't finished; he's at the beginning of his struggle, and so is Maria.

Celibacy is implicated in the departure of an estimated one hundred thousand priests who have resigned since the Second Vatican Council.

Many of them have since married. Moreover, this policy has in part contributed to almost half the world's Catholic parishes and mission stations being without a priest.[19] Such a shortage of priests has also resulted in ad hoc responses that stretch the limits of priests' endurance. Dorff states: "Our strategies of combining parishes, building mega-churches, denying priestly sabbaticals, extending the retirement age of our priests, calling priests out of retirement and importing priests from third world countries to minister to the (Western world) all have this character. For the most part, (Vatican officials are) driven less by the pastoral needs and preferences of our people than they are by the organizational need to maintain the present form of priesthood at all costs."[20] The extent of that sacrifice is exemplified by one seventy-year-old priest who is responsible for ten parishes.[21]

Yet the papacy is caught in a dilemma because celibacy is enmeshed in its belief system. Such a system deals with what gives security and what can be trusted. Thus, faith is often expressed through obedience to what a person or group discerns as God's will, and this can be measured by perseverance in times of trial. Consequently, the papacy is not about to give in and waive celibacy, particularly when it claims that its agenda comes from religious and moral principles that flow from God.

Nonetheless, this project of maintenance is being carried out under an exhaustive weight of change and is being further challenged by other beliefs and value systems. Increasing numbers of priests, in reflecting upon the signs of the times, are not convinced that God has given them the charism of celibacy, but they do believe that they have a vocation to the priesthood. These priests therefore continue to plead with the church to waive the rule because they, as one priest stated, *still want to sacrifice their lives for Christ but not be unnecessarily killed.*[22]

Sweating Blood:
The Trauma of Contracting Friendship

Priests continue to form sexually intimate friendships even though they may experience a high degree of anxiety when contemplating or engaging in such relationships. This has been illustrated by Fr. Jim's dilemma with his relationship with Maria. This concern is often focused on the problem of how to reconcile sexual behaviour with the requirement of celibacy. In paying attention to this problem, priests cope in different ways.

Some priests, for example, use their sexual experience to support celibacy by defining their own meaning of the practise.[23] Other priests are able to integrate a repertoire of roles into a plausible whole, as is the case with many of the priests who have long-term relationships. Some priests are unwilling or unable to negotiate their friendships within the priesthood and so they leave. However, during the transition phase, they are often filled with anxiety. *For the man who leaves, the acutest anguish usually comes before he decides, or before he acts on his decision. It is endured in silence and loneliness. And it can go on for years . . . it could still take "an average of four to five years" agonising . . . before walking out of the door.*[24]

A conscious clarity eventually emerges, and a priest prepares to leave. Yet for a few priests that clarity is never achieved. Often during the phase of leaving, *there are thoughts of suicide. And sometimes, the act of suicide.*[25]

Fr. Jesse was burdened by both celibacy and by the condemnation of his homosexual orientation. His was a sad tale filled with details about the difficulties of his circumstances and ambivalence towards the papacy. Torn between loyalty to the church and sexual integrity, Fr. Jesse felt he lacked a future: *There seems no hope of any change for me. I have always run away when I was faced with trouble, now there is simply nowhere left to run to.*

For three years, he struggled over his dilemma and thoughts of suicide constantly accompanied by what seemed an interminable impasse. Eventually, Fr. Jesse chose not to run to the grave: love for his friend steered him away from that action because he did not want to burden his beloved with inevitable grief and loss. He also concluded that suicide *would be a kind of slap in the face of God, who I believe gave and gives me this life, and who is responsible for none of the things that have robbed me of my backbone and curdled my joy.*

Fr. Jesse resolved his issues of loyalty and integrity by eventually leaving the priesthood. His love for the church remains, but he continues to castigate the pope, cardinals, and bishops, whom he now regards *as villains whose instincts have been twisted by society, culture, and religion, and in their search for natural fulfilment turned nasty and vicious.*

$$\rightharpoondown$$

I asked Fr. Jack if he had ever been troubled by thoughts of suicide. *Yes*, he had, and went onto say that his bishop too had been *on the edge of a pit of dark despair.* He also spoke of another priest who had a relationship with a woman that produced two children. *He never lived with her, but he went through hell and made two suicide attempts (overdoses). His parish priest at the time told me this. He also went through hell trying to protect and father and mother his assistant priest, and to help him to make up his mind to stay in the priesthood.* Fr. Jack didn't know what happened to the woman and the children, but the priest continues to minister.

Fr. Jack went on to report that he knows of priests who have committed suicide, but that alternative verdicts such as death by accident are officially given. Richard Sipe adds to this anecdotal evidence by stating, "four of the five reports of suicide we reviewed were intrinsically bound up with the sexual conflicts in pursuing the celibate idea."[26]

David Rice also cites a further incident of celibacy-related suicide. One such priest was particularly troubled by what might happen if he declared his friendship of twenty years. He was worried that people were talking about him and feared above all that his mother might know he had left orthodoxy. In not being able to resolve his love for his friend with the threat of being deprived of his priesthood, he hanged himself. In his farewell letter, his last thought was for some of his parishioners: *be more friendly and generous with your priest and do not leave him alone at the altar.*[27]

The church attempted to cover up the suicide as a sudden illness, but a confrere reported it to the media. Undoubtedly, this priest identified his solitary confinement at the altar as the nub of his considerable pain. Such isolation tormented him both in eucharistic ritual and everyday life, which he suffered under a shroud of silence. In this tragedy, the self-immolation of this priest echoes the immolation of Christ. As *alter Christus*, he ended up being sacrificed on the altar of celibacy. In upholding celibacy, such a priest pays the ultimate price.

An Official Defence of Celibacy

The papacy has a different view of the sacrifice entailed in celibacy. Any problems, it argues, with regards to its social practice do not lie with the mandate itself but with individual priests. Consequently, priests are universally called to turn their attention towards service of the church and away from their own wants, needs, and desires. Indeed, celibacy is understood by one Vatican official as reflecting "the love of God which surpasses all limits," including, seemingly, the limits of a priest's humanity.[28]

By embracing this transcendent love, a priest can overcome the difficulties that often result from concentrating on self and one's personal interests. The papacy does not acknowledge the value of embodied love that is expressed in sexually intimate friendship and how this love contributes to the wholeness and well-being of a priest. The contentment of these priests is, instead, regarded as selfishness. By taking care of their own needs and desires, or having a friend to express and receive love, these priests supposedly damage their love relationship with God. The Vatican is thoroughly convinced, it seems, that priests are to sacrifice their selfhood in order to give total service to the church.

Nor is it apparent to Vatican officials why celibacy should be considered an overwhelming problem or, for that matter, investigated. In fact, in the Vatican there is an abundance of priests who are seemingly willing to embrace celibacy. In this exclusive environment, the papacy promotes unflinching loyalty to the church, and those priests who faithfully carry out its policies are duly rewarded. This swapping of favours—of loyalty for desire of success, and vice versa—is made more effective by the celibate context. Without spouse or family to vie for their time, affection, and money, priests are not only more willing to respond to the demands of the job, they generally are more psychologically and emotionally dependent on its rewards. As a result, the sacrifices made in practising celibacy are mitigated by compensation given in the form of status and privilege.[29]

Hence, there is no hint in the Vatican that around the globe the church is suffering from the negative effects of a priest shortage. This is so because there is no lack of priests in Rome who are, at least on the face of it, willing to comply with celibacy. From the perspective of a rarefied world where there are priests aplenty, there is no need to give credit to claims and studies that assert the need for change. (Anecdotal evidence given by priests who frequently travel to Rome suggest, however, that celibacy is not being practised by a significant number of Vatican priests.)

The Vatican strongly reject claims made by those who are at the periphery of its bureaucratic centre. This is evidenced in a report entitled "New Vocations for a New Europe."[30] In its evaluation of the shortage of clergy in Western Europe, there is no mention of the most frequently cited reasons given by Europeans for their apathy and withdrawal from the pews, namely, widespread sexual misconduct among clergy and the apparent refusal of church leadership to address modern-day concerns. Included in these petitions is the request made by Catholics in nearly every European country to drop the celibacy requirement for priests.[31]

The Congregation for Catholic Education gives other reasons for the vocations shortage, such as Europe's "weak and complex culture" and the "weak" educational system both within and outside the church. Youths are also said to be at fault, because they "do not possess the 'elementary grammar' of existence, they are nomads; they are 'trying out'."[32] In blaming Europe's culture, education system, and youths for perceived weaknesses, the papacy is able to deny that celibacy is a factor in the decline of vocations. Such doctrinal tactics are unlikely to alleviate the shortage of priests or return to the pews those many Catholics who have departed.

In the infrequent instance where official studies are made of celibacy, such research is usually incapable of registering the subtleties behind the façade of celibacy. Questions geared to obtaining statistical results are insensitive to social and cultural dynamics: voting for or against celibacy can mean many things to priests.

According to Eugene Kennedy and Victor Heckler, some of those priests most resistant to a change in the celibacy law are those who are most threatened by possible contact with women.[33] These priests may wish to preserve celibacy, not for its purported advantages, but to keep at bay other members of the church.

Two religious priests whom I interviewed also advocate celibacy for religious orders even though they enjoy sexually intimate friendships. This indicates that the definition of celibacy held by a priest may contradict the definition of celibacy implied in a questionnaire.

Some homosexual priests are also unlikely to vote against celibacy. Vatican officials believe that homosexual acts are intrinsically disordered and that therefore these people should remain chaste.[34] This places homosexual men in a cultural predicament, which can be effectively resolved if they join the priesthood. Celibacy can put an end to questions about sexual orientation and provide a pragmatic rationale for their dilemma: *I'm celibate not gay*, as one homosexual priest knowingly stated. Alternatively, celibacy can provide adequate cover for the homosexual orientation, sexual practises, and relationships of a priest whilst allowing him to maintain a life of service, status, and privilege.

Given the homophobic environment of the church, it is unlikely that these priests would seriously challenge celibacy. Responses to official studies of celibacy can therefore be skewed because of reasons that are ideologically conditioned by the papacy. These also subvert the understanding of sacrifice: Celibacy is not so much about giving up something valuable; rather, it can provide social cover for the trading of self-interests.

In the rare case where official research does publicly challenge celibacy, Vatican representatives go to considerable lengths to downplay its conclusions. A well-known example of this strategy is the aggressive reaction given by the United States Catholic Conference (USCC) to the study of the priesthood conducted by Richard Schoenherr and Lawrence Young (1993). The U.S. bishops originally sponsored a nine-year sociological study based on a meticulous census registry of some 36,000 diocesan clergy in 86 dioceses from 1966 to 1984.

Research findings were gradually released through private interim reports to the U.S. hierarchy, but several bishops became irate over the gloomy projections and sought to quash the project. The USCC then ceased sponsorship but alternative funding was made available to complete the task, resulting in publication of the study. Subsequently, Cardinal Roger Mahony attacked the researcher but not the evidence. Schoenherr had been a former priest, and was accused of using the study to push his personal agenda of optional celibacy.

Schoenherr and Young insisted that they had scrupulously adhered to the data, reserving their personal conclusions to the last three pages of the book. They subsequently declared,

> . . . we believe the church is being confronted with a choice between its sacramental tradition and its commitment to an exclusively male celibate priesthood. One of the most critical aspects of this confrontation is that most church leaders have failed to accept responsibility for the choice. Instead, they focus on stopgap solutions to the ever-worsening priest shortage while hoping for a dramatic increase in vocations. . . . The need to decide whether to preserve the eucharistic tradition or to maintain compulsory celibacy and male exclusivity looms ever larger as the priest shortage grows.[35]

Though sociologists have not challenged the figures and projections in the study, criticisms similar to Cardinal Mahony's have appeared with some regularity in diocesan and other church publications.[36]

In effect, the papacy is not primarily interested in research outcomes about celibacy. Its concerns are predominantly related to doing what it perceives to be the will of God. Moreover, where there are no official numbers or no concrete information about celibacy, protests against the practise are difficult to sustain. Nonetheless, the denial of the excessive cost of celibacy and the tendency to make scapegoats of dissenting priests promote outcomes that seriously challenge compulsory celibacy.

In refusing to heed the warnings of such research, the papacy risks creating a significant gulf between official and local understandings of priesthood. Fr. David provides evidence of this likelihood: *The bishops have to start listening to the priests rather than Rome. The problem of celibacy will not be solved until bishops and priests find some way to speak honestly about sexuality and the priesthood.*

In the meantime, only bishops have the formal power to challenge compulsory celibacy. Bishops are supposed to exercise their authority for the good of the faithful, but in recent years, criticism has been levelled at the papacy for making bishops managers who only work under its instructions.

One example of the pressure for bishops to remain managers was made apparent at the European Bishops Synod (1999). The Roman curia withheld a number of controversial issues from the discussion platform, one of them being the subject of married priests. Bishops and their advisors had comprehensive discussions on this issue, but there was an oppositional lobby of curia bishops. Curia members shrewdly distributed themselves amongst the various working groups and were able, by virtue of their veto rights, to prevent the issue of married priests from figuring among the conclusions presented in the synod document.[37]

Manipulating representation, exercising prohibition, and imposing silence are the tactical devices that contribute to the maintenance of compulsory celibacy. As a result, management choices seem to lie somewhere between giving up the ideal of priest-as-pastor and closing one-third of the parishes in the Western world.[38] Significant numbers of bishops are also factoring into their management decisions facts such as illness, resignations, retirements, deaths, and very few younger priests coming into the ranks. While these bishops acknowledge that the reasons for the priest shortage are complex and cannot be reduced to a simple reaction against celibacy, what is clear is that retention of the canon renders impossible the most obvious solution: the ordination of married men and, many would argue, women.

Another way in which the papacy reduces the autonomy of bishops is by selecting those who share conservative views. Leaked documents covered by the "pontifical secret" give criteria for choosing a suitable candidate for the episcopate. They include "Fidelity and obedience to the Holy Father, the Apostolic See, the hierarchy, esteem and acceptance of priestly celibacy, as it is presented by the church's Magisterium; respect for the faithfulness to the norms concerning divine worship and ecclesiastical dress."[39] Consequently, priests who support optional celibacy will not be made bishops. Moreover, in his twenty-five-year pontificate, Pope John Paul has appointed the vast majority of the church's bishops.

Similarly, bishops who contest celibacy are reprimanded, overlooked in the selection for key positions, or removed from their dioceses, if they are not forced to resign. Bishop Eamon Casey of Ireland fathered a child, as did Bishop Hansjorg Vogel of Switzerland. Archbishop

Eugene Marino of Atlanta and Archbishop Robert Sanchez of Santa Fe were sexually involved with women: the bishops resigned. In 1995, Bishop Jacques Gaillot of Evreux, France, refused to resign and was removed from office after he publicly supported a married clergy, advocated the use of condoms to prevent AIDS, and expressed willingness to bless homosexual unions.

It follows then that few clerics are able to safely pose questions about celibacy without forfeiting their position or ambitions. Thus, the papacy does not need to listen to the concerns of priests and bishops or to the outcomes of research. Its belief system rests on the unquestioned acceptance of celibacy and the willingness of priests to sacrifice themselves to the priesthood.

Searching for Intimate Communion

Since the Second Vatican Council, scholars have looked critically at the meanings variously ascribed to the Eucharist, often using biblical exegesis and historical analysis. Theologians such as Hans Küng reject the importance that the papacy gives to expiatory sacrifice. He argues that Jesus' "sacrifice" must in fact not be understood in the Old Testament or in the pagan sense. In the New Testament, sacrifice is not taken as a conciliatory influence, putting an angry demon into a good mood. It is humanity that has to be reconciled, not God.[40]

Indeed, the only New Testament book, namely, Hebrews, which mentions both priesthood and sacrifice, separates the lineage of Jesus from the Jewish priesthood and is about ending all sacrifice. In this book, the system of Levitical sacrificing is seen as obsolete, superseded by the eternal priesthood of Christ. For the "Son who has been made perfect for ever" (Heb. 7:28) has achieved eternal continuity with the Father, and there is neither need nor possibility of future sacrifices (Heb. 7:27, 9:25-26, 10:5-10, 12, 14, 18, 26).[41]

In the search for meaning, contemporary scholars have tended to focus on the Eucharist as a communal meal. John Dominic Crossan, for example, claims that Jesus advocated radical commensality or table fellowship.[42] Jesus reflected this in his own life by eating with people who were labelled by others as tax collectors, sinners, and whores, people who were regarded as ritually impure.

Christians are likewise challenged to dispose of discriminations and separations that vertically divide people into class or rank or categorize them through prejudice and bias: they are not to exclude sinners from their table. Moreover, the belief in the equality of all people is to be honoured and practised not just in the meal of thanksgiving—Eucharist—but also in society. We are called to love our neighbour in ways that dignify our brothers and sisters' humanity.

Such an egalitarian understanding of church threatens the concept of hierarchy. Egalitarianism asserts that all people are, in principle, equal and should enjoy equal social, religious, political, and economic rights and opportunities. This ideal is in stark contrast to the current organisation of the church that is ordered by a hierarchy sustained by compulsory celibacy.

The Vatican promotes the Eucharist as the means by which the unity of the church is best signified and brought about. Consequently, when priests celebrate the Eucharist, they are also acceding to the hierarchical order. Furthermore, because the papacy regards *the Eucharist as a sign of "unity achieved,"* as Fr. Simon explains, *it also uses the Eucharist as a moral judge of people's worthiness.* Thus Catholics, including priests with friends, who do not conform to the moral code, are officially rejected. In the church, sinners are in principle excluded from the eucharistic table.

Yet such exclusion may be illusory because it does not factor into the equation those priests who continue their ministry and enjoy friendships. As a result, the pope and his supporters' continuing insistence on the truthfulness of celibacy may undermine the universal church's mission to preach the Good News. After all, the same Eucharist that unites the church may also be that which divides it.

Priests with friends who have accepted their sexuality have had to question the idea of "the sacrifice that ended all sacrifice." Clearly, that has not been the case for them. The suffering these priests have experienced and the suffering they see being endured by their confreres does not resonate with the claims made by the papacy.

This has led to a change in appreciation of their worship, in which the "Sacrifice of the Mass" has gradually shifted to a "Thanksgiving (Eucharist)."[43] These priests find that sharing around a common table is an authentic expression of what they seek to express in their relationships, both intimate and otherwise. They seek to offer thanksgiving for the love and goodness that have come into their lives, and to give to others as they have received.

Eucharist then is a sign of "unity to be achieved" and, in consequence, is used to foster community ideals rather than as a judge of private facts, says Fr. Simon. By sharing in a communal meal, a community of persons is given the opportunity to work out and celebrate its beliefs and values in a mutual, equitable, and inclusive way. A priest in this situation therefore need not be judged on whether he is celibate or not; rather, he and others present determine how sexuality, whether expressed through celibacy or sexual intimacy, builds up the person within a socially beneficent community.

Sacrifice, however, is not totally subjugated as an ideal. According to Fr. Jean-Luc, *Jesus did not redeem us by dying on the cross for us, but his death was the outcome of the beliefs and positions he took in his living of life. If Jesus can be said to have "redeemed" us, it was by showing us the way to live, so that we can work for the Kingdom fearlessly, even though the cost might be great.*

Eucharist for Fr. Jean-Luc is a celebration of what is worthwhile in life. It is also about making sacrifices to pursue what is valuable and meaningful. Consequently, *I have no regrets about my rejection of celibacy as a lifestyle because I am convinced that it is contrary to natural justice to impose celibacy as a condition for being a priest, or as a condition for entering religious life.* By emphasising a person's right to be in a loving relationship, symbolised and ritualised through a sharing at table, sacrifice is given a fresh and complementary interpretation. In effect, sacrifice continues to be expressed in the service of those who desire to build relationships built on just principles.

The experience of loving friendship also shapes Fr. Matthew's understanding of the Eucharist. *To give you some background to who I am . . . well I'm a relatively newly ordained priest. I'm in my thirties and love so very dearly the precious gift of priesthood. However, I also value very dearly this wonderful and intimate relationship with someone. Naomi and I have been close friends for nearly ten years. I knew her before entering the seminary and have always kept her friendship close. She was overseas for a short time and came back to celebrate my diaconate but couldn't be there for my priestly ordination.*

We share a number of interests, and I have always felt at home in her company. Then one evening I simply saw her differently. I fell in love with her. Since then, we have sustained a deep, fulfilling, mutual relationship. Both of us have marvelled at and valued the gift we are to each other.

My relationship with God, well, it could not be closer, deeper, or more intimate. Naomi has opened my eyes to the essence of true love. Through her, I am able to experience so deeply the beauty of the intimate God that has coloured the essence of my existence. And so in turn I have been enabled to offer a God of truly unconditional love not just through cold words or black and white symbols but through an animated, integrated, intimate, personal experience and response in a richer and truer loving faith. I constantly thank God for the precious gifts of Naomi and priesthood. When I celebrate with the parish the Eucharist and other sacraments, I celebrate and experience the essence of intimate, true love.

For Fr. Matthew, God is ultimately concerned that a priest loves. This too is a concern of the papacy. But unlike the papacy, Fr. Matthew feels that the love received and given in a friendship does not compete with the love of God; rather, it highlights the *essence of intimate, true love.*

Sacred Bread, Sacred Body

For the most part, Fr. Isaac had not endured any particular hardship with celibacy in the nearly four decades of his priesthood. Nonetheless, a long-term acquaintance with Chloe developed into a sexual relationship. For Fr. Isaac, sexual intimacy was a revelation, which led him to reassess the Eucharist in light of his experience.

With the sacraments, it is touch and sign and symbol. Sexual intimacy is also touch and sign and symbol. The basis of the sacraments is Jesus, their life and source, and I think of touching the physicality of Jesus.

Before I can tell this, please realise that I was in my midsixties before I ever touched a woman's breasts and genitals. What I did may have been the actions of a twenty-year-old but I was doing this with the wisdom, knowledge, and religious attitude of a sixty-four-year-old priest. This difference is important.

The first time we were in the bedroom, in the first week of January, she stood naked before me and said, "I didn't give you a Christmas present so I want to give you the best gift I can give you, the gift of my own body." This is Eucharist—my body given for you. Kissing and sucking her nipples helped me to see a link with the spiritual drink of Eucharist.

I saw her vagina as sacred and holy, and I saw my penis as a sacred holy part of my body, and a gift from God. In the giving and receiving, I accepted this as being similar to the Eucharist. We talked about this, my friend and I, and we spoke about circumcision as the Jewish dedication to the Lord and the most evident sign of belonging to the community of God's people. Our lovemaking was our dedication, and this was a mutual interpretation. Sexual intimacy helped me to understand Eucharist, and Eucharist helped me to understand intimacy. For Chloe, our intimacy was a healing gift from God.

Fr. Isaac forges his understanding of this sacred sexual event from years of religious reflection and prayerful knowledge. He is able to reconcile sexual intimacy with the immanent presence of God in the Eucharist.

In the language of the eucharistic ritual—*my body . . . given . . . for you*—Fr. Isaac consecrates the gift of Chloe's body, which he considers holy, as he does his own body. He then equates her nurturing body with spiritual food and drink. This he receives with thanksgiving. Intercourse—*in the giving and receiving*—is also understood eucharisically as a gift that bonds the two lovers with God and with each other.

Moreover, Fr. Isaac brings to the fore a communal-meal sense of the Eucharist. This is not just a personal event but also a sacred event that has communal ramifications. Their sexual intimacy nourished them and brought them insight and healing. Such mutuality signifies a communal sharing in both sacred bodies and sacred bread.

Difficulties and Dreams

The policy of celibacy is being worn away by questions, anomalies, and contradictions, producing much instability. The resultant ideological struggle has the potential to split priests into opposing groups that could have as its consequence the downfall of the priesthood. This possibility is currently being fuelled by discontent, as is signalled in the stories of priests with friends, and spelt out by Fr. Jean-Luc: *there is a quiet groundswell of support for systemic change. We are becoming less willing to tolerate the present system and favour a more open style of leadership where celibacy is optional.*

The notions of sacrifice held by these priests are also in the process of shifting from "giving up" the possibility of intimate friendship to making sacrifices that seek to prioritise these relationships. Such understandings are further reflected in their emphasis on the Eucharist as a communal meal in which egalitarian commensality welcomes all. This suggests a nascent social order where church members are not separated by rank but constituted in equality, each being required to coexist, cooperate, and collaborate to form an inclusive community.

These divergent views have important ramifications for the priesthood and the church. Firstly, the experience of priests with friends is having a significant impact on the understanding of celibacy. An agreement between experience and faith ensures that they will continue to surrender themselves to a relevant and meaningful vision of God. That faith is not confined to individuals or particular groups; it is also a revelation that can order the broader Catholic community. A diversity of beliefs can therefore shape new understandings of the priesthood and church in general.

Secondly, the Vatican's ability to control and influence priests can only be sustained if local priests choose to continue to uphold its uniform policies. The existence of priests with friends suggests that this is not likely. These priests are not about to give up their relationships. Their sexually intimate friendships are becoming an unchangeable reality in their lives. Moreover, due to these priests' shift from a eucharistic emphasis on sacrifice to one of gathering for a communal meal, the religious and social basis for maintaining the celibate priesthood as favoured by the papacy appears to be fading. The maintenance of hierarchy sustained by sacrifice is gradually being recognised as a form of subordination that disadvantages their lives and the lives of those they care for.

Thirdly, the expressions of disapproval by Vatican officials about sexual pluralism within the priesthood will not make the problem go away. Reiteration only reminds priests of their insecure situation and discomfort, causing them to make up their own minds about celibacy and sexual intimacy. These priests are becoming less willing to sacrifice their sexuality to what Fr. Mark calls *the golden calf of celibacy*. In considering celibacy an idolatrous practise that distracts them from their mission, they seek appropriate ways to serve God and humankind.

Finally, priests with friends are aware that the responsibility for the unnecessary sacrifice of priests' sexuality lies with the papacy: *Literally, lives are at stake, but they are at stake because of the hierarchy's fear of doing anything to address the issues of celibacy for clergy*. Failure to acknowledge that responsibility is likely to create controversies that not even the papacy can imagine.

3

Open to Change

Fr. Daniel's experience is like many priests who have developed sexually intimate friendships. Before he fell in love, he had already travelled along a path that opened him to the possibility of such a friendship.

As a kid growing up, there were men and women like my Mum and Dad and other families. And then there was another group of people that were called priests and nuns. And they were holy people. They dressed differently. They lived a different style of life. They were closer to God than us. So, if you wanted to be really good, and holy and closer to God than other people you did what Sister said.

So if you came home from school with a note for being in trouble, then you would probably get another whack from your father or mother because you must have deserved it. Because Sister would always be right. Or whatever Father said was the absolute truth.

In this Catholic environment, importance was placed on loyalty to the church. Deference was given to both priest and bishop, and their judgements were to be trusted on almost every issue. Within the parish, the priest, the brothers, and the nuns acted as moral guardians and keepers of the faith.

Mum and Dad took the faith very seriously. In our home, daily personal prayer was encouraged through our parents' example, and we said the rosary most evenings. God was no stranger in our house, and the Catholic Church was fully embraced.

That belief was further exemplified in the hope of Fr. Daniel's parents that at least he or one of his brothers would join the priesthood. To have a priest in the family indicated that a family was specially blessed.

~~~

As a child, Fr. Daniel received a full Catholic education and during that period, he developed a genuine personal piety, including *a love of the Mass, the Blessed Sacrament, and a simple devotion to Our Lady.* He was also invited to be an altar boy, and this contributed to the germination of his idea to become a priest. His teachers further encouraged the notion, and he willingly accepted their direction: *I know my vocation had its beginnings in this positive atmosphere.*

Training for celibacy began early for Fr. Daniel. *Father wasn't like my Dad or anybody else. He was a man, but he was a different sort of man. He was asexual. And that was the same for nuns. That was my only way, I suppose, of trying to understand their difference. Mum and Dad had us kids and so did every other Mum and Dad around the place. But the priests and nuns didn't.*

Sex segregation at school also conditioned him for the future. Nuns staffed the primary school, while in high school single-sex schools prevailed in which religious brothers taught the boys. This pattern was further enforced amongst the students. *The brothers warned us about girls, and there were all sorts of rules forbidding us to associate with the girls from the convent school. So us boys would be into playing sport and studying. Girls really didn't figure in my life.*

Fr. Daniel summed up his youthful years by saying that he was *innocent, sometimes naive, now and again confused, often curious, but never scrupulous. I thank God that the adolescent turmoil of unruly feelings, masturbation, and excessive preoccupation with girls mainly passed me by.* His was a generally smooth sexual passage through adolescence, directed by the moral rigour of the church.

~~~

The young Daniel did well at school, and in a period where there was a high intake of vocations, his excellent academic record ensured that he would be thought of as a candidate for the priesthood. He subsequently entered a diocesan seminary, encouraged by his parish priest, a generous and warm character, who put a good word in for him to the bishop.

Having left his family, this youth entered into a regimented environment for seven years. *For the first few years, I slept in a dormitory with a dozen other men. And we had to study in the study hall; we couldn't study in our rooms. At night, one of the priests would come around with the torch and check that we were in our beds.*

Later in the major seminary, we all had private rooms with a hand-basin, robe and desk, and we studied in our rooms. But we were forbidden to go into each other's rooms. Though we did sometimes. I remember two of us were discussing something one night, and we heard one of the priests come in to check on everyone. So my visitor hid under the bed.

When the priest came in to say hello, he sat down on the bed with this guy underneath. Thinking "Oh God, . . ." we were sure that the priest knew he was there but was just making us sweat!

During his seminary years, Daniel's wardrobe consisted of black cassocks, black shoes, and a white clerical collar. The colour black served as a symbol of death to worldliness and to sexuality; conversely, the colour white symbolized purity, indeed, celibate purity. Another example of this separation from the world was reflected in the control of communications: newspapers and radios were excluded, letters were opened and screened by the rector, phone calls were limited, and familial contact was restricted even in the case of a family crisis.

A couple of years before I was ordained a priest, I was called into the president's office, . . . "Daniel, please sit down." And I sat down. "Daniel you have a sister." And he talked about her, and he talked about her having five young children, and then he said, "I'm afraid I have to tell you some bad news Daniel. Your sister was killed in a car accident this morning." And he told me the circumstances, and then after we talked about it for a little while, he said very considerately, "Well Daniel, I want you to consider this, I want to know whether there's any reason that makes it imperative that you go home." I said, "No, Father." So I went back to choir practice.

Another calamity unfolded within the seminary. One of Daniel's fellow seminarians had tried to tame his sexuality by castrating himself. The botched operation led to massive bleeding. He was whisked away to a hospital, never to be seen again. Daniel confided that he had himself used his pyjama strings for the same reason.

Daniel's life essentially revolved around a regulated and monitored pattern of community prayer, study, and exercise: *especially sport, which was my salvation.* But forming close friendships, customarily referred to as "particular friendships," was frowned upon.

If you were seen associating with one person exclusively, one of the staff would say that you need to widen your range of friends because it was perceived as perhaps entering into a semi- or close homosexual type of relationship.

There was also a total absence of women. So our whole ability to relate as a normal young male to a young woman just didn't happen. The only people you ever related to were people of your own sex: males. The only women we had were the nuns who cooked for us, and they were very remote.

The temptations of women were also addressed through adages such as, *keep guard on your heart, and you will not stray,* and *numquam solus cum sola* (never one male alone with one female). One spiritual director advised Daniel and his fellow seminarians: *If you see a very beautiful woman and she tempts you, look around for her mother. That's what she'll become.* Another told them, when feeling tempted, to think of women as *rotting flesh.*

Other adages further underscored deference and uniformity: *be all things to all people; conceal what you feel; keep the rule and the rule will keep you.* Such thinking reveals past thinking about man-woman friendship and intimacy in the life of a priest: *Intimacy in those days only meant being naughty.*

Opposition to close friendships between confreres ensured control of seminarians. As individuals, their sexual energies were harnessed for priesthood and their isolated priestly character ensured there would be no banding together that would challenge ecclesiastical authority.

⌇

While the slur of particular friendships officially ceased to be part of seminary life after 1968, the atmosphere of caution still lingered. Fr. Simon, for example, was *taught Jesus had a special friendship with John, the Beloved Disciple, and with Mary Magdalene, and this was considered natural and healthy. But we were warned that friendship was not to be possessive or exclusive. In other words, don't make third parties feel rejected or left out.* This proved to be the essential challenge to a seminarian's impending commitment to celibacy.

Our understanding of love toward another person didn't allow for exclusive love. And besides, I was becoming aware of a strong homosexual strain in my makeup, though THAT was well and truly repressed, I can tell you. Nothing was taught about homosexuality.

Interestingly, I had my first "in-your-face" encounter with my own homosexuality in my last year at the seminary. There was a priest in the seminary who was quite clearly homosexual. My reaction was to run from the massive challenge that his very presence posed for me (Years later, when I finally came to encounter my homosexual orientation, I did wonder whether I had unconsciously opted for priesthood because it might be a way of "dealing with" my sexuality without having to face it directly. But in the years leading up immediately to priesthood, I was not consciously moved to take on priesthood to cope with my homosexuality.) At that time, I considered that ALL sexuality was a no-go area for me as a man who was trying to prepare myself for a vow of chastity. The initial decision and the earlier years were motivated almost exclusively by a desire to offer myself for service within the church. I wanted to be a priest and celibacy was part of the deal.

Fr. Daniel and Fr. Simon both aspired to a life of holiness and service. Priesthood was therefore a very desirable profession, offering opportunities of ministry, status, and a lifestyle that they would not otherwise have had.

Questioning Celibacy

When Fr. Daniel was newly ordained, he was sent to a parish to assist a senior parish priest, but again his life was supervised both publicly and privately. As a neophyte priest, he experienced an initial sense of disappointment. *Eager to roll up our sleeves, and get right into the Lord's vineyard, I became, instead, a junior at the bottom of the hierarchical heap in the home of an elderly priest.*

In this milieu, Fr. Daniel also came to a new understanding of celibacy. *Gradually the whole of what celibacy meant was realized. It was not about consecration of your life, or commitment of your life to the church and God, rather, celibacy brought about a sense of loneliness. And I think that is why I would start to fall in love and all of a sudden I would say, "Oh no, this can't happen."*

I related fairly well to women, but if it started to get more intimate, I would pull down the shutters, and they would be just left out in the cold. Somebody said years ago that it would be better to kiss a fridge than kiss me. I was a sort of consecrated refrigerator. The tragedy though is that I would have hurt a number of women during those early years. Looking back, my ministry to women must have also been severely hampered.

Fr. Daniel had been trained in the "good Father" image, a loyal and obedient priest of the church. But his experiences reflected a mismatch between what he had learnt in the seminary and what he was encountering in the priesthood. The image of a priest giving total service was contradicted by consequences that had not been earlier imagined. Previously unknown emotions surfaced, including loneliness and sexual desire, sometimes leaving him feeling powerless and confused with needs of his own that he could not assuage.

These dilemmas were also compounded by a change in the climate of the church. As mentioned in chapter 2, the Second Vatican Council endeavoured to modernise the church. Priests were now encouraged to be open to these internal changes and to engage with the outside world, but such a turnaround made it difficult for significant numbers of priests to observe celibacy.

Fr. Daniel gradually became aware of the massive exodus of priests from the priesthood. *Guys I went through the seminary with were leaving the priesthood. Now I said, "What's going on? Why them and not me?" You started to question not only your ministry but your whole personal approach to life.*

He also started to question the hierarchical order of the church, which he now thought *had an enormous bureaucracy, the Vatican Curia—and I was expected to exercise authority in the name of the bishop and the pope. So I started to object to it, revolt against it.*

~

Fr. Marcus also had to cope with this change. As a seminary professor during that period, he taught much the same things that he had been taught, but he was challenged by some of his students. *They pressured me to think more deeply about many things, about some dogmas, and about relationships.*

He especially considered the argument that suggests that *we can love everyone in general if we love no one in particular. It is however countered by the observation that we all build an inner circle of friends with different levels of intimacy and trust. If we do not have these, generally we don't have companions either. Special relationships usually help rather than hinder other relationships. Then it is put that we can have particular friends and intimacy, but should refrain from sexual expression. But this counsel only makes sense if we establish that there is some valid reason to abstain from sexual expression. Is there something wrong with it? No one wants to say this nowadays. If not, then why exclude it? In fact, we often hear that the best way for sexuality to find its proper expression is for it to be grounded in one relationship rather than in many or none. In these circumstances, the condition of being denied legitimate expression has priests feeling more disadvantaged than advantaged. They are in the silly position of being expected to understand sexuality without experience. It is one reason why many are inclined to do their own research.*[1]

Some years later, Fr. Marcus lectured some nuns: *It was the first time that women became important in my life; they contributed to much that I could not have thought of, complementing the things that I wanted to say. I had to admit that for a certain wholeness in my life—I needed women!*

Events followed, and he lost his *fear* of women: *I have tried to bring them into my life, knowing that I could only benefit.* Fr. Marcus then met a woman with whom he *now enjoys a special sexual relationship.*

Significant numbers of priests experienced considerable turmoil in the postconciliar church and continue to do so. These priests have reappraised their celibacy in light of their experiences and, consequently, they have shifted to a position where they disapprove of the way the Vatican administers control and exercises authority in the church. This includes the enforcement of celibacy.

Officially, Love Is Conditional

The centralised authority of the church means that the pope and the curia are able to control the meaning of celibacy. Without regard to the viewpoints of priests, and unwilling to give appropriate attention to the effects of their policies, they argue from stereotypes to ensure that celibacy is publicly maintained.

This is demonstrated in the document *I Will Give You Shepherds* in which the pope reduces love to his own basic formulation, neatly fitting his preference for celibacy. According to the pope, "without love. . . life is meaningless." Such love "involves the entire person," and can be expressed in the "'nuptial meaning' of the human body, thanks to which a person gives oneself to another and takes the other to oneself."[2] The pope asserts that sexual love can only be properly expressed in marriage. This view is reinforced by his condemnation of "a widespread social and cultural atmosphere, which 'largely reduces human sexuality to the level of something commonplace, since it interprets and lives it in a reductive and impoverished way by linking it solely with the body and with selfish pleasure.'"[3] Sexual expression outside marriage is deemed unacceptable; it has no place in the pope's belief system.

Nevertheless, the pope asserts that a priest is required to love and be loved with an "affective maturity which is prudent, able to renounce *anything* that is a threat to [his celibacy]" (emphasis added).[4] A priest can have a "true friendship" as long as it does not detract from his celibacy. But, in the case where obedience is threatened, a priest is required "to fight and overcome . . . selfishness and individualism," and as curative to this threat, a priest must submit himself "to a suitable education to true friendship."[5] The pope's notion of love is used to support celibacy, and vice versa. Anything that tarnishes this practise is renounced.

However, *anything* can include a priest's love for his friend, and the friend as well. The pope reduces a priest's friend to an object, while his affection for his friend is discredited and dismissed as a distraction to his love of God. The pope is unable to accommodate the idea that a "true friendship" could be nurtured and nourished by sexual intimacy or can enhance a priest's relationship with God. Consequently, he is able to maintain a position that seems dispassionately objective, a stance that erases any alternative understandings of love that may be held by priests with friends.

Unofficially, Vatican representatives also offer blunt comments about priests who do not practice celibacy: "There are some priests who, probably as the Lord said, entered, not through the front door, but through the back door. They were not really called to the priesthood."[6] Behind the official façade of celibacy, prejudices are unmasked in blatant condescension and contempt. Priesthood, in the papacy's view, is synonymous with celibacy. Any other sexual state is considered deceitful and profane, a condition that seemingly invalidates priesthood for the individual concerned.

In the case where a priest asserts that celibacy should be made optional or that sexual intimacy is a grace, the pope is able to criticise this dissident by asserting that such a person is "acting against the will of Christ . . . [for] in reality, the church as mystery is not 'ours' but 'His.'"[7] In effect, the pope and the curia harness the divine to their own belief in celibacy by assuming that they state the absolute and eternal will of God; the corollary being that priests with friends do not, for they have failed to plumb the mysterious depths of celibacy. Belief, after all, is not based upon superrational understanding but on trust that does not always yield answers. Vatican opinion therefore holds that humankind always has something to learn about celibacy and that no one knows all about its practise, and never will.

Furthermore, when the papacy uses the strategy of mystery, it reduces other arguments to nonsense, and proffers in its place arcane knowledge. Such knowledge is inexplicable and secret. Only Vatican officials can know the will of God, which they determine to be for celibacy.

For many people, the belief system of the papacy, wedded to such arcane and abstract concepts of celibacy, is quite inadequate. In contrast, the belief system of priests with friends is formed by their experience of relationships. Such experience yields thoughts, feelings, images, and intuitions about the presence and guidance of God in their lives and ministry. Thus, the "mystery" of celibacy and the rejection of sexual intimacy by church authorities are simply explained: it is about the papacy wanting to maintain vested interests.

A Critique of Canon Law

Canon law is generally understood as being a means to shore up the social design demanded by God for the church. Such a law is intended to bring the community together so that the Spirit might hold it in unity. That law is also designed on an idea of ordered reason, and duly promulgated by the one who is in charge of the community, namely, the pope.

In this collective scenario, the pope and God are effectively aligned with each other, creating a powerful force that brooks no challenge. Whilst at best these canon laws are supposed to benefit all in the church, in reality they often serve the papacy, upholding its own beliefs at the expense of local needs and personal ethics.

In the documents of the Second Vatican Council, celibacy is referred to as a discipline and is therefore not demanded by the very nature of priesthood.[8] Yet the papacy absolutises celibacy in canon law, particularly canon 277, and thus effectively negates any objections to its arbitrary character.

The overarching effect of this law makes celibacy appear essential to the priesthood and, as well, ensures formal observance and public enforcement. In effect, canon law ensures that sexual deviance is locally policed and rectified. The purposes of the Vatican are therefore fulfilled, for the law promotes celibacy as being necessary for social order in the church.

Despite the best efforts of Vatican officials to promote celibacy, the crossing of the celibate-sexual boundaries is certain to continue. This is most likely to occur more obviously in democratic countries, where much of the impetus for reform of celibacy has been expressed. Democracy has germinated favourable conditions for personal autonomy and local determinations over universal values and the ethic of dominance. In its emphasis on the equality and respect for the individual within the community, it is to be expected that it will further undermine the foundations of compulsory celibacy.

However, given the top-heavy allocation of power and resources in the church, reformers may be required to expend considerable energy and to make huge sacrifices to bring about other forms of sexual practise in the priesthood. Meanwhile, celibacy continues to exist, but it is not the same celibacy that the papacy promulgates. Rather, the practise is governed by priests' definitions that embrace diverse sexual behaviours in the priesthood, some of which could eventually become acceptable to the church.

Media and Dissent

The papacy faces an enormous challenge in maintaining celibacy, for the erosion of faith in this practise is also being fuelled by the secular media. Before the 1970s, the film industry seldom portrayed a priest in anything other than a heroic or saintly guise, and the best-known images included such near-hagiography as *The Keys of the Kingdom, Going My Way, Boys Town, The Bells of St. Mary's,* and *Angels with Dirty Faces,* all made between 1938 and 1944.[9] This deferential attitude reflected concern about offending powerful interests in the church.

Similarly, the media exercised considerable restraint in investigating or reporting news stories that involved scandals in the church. To reveal the shortcomings of a priest was akin to blasphemy in the eyes of diocesan officials and they were ever vigilant against such disclosures. These Catholic watchdogs also had the ability to exercise sanctions if the code of silence was broken, including withdrawal of advertising, loss of circulation, and revenue.[10]

A change in media representations of the priesthood began to occur in the mid- to late seventies. This change in media values was due in part to the influence of international media magnates who encouraged a shift towards sensationalist coverage in tabloid television news and prurient talk shows, fanning peoples' interest in the sexuality of priests. Once taboos limiting attacks on the church were lifted, the media realised that reprisals were no longer as severe as they had been, and that exposure did not in itself conspicuously offend public taste.[11] *The Thorn Birds,* the 1977 novel that was an international best-seller and was later made into a TV miniseries that proved immensely popular, further illustrates this change. The sexuality of priests is also the theme of films such as *Monsignor* (1982) and *Agnes of God* (1985). In the 1990s, these sexual themes became more explicitly expressed in the film *Priest* (1995).

During the 1970s and early 1980s, secular and independent Catholic newspapers also began to cover stories of sexual abuse by priests and newsworthy tales about priests and bishops, especially those who renounced celibacy. A recent and prominent case is that of Emmanuel Milingo, archbishop emeritus of Lusaka, Zambia, who married a forty-three-year old Korean acupuncturist in a widely publicised group wedding led by Reverend Sun Myung Moon in May 2001. He later ended his marriage and returned to the church, events that have been equally publicised.

In recent years, the global media has given massive exposure to multiple sexual abuse claims and the mishandling of these cases by certain bishops and cardinals. This has further increased the level of criticism given to celibacy. These revelations of fact and fiction reduce the mystique of celibacy, diminishing the religious and social expectations for priests to be celibate.

Some Catholic reform movements further undermine compulsory celibacy. Priests who have left the official ministry promote one such movement. During the mid-1970s, some of these priests began to resist the demands for silence and anonymity placed on them by the papacy of Paul VI, followed by that of John Paul II. The policy of forbidding such men from being publicly involved in Catholic institutions, and insisting that they move away from the places where they were known to be priests, created conditions that led them to believe that they were isolated in their struggle to leave the priesthood.[12] However, as local support groups were organised, followed by the emergence of national groups, this sense of isolation gave way to an awareness that they shared in a worldwide predicament.

In 1986, the International Federation of Married Catholic Priests (IFMCP) was convened, which, in turn, successfully encouraged the organisation of new national groups. These national bodies, as well as the IFMCP, publish newsletters to promote changes in the law of celibacy and to organise events and create forums to promote their cause.

More recently, the IFMCP has begun to liaise with other well-organized and well-resourced reform groups such as "We Are the Church," "Call to Action," "FutureChurch," "Association for the Rights of Catholics in the Church," "Women's Ordination Worldwide," "Catholics for Free Choice," and "Communidades de Base."[13] In networking with each other, these Catholics, priest and lay alike, are endeavouring to bring about a church that is structurally decentralised, more open to contemporary understandings of sexuality, and one that does not insist on compulsory celibacy.

There are also individual priests who have left the official priesthood and have found ways to creatively engage in the celibacy debate. For instance, the following priests have published their autobiographies. David Mackay's three-part roman à clef *In Memoriam J.N.A.R* reflects on his life as a homosexual priest in Africa.[14] Jim Madden, the founder of Epiphany, Australia, an affiliate of the IFMCP, has also written an account of his priesthood.[15] The biographies and autobiographies of friends of priests are also in circulation.[16]

Other priests who have left the ranks of the clergy have used their professions to further the debate on celibacy. David Rice, a former priest and investigative journalist, reported the global phenomenon of resigned priests.[17] Richard Sipe, a psychotherapist, published his study based upon interviews with, and reports from, fifteen hundred people who have firsthand knowledge of the sexual/celibate adjustment of priests.[18]

As well, dissident theologians, many of whom criticise the sexual policies of the Vatican, promote their works through various media. Listed in Paul Collins's book *From Inquisition to Freedom* (2001) are seven prominent Catholics priests and religious sisters who have undergone examination by the Congregation for the Doctrine of Faith over issues that relate directly or indirectly to sexuality.

The Internet further contributes to wearing away people's belief in celibacy by providing a level playing field for those Catholics who wish to promote their disparate ideologies. While the papacy also asserts its ideology by using these diverse media, it must compete with others in these fields. Thus, the contest over celibacy continues to ensure that rather than being unquestionably accepted, it remains an ideal, one option amongst many that is promoted in cinema, print, television, and cyberspace.

The use of the media by dissident individuals and groups has contributed to uncovering the stereotype of celibacy to such an extent that significant numbers of Catholics no longer give broad social approval to its practice. For example, in a six-nation study conducted circa 1998, the majority signified that they would favour married priests: Spain 79 percent, Ireland 82 percent, the United States 69 percent, Italy 67 percent, Poland 50 percent, and the Philippines 21 percent.[19] In 1994, another survey was conducted in the United States and Canada. Less than one-third of the respondents agreed with the view that priests should be required to live a celibate life.[20]

Once upon a time, the idea of reforming celibacy was so unthinkable that the Catholic population would not speak of it. Yet now the idea has become widely accepted.

Problems of Disclosure

Despite the breakdown in the belief that priests should be obliged to live celibate lives, those who have already made changes in their own lives are not in a position to disclose their friendships. These priests continue to be constrained by Vatican controls, as well as by clericalism. Clericalism is principally concerned with maintaining the distinction between clergy and laity and putting the interests of celibate priests before others in the church. In doing so, it denies alternative perspectives and loathes criticism, leaving it defensive and self-protective.[21]

Some priests who do consider disclosing news of their friendships are faced with key issues, such as their sexual orientation. This was the case for Fr. Simon. For years he simply didn't bother with general questions about his homosexuality, but this had unwanted consequences. *In shutting off from the personal, I completely repressed emotional expression (with the exception of anger) for many years. I could laugh but not cry, become angry but never show fear, and partly, by way of compensation, I developed a cynical shell and an ability to exercise an absolutely biting tongue—a sort of defence and distancing mechanism.*

After several decades, I became friends with a confrere who helped me to deal with the effects of years of emotional repression and denial: his warm encouragement of my stumbling efforts to grow and his confrontation of my reticence to face areas of need in my life have pushed that growth on remarkably. Then two women friends of great insight helped me to clarify and tighten up thoughts about my own inner journey. They also helped me to loosen up with respect to expressions of familiarity and intimacy. By that, I don't mean cheeky greetings when meeting, or genital intimacy. Rather, I mean easily taking up conversation with them, and later, we would hug and/or kiss in ways that were appropriate signs of affection between us.

Later, Fr. Simon decided to disclose to his religious order the fact that he was gay. This revelation brought unexpected consequences.

Having "come out" to my religious superiors as a gay man, I was quickly made aware that any trust they had previously put in me had evaporated—overnight, as it were. The ministry I was now to be engaged in was hedged around with conditions about, for example, being in every night by 6:00 pm, not being given any money for bus/train fares, formal fortnightly reports to the local superior detailing what I was doing—and so on. My conscious thought was, "When my honesty and sexual integrity were not declared, I was given major responsibilities for administration and finance as well as great freedom. Now that I have been honest and adult, I am being punished, treated like an irresponsible boy."

In the priesthood, clericalism encourages a code of silence with respect to the homosexual orientation of priests. Because homosexual persons are suspect, they are dissuaded from declaring their sexual orientation (a subject that is discussed further in chapter 6). In addition, because the hierarchical structure keeps priests independent from other priests, any possibility of formal support and overt compassion by confreres is suspended.

When it comes to revealing secret information about one's self, a priest may also need to take into consideration the stance his particular bishop or provincial takes on celibacy. One such priest is under the impression *that most priests who are not happy with the situation of celibacy simply do what they believe is appropriate, but do not discuss it much with others. It seems clear in this archdiocese that any priest who publicly announced that he had any intimate relationship with a woman would be immediately suspended. The archbishop made that clear in an interview with a confrere who was thinking of resigning from the ministry. To speak out would mean priestly suicide!*

Similarly, another priest reports that his bishop has launched a witch-hunt for any priest who might not be practising celibacy and furthermore, any priest who was known to be homosexual *would be got rid of.*

However, this stance is not universal amongst bishops. One priest who shared some news of his friendship with his bishop indicated that the bishop was also enduring difficulties: *he's paining too; he can see the pain of what is happening.* Not only do some bishops struggle with celibacy themselves, they also feel powerless to do anything for their confreres at an official level. These bishops are convinced they will not be respectfully listened to, and they fear being chastised by their fellow bishops and the consequences that go with such a reprimand.

Nonetheless, a few bishops do exercise power at the local level in discreet and considerate ways. If, for example, a priest is careful about his friendship or is homosexual, the relationship or orientation may be overlooked. After all, the issue is not what does or does not happen in the priesthood, but rather what appears to be seemly.

Behind this ruse lies the pragmatics of realpolitik. One consideration might be that bishops count these priests amongst their closest friends, as is the case for Fr. Jordan: *The arch knows about Tabatha and me. He's not happy about it, but he lets us be. He basically pretends our relationship doesn't exist, even though he is fully aware that it does exist.* By refusing to recognize the loving friendship of his confrere, this archbishop obviates the necessity for taking action, thus maintaining a trusted friend and an experienced parish priest—both valued commodities in today's priesthood and church.

***

Disclosure may be further inhibited by a complex set of dynamics. Fr. Nathaniel made a list of reasons why he does not speak about his intimate friendship,

a) Guilt;
b) Concern for protecting privacy/confidentiality of my friend;
c) Sharing about my "successful" relationship will only make my priest mates jealous;
d) Sharing about my "failures" will discourage and disappoint them;
e) Others don't share very much with me, and so if I share my story they may feel pressured to reciprocate.

Fr. Nathaniel is conscious of wrongdoing as evidenced by his admission of guilt and is additionally concerned that there might be sanctions levelled at his friend. This priest also responds to the agendas of different groups of priests by describing his relationship as both a success and a failure. Given the problems and politics of sharing news of his friendship, Fr. Nathaniel concludes that nondisclosure is a characteristic of the priesthood and chooses to take shelter in the culture of secrecy.

Fr. Mark, on the other hand, feels there are different reasons as to why priests don't talk about celibacy, sexuality, and their friendships.

My confreres and I have been playing golf for nearly thirty years and we never speak to each other about real concerns: about life, about how we're going, or the pain we're suffering, or about loneliness, or how we combat loneliness. We can talk about football, golf, or cricket until the cows come home, but never about ourselves.

The unspoken rules of silence and secrecy are also echoed in the thoughts of Fr. Pierre: *It is rather difficult to become good friends with other priests, for they were trained in much the same way as I. While there are times when we do share some deep moments, we never really pour ourselves out completely to others. We don't share vulnerability. And even if a priest would like to share his human frailty with other priests, often he doesn't know how or where to begin. I would have seen myself as one of this type of priest until I decided that I **had** to share my problems with another priest.*

Ingrained forces of yesteryear, ideological pressures of the present, the negation or denial of personhood, an inability to share details of the inner self, and fear of sanctions appear to prevent priests from talking about their difficulties with celibacy.

⌐⌐

As Fr. Pierre mentioned, he felt compelled to share his story, but he considers himself lucky to find confreres who are prepared to listen. *One of these has walked with me through a great deal of pain and anguish—and I'd walk through fire for him! These men have cared for me as I do for them in a truly "brotherly" manner and I regard their friendship as a wonderful blessing.*

Fr. Matthew (whom we met in chapter 2) was not so fortunate with his selection of clerical confidantes.

Some priests have really brought down the letter of the law and have reinforced the fact that I am ". . . therefore bound to celibacy" (canon 277). To them it seems that an intimate relationship would only "eat away" at my priesthood, and so only "lead to scandal of the faithful" (canon 277.2). Then there are those who simply believe I am endangering the talents, gifts, and blessings that God has bestowed on me. In these few, there is no concept of an enrichment of these gifts.

His confreres deny him an opportunity to put forward a positive view of his friendship with Naomi. They have on their side the weight of doctrine and canon law. Fr. Matthew only has experience, a knowledge that is discounted by his confreres and by the papacy. As a result, the choices of Fr. Matthew are limited. He can either end the relationship or foster it under a shroud of silence and a veil of secrecy.

In contrast, when Fr. Thomas shared news of his friendship with his confrere, he found that he was permitted to have a relationship until he mentioned that he was thinking about leaving the priesthood and marrying.

The mistake I had made was to continue what should have been only an affair. When I stressed that I actually preferred to marry, he thought it ludicrous that I would think such a thing. How could I abandon priesthood for that? How could I let myself be tied to someone who would restrict my freedom and "spend all her time talking about her varicose veins." When I said I resented having to make the choice between priesthood and marriage, he was not interested in arguing the issue because the rule would not change in our lifetime. So his position was that I get rid of her and he would support me, or else I could do something silly and leave.[22]

Celibacy is maintained by many formal and informal rules that rigidly control what a priest says and does; hence, the majority of priests do not disclose their friendships. However, for a priest who does tell, he must rely on the continual charity and understanding of his confreres, bishop, or provincial. Yet any disclosure remains risky, for sometimes a priest is unaware of the informal rules or the level of attachment a confrere may have to celibacy.

Consequently, bishops and priests who do desire reform of celibacy find themselves *between a rock and a hard place.* They cannot afford to admit to the Vatican that there are internal disunities within the priesthood. Yet their refusal to acknowledge such fissures diminishes their credibility within the church. Nonetheless, these clerics continue to invest in the official rhetoric of celibacy because it is crucial for their respective episcopal and priestly survival—an action that is supported by another informal rule of the priesthood: *you should never crap in your own nest.* In refusing to crap in each other's nests, certain bishops and priests are able to maintain their privileges and prerogatives and their friendships as well.

The Pope's Policemen

At the parish level, there exist self-appointed custodians of priests' celibacy who are sometimes referred to as *the Pope's Policemen, the God Squad, the Catholic Mafia, God's Gestapo* and, more recently, *the Catholic Taliban.* These parishioners keep watch over their local priest and threaten social and political violence if he fails to comply with their rigid expectations of how he should conduct his life and ministry.

Such expectations are generally coupled with various self-interests, including the maintenance of religious security, social status, economic privilege, and political favour, each of which could be eroded if the reputation of their priest becomes tarnished. As well, these custodians often assume, or do have intimate knowledge of the everyday comings and goings of their priest. This privileged association ensures that these people will have a share in the priest's harvest of rewards.

Fr. Elisha lives in the same town as his sisters, Mary and Martha. These sisters constantly police those who provide their brother with domestic service and who come into his social and religious circle. They were therefore none too impressed when an attractive divorcée began to work in the parish and later started to enjoy their brother's company on a regular basis.

The sisters felt some anxiety about this situation. They felt they could no longer visit the presbytery as freely as they once had. Nor did it appear that they were being listened to in the same way. Whereas, "she" was being allowed into his home, and he seemed to frequently seek advice from her on parish and other matters.

Mary and Martha became so threatened by the newly acquired friendship of their brother that they started to voice their concerns to others: "she" goes shopping for him; "she's" been seen walking with him. And so the seeds of disfavour were sown. Those who listened to the gossip also had investments in the previous arrangement and "the news" spread to such an extent that it inhibited the ability of the woman to work within the parish.

Then one day, the constraint took on another dimension. The sisters and a few other parishioners approached Fr. Elisha with "the problem" of his "affair." This was news to Fr. Elisha, and not being able to get over the shock of such vehement accusations, he was forced to suspend the relationship with his friend. This reinstated his celibate reputation but the previous set of relationships with his sisters and particular parishioners could not be fully restored because he felt betrayed by their actions.

Mary and Martha were envious of Fr. Elisha's association with the parish worker because it eroded their own exclusive position in his life. As a result, his sisters decided to denigrate the achievements of the woman and make disparaging remarks about her being divorced.

For a while, the sisters felt a sense of power over their brother and over the parish worker, and experienced a temporary bonding with their listeners. But, in gossiping, they avoided having to face serious issues within themselves. They did not ask critical questions about their motivations and prejudices. They also failed to speak to their brother and priest and to share their concerns and difficulties. The effects of their gossip were, however, disastrous for all concerned. Fr. Elisha was forced to put on hold a friendship that he valued, and the ministry and reputation of the woman were damaged.

Gossip intensifies in times of cultural upheaval or chaos. Once social order disintegrates, people are no longer clear about their identity and place, and so they must compete for status and power. Gossip is one way for them to achieve, at least fleetingly, personal well-being and superiority.[23] The current social disorder in the church provides such an environment in which gossip can flourish. In this scenario, the gossip discouraged Fr. Elisha and left him unable to challenge the behaviour of his sisters and particular parishioners. Neither was he able to assess his relationship with the parish worker without fear of negative consequences. His assent to their gossip also made the woman a scapegoat. In consequence, everything changed, yet nothing changed, because serious questions about celibacy and the social relationships that it engenders remained unanswered.

~

Some priests with friends feel considerably constrained by what the laity thinks, as does Fr. Aaron: *I worry about what my lay colleagues know of my relationship. I treasure my friendship—but in this atmosphere, I feel so constrained to act in the "expected way" —I feel really dehumanised by it all—I can't be myself. I'm living a celibate life because it's demanded of me, not because I now choose it.*

Essentially, the expectations of the laity restrict Fr. Aaron to the practise of a particular version of celibacy, one that upholds the public appearance of singleness, whilst in his private life, he considers himself a part of a loving and committed relationship. Such priests retain a burden of frustration that they are unable to resolve.

Yet, some family members and lay friends appear to be reassessing the intimate friendship of their priest, viewing it as beneficial to his life and ministry. This new perspective is frequently in tandem with their changing views of the church. This is apparent in Fr. Joshua's comments:

Some friends consider my friendship with Susan as healthy. They see her as my source of support and encouragement, which she is. I don't think I could live without her. Of course, a lot of my friends would say go and get married. Even my family would say that. But I like ministering to others, and I thoroughly enjoy what I do, even though I've got problems with some of the church's teachings. The trouble with the church is that it makes you buy the whole package.

The friends and family of this priest do not buy the whole package either and are convinced that Fr. Joshua would be well served if he were to marry his friend. *Right now, my relationship is the biggest issue in my life. I can't see why I can't function as a priest and as a married person. I would have a lot of stress taken out of my life, I can tell you that, just to have a friend or a partner on an everyday basis.*

~~~

Some priests feel compelled to make a choice between priesthood and their friendships, as was the case for Fr. Mahlon. The following is a brief record of his resignation.

At the weekend Masses, a parish councilor briefly announced that Fr. Mahlon was finishing his ministry in the parish and would not be returning. He would also like to make an address to the parish at an open meeting on Sunday evening to notify the parish personally and officially of his decision.

A parish meeting was held on Sunday evening, which was attended by more than three hundred fifty parishioners. When Fr. Mahlon entered with the parish council chairperson, he was given a standing ovation. Fr. Mahlon's letter was then distributed and read:

My dear friends and fellow parishioners,

It is with a heavy heart that I announce to you that I am no longer the pastor of our parish. I took the decision to approach the archbishop seeking leave of absence from the active ministry. I agreed with him that for the sake of the parish community, as well as for my own sake, the best course of action is to step down immediately. I wanted to personally inform you of my decision, as well as to be very clear about the reasons behind it.

The reasons behind my decision are deeply personal. I have loved the ministry of priest and believe I have exercised it with a degree of effectiveness. The church and its mission have been a major part of my life over the eighteen years since beginning at the seminary. But it has not been the only part of my life. I find myself in good faith not being able to live life as a priest in the manner the church expects. I know I cannot live the rest of my life alone. I yearn for the meaning and support that a relationship with a "special other" can bring; a richness that many of you experience in your marriages. However, I understand this is incompatible with the church's discipline of celibacy, and because I acknowledge and respect the church's authority to regulate these matters, I step down.

I know my decision has consequences far beyond my own self, and that there will be repercussions in parish life for some time. I am sorry to put you through this; it is not my intention, but as an outcome, it is inevitable. I know you well enough to have every confidence that you will be able to regroup and build on the good work we have accomplished together. In time, the archbishop will appoint a new pastor for this parish community. I know you will lend him the same enthusiastic and sensitive support that you have given me over these nearly five years. At this significant personal moment allow me to express my gratitude for the excellent opportunities and privileges I have been afforded, not only here in this parish, but over the nearly two decades I spent within the church. I consider myself a very fortunate person indeed.

I now move on to seek a new "expression of myself in the world." There is so much I will miss, as there is so much waiting to be discovered. I wish you well and God's blessings in your endeavours. I would be grateful for an occasional remembrance in your prayers. And so now as your pastor, I say goodbye.

A number of parishioners replied (a travelling microphone was available). The main response was one of warm understanding and acceptance of Fr. Mahlon's decision; also, appreciation of what he had brought to the parish community and given to people individually. The meeting affirmed his decision, but it also assured him that he would always be welcomed back.

The parish response to Fr. Mahlon's departure highlights the difficulties that some laypersons are experiencing with celibacy. These people, who have been the conventional custodians of their parish priest's celibacy, are slowly changing their understanding and becoming aware of a complex set of variables that they have not previously considered.

Celibacy is proving very costly because it is creating increasing tension among those who are the most loyal and committed members of the church. These people, who have continued to spiritually, socially, and financially support the church, are finding less satisfaction and insufficient returns for their involvement. Not only are their relationships with particular priests being jeopardised, they are also losing quality pastors. With no concessions in sight, the interests of these people may now lie in pressing for reform of the celibacy law.

The Pope: A Force to Be Reckoned With

By asserting that celibacy is willed by God and by inculcating this practice into centralist policies, the papacy is able to exercise enormous control over the church.

The extent of that control is well articulated by Thomas Reese. "The papacy touches the moral and spiritual lives of millions of people through the pope's pastoral visits to scores of countries, his comprehensive teachings on doctrine and morals, his appointment of bishops, and his supervision of local churches. His decisions can foster unity in a multinational and multicultural church by reminding far-flung local churches that they are part of one communion. His decisions can also divide the church when he insists on teachings or practices that alienate or polarise the faithful. . . . As the leader of this constituency, he is a force to be reckoned with."[24]

That force also enables the papacy to demand that priests submit to celibacy, at least publicly, and expect broad agreement by the global Catholic community. In doing so, Vatican officials deny collective responsibility for a celibate priesthood. Synods, conferences, and diocesan and parish meetings are not deemed suitable avenues for attending to problems relating to celibacy.

Thus the convention of celibacy is maintained, and papal influence continues to permeate the local church. Despite consistent and studious criticism of celibacy and popular dissent, the Vatican remains unyielding.

The Vatican shrewdly uses various strategies to dampen the effects of dissent. For instance, it occasionally suggests that celibacy is of secondary importance. This is evident when it states that celibacy does not belong to the essence of priesthood.[25] Then there are the extended periods of public silence on the issue, again suggesting the unimportance of celibacy.

Yet, within the realm of policy and control, the papacy is deeply preoccupied with celibacy. The pope and other clerical officials remain anxious because of the influences of the media, dissident individuals, reform groups and questioning laity. Once upon a time, these people were the papacy's allies and significantly helped to maintain official policy. Now they have become ideological foes.

Threats to celibacy are found not only in the resistance of reform-minded Catholics, but also in the encroachment of the laity upon the priesthood. With the growing shortage of priests, permanent deacons and laypeople, especially religious women, have stepped into parish administration. Priests who have left to marry are also known to discreetly fill the breach. Many of these laypersons and clerics minister effectively to the needs of the parish, but with the exceptions denied to them: key sacramental ministries, namely, the sacraments of Eucharist, reconciliation, and anointing of the sick. Consequently, certain people, particularly those in parish positions of leadership, are challenging compulsory celibacy and related sexual policies and demanding an overhaul of the centralised bureaucratic system.

The papacy, however, has determined that these developments are not in the best interests of the church. By using various avenues—religious, social, political, and economic—that consolidate its control over celibacy, it is able to monitor the actions of priests and to mobilise defences to ensure that this practise is publicly maintained.

This mobilisation and defence has had one consequence in a massive eucharistic famine. The requirement of celibacy has created a situation in which there are insufficient priests to celebrate the sacraments. Another consequence is the loss of services and goodwill that many priests who have left to marry, and their partners, are prepared to give. Such people are prevented from doing so because they are excluded from leadership and decision-making roles in the church.

Nevertheless, the papacy feels that it must withstand these massive costs, for it is aware that without celibacy the entire hierarchical order is jeopardised. This is a view that is echoed by Fr. Ben: *The Vatican is not about to give away its allegiance to the cultic model—for without it, the very structure of the Vatican itself would be undermined. What man would crawl under his own home and dig out the foundations? Only a mad man—and that's how the Vatican perceives those who argue for a change in the laws governing celibacy and priesthood.*

At risk, then, is the priest, clearly the victim in this, indeed, a sacrificial victim. For if the papacy's solution to the predicament is to continually suppress expressions of sexual intimacy, then the priesthood of the future will have a very old face. It is not a comforting thought. On the other hand, if change is to occur, then a great deal hinges on establishing different kinds of relationship with and for priests.

The real test of priestly identity, though, lies in breaking out of patterns of condescension, bigotry, and discrimination. Unfortunately, these patterns are largely invisible and, therefore, all the more insidious. How many people, for example, will recognise the menace in the constant humourous digs at sexuality that I have witnessed on a number of occasions? One incident stands out in particular.

I was invited to a dinner-function for priests and was seated at a table with seven other people, six of whom were priests. At the end of our meal, a waiter approached one of the priests and said: *A lady is in the reception and would like to speak with you.* As the priest rose to meet her, his confreres chuckled and one said, *Meeting with a woman, what will the bishop say?*

The implication was clearly that there was something sexually improper about this meeting.[26] Such a response plays on a particular stereotype of celibacy, indicating how priests are locked into a seemingly inflexible grid. This rigid clerical framework subverts the goals of those priests who seek a meaningful sexual identity. This behaviour also illustrates how compulsory celibacy is perpetuated.

To break away from such manipulation is fraught with difficulties. Due to Vatican policy there are limited opportunities for priests to come together to openly discuss issues relating to celibacy. As a result each priest must suffer his own private turmoil when it comes to dealing with such personal issues.

Thus, the true test of celibacy will be played out on the margins of the priesthood, where Vatican officials continue to confine the debate. Will church demands give way to a respect for what the local priesthood is today rather than what it was in the past? The answer seems directly tied to the extent to which the local bishop will be able and willing to develop a corresponding respect for disenfranchised voices in the local church. This, in part, also depends on the preparedness and the courage of priests and others to share their concerns and difficulties about celibacy. These are, after all, not issues for the papacy alone. Unless both of these processes occur, priests will continue to search for meaning in ways that they have been forbidden to seek; yet, that may be what will propel the priesthood, and the church, forward.

4

Moral Dilemmas

It was at the end of another busy day when Fr. Lucas sat down to his evening meal. On his plate were the leftovers from a parish function of the previous evening, which he washed down with a glass of cask red. His dinner companion was a pile of church magazines that he read more out of habit than interest. There was nothing really being said in their pages that hadn't been said many times before. After a short while, he pushed them aside.

When he had finished his supper, he turned on the TV. He was annoyed with the soapie that traded in tears and tragedy so he flicked over to another channel, only to find just another version of the same domestic drama. Irritated, Fr. Lucas turned the box off.

Fr. Lucas sat there without the comfort of the usual distractions. Deep down he knew this was a day just like many that had gone before: the routine and loneliness were eating into his soul. While his life as a priest was busy and fulfilled, within himself, he was withering away. *I began to see myself as being alone and lonely. I had some good friends, but never allowed myself to get really close to anyone. My religious convictions and self-image as a priest had built a fortress around me.* A year or two passed by and finally his term in the parish ended. He packed up his belongings, farewelled his parishioners, and moved on to yet another place.

No one had recognized how his soul was drying up, how his footsteps had slowed down, or how his heart was starved of love. Fr. Lucas didn't expect it would be any different in his new parish. Why should it be? He had barely finished unpacking his case when the presbytery doorbell rang. Fr. Lucas heaved a great big sigh and readied himself to begin his ministry.

Sr. Johanna, the pastoral associate, called by to greet the new priest. She welcomed him, enquired whether he needed anything, and then suggested that they might meet up soon to discuss the parish. Fr. Lucas appreciated the warm reception. The offerings of assistance and information helped him to settle in quickly and they signalled the beginnings of a much-needed friendship.

Fr. Lucas and Sr. Johanna often had coffee together. He shared with her ideas for sermons and plans for the parish, while she discussed her own ministry and thoughts about life and the church: *We were completely on the same wavelength, spiritually, and emotionally.*

But after many, many months, Fr. Lucas realized that he was becoming attracted to Johanna in ways that troubled him. They had started embracing each other and while holding and being held by her was a beautiful experience, he was fearful of the desire that seemed to be welling up inside him. Eventually, he decided that he needed to talk openly and honestly with Johanna. So one Sunday afternoon they went for a drive. Away out in the bush they found a quiet spot where they could talk about their feelings for each other.

We also talked about the risk of our sexual attraction for each other. So I suggested the way to beat the problem was to deal with the attraction while we were still in control. We came to a decision that embracing, touching, intimacy, nakedness, all this was acceptable, but under no circumstance was there to be sexual intercourse.

Even as I write this, I wonder, did this really happen? What on earth did I think I was trying to do? I can answer that latter part quite truthfully: I was trying to survive. Time passed. *We weathered the storms of intense feeling that our friendship naturally aroused in us, somehow.* During that time, Sr. Johanna salved his deep need for companionship and love. But a new set of traumas began to emerge.

My friendship with Johanna created an enormous inner conflict. There was the obvious ambivalence over the sexual connotations of our friendship, of "living a double life." At the same time, there was the fear of discovery and the consequent "sham" of not abiding by the external standards of the church's professed moral code. *This moral crisis brought with it unhappiness and misery, coped with by a state of numbness in which moral issues were consciously repressed: "put into the too-hard basket."*

Many months passed. Then one day, Sr. Johanna asked Fr. Lucas to take her for a drive to the place where they had first talked to each other. She was quite distraught when she broke the news to him. She had been given a new assignment overseas. Now they had to make some decisions.

In a "Mills & Boon" style romance, we should have both departed and married. We didn't, for we both believed in our 'primary' commitments to ministry.

They agreed to face up to and live out what was being demanded of them: with deep sorrow, Fr. Lucas and Sr. Johanna farewelled each other. After the first pangs of grief had subsided, Fr. Lucas started reading about Christian and human morality by non-Catholic authors.

These authors led me to a reexamination of the nature and moral gravity of sexual behaviour in terms of relationship. I came to realise that in such a relationship, responsibility for my actions (and for my unloving ones, too) lies with me and the person whom I love. Whereas the church fixes general principles from which external norms are derived. The trouble is these abstract standards do not have their origins in a consideration of the total person.

I am, at this moment, working towards an honest and integral response to these matters. I cannot, however, subscribe to the unbalanced, impersonal emphasis placed by the official church on sexuality and sexual behaviour. It is very important, but it is not so important as to be elevated to a unique position in moral theory and divorced from other areas of morality.

Sometimes Fr. Lucas drives to the place where he and Sr. Johanna shared so much. It is there where he reads her letters and remembers her being close and intimate. It is there where he aches for the company he can no longer touch. It is also there where he prays that things might one day be different.

⸺

Fr. Lucas found himself in a dilemma with regards to his friendship with Sr. Johanna, a quandary that took considerable heartache, sacrifice, and time to work through. He came to realize that morality could be understood in a way that is much more accommodating of his personhood, relationships, and particular circumstances than what church doctrine currently allows.

Nevertheless, Fr. Lucas is also aware that if he wants to continue to be a priest, he has to present himself as celibate, because the papacy considers this practise a nonnegotiable moral condition of the priesthood. By fixing this moral position in doctrine and canon law, it is able to keep any discussion of celibacy off the official agenda of the church, thereby leaving priests like Fr. Lucas in an insidious situation.

The Moral Position of the Papacy

The papacy contends that its understanding of God's will is the norm. The practical consequence of this belief is that it also claims the exclusive right and responsibility for giving moral guidance. As a result, it puts itself in the position of being ultimately accountable if its moral code is not upheld. Thus, the pope and the curia refuse to take into account beliefs and opinions or experiences that differ from their own.

In the official view, morality is fixed by a set of ideas about right and wrong. It is right for a priest to be celibate and wrong to be sexually intimate. The papacy goes about justifying this particular moral construction by gathering the many claims made about celibacy by previous papacies. On such a seemingly indisputable bedrock of historical fact, it is then able to declare that celibacy is a tradition of the priesthood.[1] Consequently, the pope and the curia are able to reinforce the message that celibacy is "a gift of God to the church."[2] Yet behind this triumphalist rhetoric there are details of history that contest this claim.

⸺

From the time of Jesus and the apostles until the fourth century, the church imposed no known celibacy-related restrictions on priests. For the first four hundred years, marriage was the norm for Christian ministers, with celibates working alongside these men and women. But from the second century, ascetic movements urged religious leaders to recognise the superiority of sexual continence.[3] By establishing this exceptional sexual discipline, Christians were able to express the moral difference between themselves and the pagan world.

By the third century, parallels between the Christian priesthood and the Jewish priesthood were assumed to exist. This development saw women being phased out as leaders and decision-makers and male priests being required to observe ritual purity in daily altar service. Zealots then pressured for legislation to insure that such demands were upheld. Subsequently, at the local Council of Elvira, ca. 305, a canon was enacted that required all concerned in the ministry of the altar to maintain abstinence from their wives under pain of forfeiting their positions.[4]

In 324, Constantine made Christianity the state religion of the Roman Empire. With the end of Roman persecution, martyrdom became obsolete and was replaced with sexual renunciation, a new form of sacrifice.[5] Priests were consequently pressured to become the leading moral exemplars, reflecting the ideal for Christianity in celibacy.

At this time, priesthood also became a privileged position that offered substantially increased temporal advantages. The papacies of Damasus I (366-384) and Siricius (384-399) were keen on regulating the sexual behaviours of priests in order to uphold the moral reputation of the priesthood, as well as to safeguard the growing wealth of the church that was under clerical control.

The church of this period received vast accessions of property from the pious zeal of its wealthy members, the deathbed repentance of despairing sinners, and the munificence of emperors and prefects. Such acquisitions, however, were exposed to a risk of depreciation when the priests in charge of these riches had families to provide for. To avert this, priests were simply relieved of paternity.[6] The papacies initiated programs to ensure that priests maintained sexual continence, and thereafter canonical injunctions against sexual relations within the marriages of priests multiplied. Nonetheless, these and consecutive papacies had limited jurisdiction, and without the means to implement these standards, the practise of sexual continence was limited.

The second period of concentrated efforts to impose celibacy occurred in the Middle Ages. Between 800 and 1000, Europe experienced cultural and civil upheaval. The church also underwent a period of widespread corruption and new factors such as imperial interference, factionalism, and simony regulated the priesthood. Such activity fuelled a reform movement that in part envisaged the remedy of a celibate clergy. Centralisation of papal authority was also considered an answer to the problems of the church. A succession of determined papacies, commonly referred to as the Gregorian reform, endeavoured to reorganize the priesthood by stressing papal primacy and the requirement that bishops were to enforce church decrees.[7]

The Gregorian reform was significantly assisted by clerical reformers who reemphasised ritual purity in the administration of the Eucharist. These reformers asserted that priests who stood by the altar were a race apart from the laity. Their superior status therefore required them to uphold the greater moral integrity of celibacy.[8] With this theological premise established, priestly marriage was subsequently denounced as not only illicit but invalid. At the Second Lateran Council (1139) the first universal law of celibacy was passed, which required priests to give up their wives, a decree that was often violently rejected by priests. In many parts of the church, papal messengers were maltreated, imprisoned, and even burned.[9]

The reformers persisted. To ensure that the law was observed, regulations were reiterated in 1179 at the Third Lateran Council with an added penalty for noncompliance: loss of ministry and all related and accrued revenue. At the Fourth Lateran Council (1215), Innocent III (1160–1216) supplemented the previous legislation with a canonical ruling that provided for the removal of priests guilty of sexual incontinence. Ecclesiastical authorities that maintained the services of such priests also incurred the same sanction.[10]

The canon, however, was still unable to win general acceptance, and by the fifteenth century, significant numbers of priests had "wives" and families.[11] The flouting of the law also extended to popes. Between 1484 and 1585, six popes fathered children.[12]

During this period, generally known as the Renaissance, there was a revival of classical art, literature, and learning, which made Europeans rethink their relationships with God and with each other. The rise of national states, the discovery of the New World, the invention of the printing press, and proof of Copernican theory threatened to displace the temporal and spiritual supremacy of the pope. Within the church, diverse factors contributed to instability, including financial abuses of ecclesiastical taxes that placed heavy burdens on priests and the laity. The arguments of reformers such as Luther further weakened the credibility of the hierarchical church. These reformers insisted that since the Eucharist was not a sacrifice (Calvary cannot be repeated), there was no need for a cultic priesthood and its associated celibacy. The convergence of these complex forces precipitated reform movements that moderated or dismissed ecclesiastical tradition, emphasised the pastoral dimensions of priesthood, and repudiated celibacy.

To counter these challenges, Pope Paul III (1534-1549) convened the Council of Trent (1545–1562). This Council reasserted papal authority, reiterated the ban on marriage for priests, and reinforced the cultic dimensions of the priesthood. These promulgations also ensured that benefices and other revenues were kept within the church.

Mandatory and uniform seminary formation was later introduced that set priests further apart from the laity. Boys and young men were chosen and isolated from the world, shaped and locked into a cultic vision of priesthood. Ritual purity emphasised belief in the superiority of celibacy, which could now be rigorously administered by the central authority of the Vatican, a pattern that ostensibly remained for the next four centuries except where the control of a particular papacy was weakened.[13]

In this brief resume of history, key political forces that have shaped the construction of celibacy have been identified. In each period respective papacies have attempted to control the sexuality of priests and to preserve the patrimony and the wealth of the church. Nevertheless, priests through their protests, relationships, and sexual practises have consistently challenged these canons. It is only when a papacy has exercised tight social control that priests have observed celibacy.

These historical details challenge the claims of tradition made by the current papacy. John Paul II, for example, states: "It was not merely the consequence of a juridical and disciplinary fact: it was the growth of the church's realization of the appropriateness of priestly celibacy."[14] The claim of "appropriateness" is, however, disputed by a substantial number of priests throughout history.

Furthermore, previous papacies, like the current papacy, have instituted and maintained canons by marginalising and demonising those priests who challenge the official claims made for celibacy. In effect, these papacies have attempted to erase the moral viewpoints of these priests and the details of their lives from the annals of history. By ignoring the social conditions in which these priests have challenged celibacy and insisting that celibacy has always been the norm, church leadership distorts and weakens the argument of tradition.

Multiple Traditions of Celibacy

Priests with friends hold different views as to whether celibacy is or is not a part of the tradition of the church, but what they do contest is the absolute nature of these claims. Fr. David, for instance, recognizes the ambiguity of the claim made for celibacy. *Celibacy had a use for a time and place, but it has outlived that usefulness, and now we have to put it aside. For hundreds of years tradition in the church has encompassed both optional and obligatory celibacy. It all depends on which era you want to base your argument. I believe that we should go back to the pre-twelfth century where celibacy was encouraged but not obligatory.*

Fr. Luke is angrily dismissive of celibacy as a tradition. *It was only after celibacy was enforced in the church that the real time of Christian darkness began. It was in the twelfth century that celibacy became mandatory. And all sorts of things began after that. First came the crusades, then the burnings, all due to a huge power play. Next, we see the horrific escalation of persecution of Jews and Muslims and homosexuals. Mandatory celibacy had a lot to do with turning everything sour.*

Fr. Thomas takes a different stance. He contends that the argument for celibacy as a tradition *is convincing only if we believe that history is always progressive and the church can never regress in ideas and practices. There are, sadly, numerous instances that contradict this hypothesis. Tradition, then, is no sure validation.*[15]

Priests such as Fr. Aaron emphasise people over tradition. *Jesus reminds us that moral laws are intended to serve the needs and well-being of people, and when a moral law stands in the way of doing the loving thing for a person, that rule loses its power.* Another priest adds to this argument by asserting the inappropriateness of celibacy for today's priests. *We live in a very couple-oriented society; the celibate life is no longer considered a greater calling than the married state. When my colleagues and I joined the priesthood in the early 1970s, we felt we were being called to a greater state. Today, that kind of thinking would be considered an insult to the sacrament of marriage.*[16]

Priests also gave reasons why they thought the church continues to maintain celibacy. *The reason behind the official stonewalling on the law about celibacy probably has little to do with doctrine since there is, in fact, no doctrinal obstacle to a married clergy, but rather to the fact that a married clergy would cost more than a celibate one, and also be less amenable to episcopal control in matters such as transfers. Money and power may have more to do with the law on celibacy than doctrine or tradition.*[17]

The church doesn't want to pay for a guy with a wife and kids, says Fr. Daniel. *Neither could they move them around as easily because of the kids' schooling or the wife's job. They don't want to deal with all the practicalities or difficulties that become part of a team of people.* By avoiding everyday realities through not having to consider personal relationships, the papacy is able to divest priests of potentially competitive loyalties and responsibilities that might deflect from what it regards as important for the church. At the same time, it also secures and maintains a permanent, committed, and cheap labour force, thereby protecting the wealth of the church.

Priests with friends recognise many contradictions in this official position. Having become responsive to the ordinary rhythms of life, they argue that the realities of sexual partnerships and family life should be accommodated in the moral vision of the church. Indeed, one priest commented that in the face of the many struggling families he ministered to, *my lifestyle looks like selfish luxury. Celibacy doesn't help me to relate emotionally or financially to members of my parish. In some ways my ministry suffers from not having those experiences.*

In summary, for priests with friends, the official claims made for the tradition are spurious and have deleterious effects on their ministry and on the life of the church. As a result, the centralised authority of the papacy will continue to be questioned as long as universal morality is maintained at the expense of people's lives.

Reading the Moral Barometer

By treating celibacy as a tradition of the priesthood, the pope and the curia are able to absolutise this practice. In this way, the relativism of celibacy, a practise that is continuously shaped and changed by history and culture, is transformed into an eternal verity.

Nevertheless, this absolutist stance can create genuine embarrassments for the Vatican. Within the North American priesthood, perhaps as many as half of the priests are engaged in sexual relationships; and in other countries, studies confirm that significant numbers of priests are sexually active.[18] In South Africa, for instance, research has found that 40.5 percent of priests had, at sometime in the two years before the study, engaged in "casual sexual encounters," 43.1 percent of priests were involved in "a love relationship," and 37.7 percent had recently "ended love relationships."[19] Two missionary priests whom I interviewed both claimed that this situation is common not just in particular African countries but throughout the continent: *Celibacy, by and large, has ceased for indigenous clergy. It's a real, real problem. They are not living with women, because they couldn't get away with that. They would be immediately suspended if they did. But a lot of them have girlfriends, and quite a few would have children.*

This situation is not only confined to the United States and Africa. One priest who frequents Rome reported to me a conversation that he had with the superior general of a major religious order. *He told me that the Vatican had just sought his recommendation. It wanted a priest from his order to serve as bishop of an unnamed diocese in Latin America. Reason: of the sixty-three diocesan priests in that area who had the education background to be a bishop, none of them was celibate. They all had wives and families.* My correspondent then went on to say that the ubiquity of this phenomenon could be checked out in the *Annuario Pontificio*, the Vatican Yearbook, where one can see just how many bishops in Latin America are religious.

David Rice also documents anecdotal evidence that the majority of priests in South America are not observing celibacy, and that this phenomenon is widespread in European countries as well.[20] The members of the International Federation of Married Catholic Priests makes the same observation. Recently, a poll showed that more than 50 percent of Swiss priests did not observe the celibacy rule.[21] Support groups for partners of priests in the United Statesd and Europe are further testament to priests not practising celibacy.[22]

Other ambiguities also exist, such as the admission of married priests from the Anglican and Lutheran churches into the Catholic priesthood. These exemptions, according to one priest, *have left some priests angry and bewildered at the double standards.* As well, a few Catholic married men are being ordained after they have promised to refrain from sexual intercourse with their wives. Pope John Paul approved the ordination of two Brazilian men in this situation. The Vatican issued a statement listing conditions for "a dispensation from the impediment of the marriage bond in view of ordination to the priesthood."[23] Fr. Aaron contends that this turn of events *makes the teaching about the sanctity of marriage hollow and insincere, and it takes the soul out of celibacy.* Such embarrassments ensure that the papacy's control over priests is diminished, and they tarnish its role as moral arbiter.

The Immorality of Compulsory Celibacy

As the papacy's moral rein on priests diminishes, diversity over the meaning of celibacy is expressed. Some orthodox priests, for instance, argue that the church is universal and unchanging and that therefore priests should remain celibate. In this view, the historical and social context is waived and the individual priest entirely subordinated. For these priests, the meaning of celibacy is established before life itself.

In contrast, other priests regard celibacy as a complex phenomenon. Fr. Cain originally took refuge from his homosexuality by hiding in the priesthood. For twenty-six years, he avoided human warmth and interest. All he wanted to do was preach and teach. Fr. Cain always had the answer, or rationalised his version of what others were saying.

While his head took charge, his heart had other plans. He fell in love with four handsome young men, *John, the brilliant student; Luke, on trial for murder; Mark, consumed by raw emotions, and Matthew, the*

*golden-hearted friend, full of tenderness, passion and simple, sane human-
ity. Each helped resolve the contradictions in my life: flesh vs. spirit, word
vs. deed, thought vs. matter. And so it is that love brings me home to Eden,
where mind and body become as one, and faith and lust can somehow be
reconciled.*[24]

Fr. Cain suffered deeply, yet he found the blessings of love that
knitted his fragmented self back together again. Yet apart from sharing
in affections, he still considered himself within the bounds of the
celibacy law.

Time passed, passions mellowed, and a move away from his
beloved friends shaped Fr. Cain's personal decision to remain celibate. While he considers the rule of celibacy malevolent, his practise
leaves him relatively content. *God has placed a no parking sign across
my forehead!*

Fr. Samson is also committed to celibacy. *I have never touched a woman
sexually. I am physically a virgin, to put it bluntly. I'm quite happy that
way. I believe I have that gift.*

*From talking to priests, I'm rather unusual. I come from a very religious
family. But when I was fifteen and living at a boarding school, I remember
having this unmistakable experience. I was in bed and it was almost as if
a voice said I was to be a priest. If you had asked me that night before I
went to bed what I wanted to be, I wouldn't have known. But the next
morning I would have definitely said I would want to be a priest. In some
way, I think there is a gift of God there.*

*In my seminary days I never had any doubts about my vocation,
never thought of leaving, never struck a lot of the problems the other students seemed to have. Since I've been a priest, I have never had major
problems, even though I have had some very good women friends over
the years.*

*But I've seen so many of my brother priests, who are my friends, have
genuine problems with celibacy. Some of them definitely are called to
priesthood. Some of them are fantastic priests and wonderful ministers.
But they don't have that gift of celibacy. In fact, the finest priest I have
known, one who struggles all the time with celibacy, finds it very difficult.*

Fr. Samson is concerned for other priests who are suffering because of the rule of celibacy and for the credibility of celibacy itself. *The celibacy law has to go if celibacy is to retain its value as a way of Christian service.*

Some priests are convinced that homosexual priests should not be obliged to be celibate. As Fr. Joshua says, *they struggle and have just the same needs as we heterosexuals do.* The need for intimacy and for the freedom to be able to express that in a sexual manner within loving friendship should not be precluded because of sexual orientation.

Fr. Malachy, who has a serious medical condition, also argues that *an intimate and ongoing relationship with someone else would not only help us relate and minister to our parishioners, it would also help when we have personal needs that require care.*

Meanwhile, Fr. Daniel maintains that a married priesthood is a fait accompli. *What will happen when some day husbands, wives, and children run through the passages of the presbytery? Surely, it will change the dynamics of the church's understanding of itself, its teachings and so forth. In fact, celibacy will be looked on with some suspicion.* Fr. Samson, though, puts a humourous spin on the issue: *Marriage is fine, as long as they don't make it mandatory!*

The question of whether religious priests should remain celibate was also specifically mentioned. Fr. Jonathan, a provincial of a religious order, thought that such priests should remain celibate because they generally live in community, and sexually intimate friendship in this context might pose a threat to group cohesion. However, Fr. Jonathan concedes *some might revise their preferences if they knew that marriage was an option for the diocesan priesthood, which would make it a more attractive option.* When I asked him if this was the general position of those in religious orders, Fr. Jonathan responded: *a number of older priests would see clerical celibacy as a* sine qua non *not only for religious priests but for priesthood generally. In the middle years and the younger years, they would be more likely to see a married priesthood as a possibility.*

Fr. Stephen, a religious priest, contends that it is unethical to reduce a religious order's vision of service to celibacy: *We need communities whose members are single, single and vowed to chastity, and married, from which a priest would be chosen regardless of marital status.*

Priests who seek reform evaluate the morality of celibacy not as a given, as does the papacy, but in terms of experience. These priests make their assessments from an historically conscious perspective that takes into account personal and social considerations. Such priests recognise that they belong to a shifting and fragmentary world, and, as a result, they constantly subject celibacy to readjustment and reevaluation. This social flexibility contrasts with the inflexibility of the papacy, which uses the abstract ideal of celibacy to fix the boundaries of the priesthood. This difference in understanding obviously creates tension because priests are required to locate this abstraction in their ordinary everyday lives. Fr. Pete considers this a difficult task: *We are busting our guts to put into practical terms what the bishops, cardinals, and pope decide. They hardly have to live out the reality. Whereas we, the underclass, the priests who are the lower class, have to grapple with the reality.*

Fr. Jesse considers celibacy not only problematic but surreal: *What would we be doing if we weren't expending so much energy contesting an unreality or coping with a reality in an environment of unreality?*

After much reading and listening to the arguments for and against celibacy, another priest in Fr. Jesse's diocese came to be convinced that the imposition of celibacy as a prerequisite for priesthood is an injustice. *No one has the right or the power to take away from anyone what is a fundamental human right. If someone wishes to be celibate for the right reasons, I would applaud that. But to make celibacy a condition of priesthood is an injustice and repugnant. Consequently, I would not consider myself bound by Canon 277.*

Constructing Contemporary Moralities

All priests are left to their own devices to construct a moral universe in which to live out their celibacy. For instance, Fr. Reuben used to cope with celibacy by keeping his distance from the laity. *Looking back, I had an unspoken sense of superiority. Not spoken of course. Most priests are not even aware of it. You have this sense of superiority when it comes to women and when it comes to people in general because when you are a priest, you think you are better than other people. It's almost as though when you become a priest you leave the human race! Although we would be the last to see it that way.*

Other priests find different ways to work out their celibacy, as Fr. Thomas has observed. *Though it is a rough sketch, and one derived in part from the language of priests, some of the lifestyle choices we encounter in the priesthood include those of "bachelors", boyos", "mummy's boys", "affairs men" or "career men".* Bachelors *are those who would, even if they were not in the priesthood, most likely not marry. They simply do not want that sort of relationship with anyone.* Boyos *love nothing better than to go golfing, drinking, to the football, or racing with a group of blokes.* For Mummy's Boys *mother supplies the governing relationship. Often they feel a need to make up to their mothers for the deficiencies of their father. She is very proud of them and cannot help speaking of and for them. They are torn between feelings of affection and oppression.* Career men *shelve the question of relationships because it is detrimental to their accession to power or to their accumulation of assets.*[25]

Some priests who cannot assuage their needs for intimacy project their needs onto their parishioners: *He spends long hours with them, more to fulfil his desires than theirs,* observed one priest.[26] Alternatively, priests may use the *celibacy vaccine,* a priestly euphemism for alcohol, to quell their desires. One priest, at the beginning of his priesthood, was advised to choose *Punch* over *Judy,* meaning alcohol over women. Tim Unsworth also highlights this problem. In his book *The Last Priests in America: Conversations with Remarkable Men,* one priest suggested that in an ordination class of twenty, between 18 percent and 27 percent would have a problem with drink. *It's the only thing that wasn't a sin. Drink is the first thing you're offered when you get upstairs in a rectory.*[27] Substances such as food and drugs are also included in these self-prescribed vaccinating programs.

These means for working out celibacy may also be combined with various sexual behaviours. Priests may elect to be single and sexually abstinent either by choice or because their preferred type of relationship is unavailable. Alternatively, a priest might choose to have occasional or rare sexual encounters, or become a *promiscuous Tomcat,* avoiding a sustained relationship because of its demands, or because of other perceived problems. This choice may also include the use of pornography and prostitutes. Another possibility is to be companioned in monogamous or serially monogamous relationships. One such priest considers these latter relationships a gift of God, in which *the Lord gives, and the Lord takes away. I'm simply saying, occasionally someone comes along, stands by you and becomes your mate, and things work out.* Priests are highly creative in dealing with their celibacy. They ensure that the abstract notion promoted by a faraway Vatican is maintained, but in a fashion that can be locally managed.

Not surprisingly, the imposition of celibacy produces a considerable degree of antagonism, which is often directed towards the pope. *Celibacy could be abolished today. You wouldn't have to wait until midnight if we had someone with a bit of sense who was pope,* says Fr. Barnabas, a critical thinker who has taken leave to consider his future in the priesthood. Later he commented: *If the pope had had sex he wouldn't be so concerned, but the trouble is he has only known sexual fantasy, masturbation, and struggle. So, we too are forced to live out our sexuality like that.*

Priests like Fr. Barnabas consider celibacy as impractical, unrealistic, and unrelated to the contemporary realities of priesthood, a view that is reiterated by Fr. Joshua: *If I had to stand with the pope before the Lord, my wisdom would say that we ought to make it optional.* Fr. Luke raised the bar of resentment one more notch: *I think mandated celibacy is mischievous, dangerous, and arrogant. It would be hard for me to say everything I feel about it. I think it's demonic.*

Handling Tricky Situations

In viewing the imposition of celibacy as immoral, priests with friends find themselves in the awkward position of having to invent ways to negotiate their relationships. One of the ways in which they manage this task is by using shifters. A shifter is an ingenuous trick that enables a priest to express in various ways the conviction that his friendship is moral. At the same time, this trick also allows him to ostensibly defer to official expectations.

A shifter can become operative in the interaction between a priest and his bishop. A priest in speaking to his bishop may refer to his friend as "a parishioner," "the housekeeper," "the parish secretary," "sister," or "brother." When he characterises his friend in such a way, he obscures the intimate nature of their relationship. However, from the bishop's perspective, these characterisations suggest that there is an absence of personal closeness.

The strategy of the shifter is also made effective by the formal relationship the bishop has with the priest. By maintaining a conventionally correct regard for the priest, the bishop remains removed from his everyday life. Without an awareness that comes from being closely connected to a particular situation, the bishop is not privy to the subtleties of speech. He therefore interprets the characterisation of a priest's friend according to the fixed parameters that are outlined by doctrine and canon law.

Nevertheless, in assuming his interpretation of the priest's relationship with the particular person is correct, the bishop creates a danger. When shifters are used in such interactions, they are co-opted and subsumed into the bureaucratic processes of the church. By accepting and accommodating a certain characterisation of a priest's friend, the bishop undermines the papacy's ability to manage the priesthood.

Fr. Jethro uses a shifter in another situation. Although sexual intimacy is conventionally associated with married laity, he is able to transfer this abstract notion to his own circumstance and regard it as a part of his preferred way of living.

Fr. Jethro complained about the need for intimacy in his life. *The thing that is so difficult is that Catholics don't encourage a priest to experience intimacy at all. They all think a priest is screwing. Actually, I was out to dinner last night with a friend, and I was saying that the greatest thing I miss is having someone to snuggle into. But if I spoke to my fellow priests openly about that, most of them would think you just want a fuck, and yet it really isn't about having sex.*

When terms such as *intimacy* are recognised as having multiple meanings, they can be used in ways that suit the circumstance in which the conversation is being conducted. Thus, Fr. Jethro is able to acknowledge his need for intimacy without precluding sexual intimacy. By discreetly including sexual intimacy, he is able to subtly expand on official definitions of intimacy in ways that meet his own needs. But to the unaware Catholic listening to a priest talking about intimacy, he or she might interpret what he says to mean an intimacy that excludes sexual intimacy.

Fr. Jethro also complains about the way in which his confreres and parishioners define intimacy. They are criticised for reducing the term to the function of an object, *screwing*. By downgrading sexual intimacy in this way, he argues that Catholics in general remove from a priest's sexual encounter valued attributes such as personal comfort and cherished closeness. For Fr. Jethro, it is not primarily about *having sex*. To him, it is a way of expressing a deep need for intimacy and bonding with someone he loves.

Fr. Jethro therefore regards the enjoyment of relational closeness with a trusted and loved friend as a moral good, a moral good that the papacy recognises as ideally existing in marriage, but that this priest transfers to an intimate friendship.

Of further interest is the fact that Fr. Jethro is homosexual, a state that, according to the papacy, precludes him from enjoying sexual intimacy. This priest has, however, taken the notion of intimacy beyond heterosexual marriage to include other relationships. Indeed, intimacy is perceived by Fr. Jethro to be a moral good for all priests and should be encouraged.

Discovering the Morality of Friendship

Fr. Joseph had always wanted to be a priest, and even in his primary school days, girls really had no place in his life. *I wanted to be a priest, and priests lived apart.* As a secondary student and as a seminarian he lived and studied in an all-male environment. Then after he was ordained, he lived in an all-male community and taught in a boy's boarding school for twelve years followed by eight years of teaching in a seminary. After four decades of living in an institutional setting, Fr. Joseph went overseas to take a course in pastoral theology.

There were quite a few on the same course, both men and women, and there was quite a bit of interaction between some of us. I began making sure I was always dressed in clericals, the proper uniform. I was deter-mined to make sure that others respected my priestly dignity; feminists had me very worried. It took me about three weeks to ask myself the question about what I was trying to prove. So I doffed the clerical clothing and didn't wear it again. For me that was quite a decision. I soon began to act in a more human fashion (less clerical) with the women on the course.

After a few months, one of the women told me she loved me. It was a great shock, something I never expected. That night I couldn't get to sleep. I was overjoyed that someone loved me. Just to know that I was loved for myself, that I was lovable. That was a real breakthrough for me. Knowing that I was lovable has been a great strength.

～

Unlike Fr. Joseph, some priests find it difficult to hinge their changing moral position on celibacy to the formal expectations of how they should behave as priests. One such priest struggled with the question of how to express his feelings towards his friend: *What is affection and not yet sin?* In effect, the nebulous line of celibacy between priesthood and friendship can create a quandary, leaving a priest in a state of un-certainty or indecision about what to do or say. Fr. Sergio also suffered greatly with this problem. *Inner conflict? Frustration? I'm aware of my mixed messages.* For this priest, the difficulty was too much. After eight years of friendship, he said to Felicity: *I love you, but I treasure the priesthood.* And so ended the relationship. Fr. Jacob also feels that his previous attempts to change his understanding of celibacy were morally suspect.

After ordination, Fr. Jacob found himself in a parish that was vi-brant and diverse. *I was working in hospitals, youth groups, and the local schools. Everything was going really well. The relationship with the parish priest was mutually supportive; I was relating to many women of all ages on a warm and professional level. I had feelings of attraction to many and believed that was normal.*

There were three women in that parish that I enjoyed a close relation-ship with. It sounds exploitative, but there was a similar pattern in our meetings. I listened, and that is what they longed for. We would hug. But each meeting we would go a little further. Never sex (intercourse), never demanding, just relaxing, pleasurable, affirming. A breath of fresh air in an otherwise straight and proper life. I think of them now as half-affairs. They were technically wrong but not technically breaking vows. The problem with half-affairs is that they go nowhere, and eventually the risk outweighs the pleasure. It is like investing in a venture that is almost guaranteed to fail.

In the second parish, the pattern continued to be the same. The circumstances are in the system: lonely women, usually taken for granted, talk about their feelings; the young priest listens attentively. A friendship forms. The kiss goodbye becomes a kiss hello. Nothing is said but both know it has changed. Both know it is wrong, doomed to failure, but it fills a gap in your guts.

Fr. Tim had to work through the difficulty of moral attribution in his relationship with Priscilla. Fr. Tim had known Priscilla for almost as long as he had been a priest. *It wasn't always an intensive sort of relationship; it was sort of a friendship like that which I had with a number of other people too, men and women. Up until fourteen years ago, that was the sort of friendship we had.* Fr. Tim then moved to a parish that was closer to where Priscilla lived. *We'd often have a meal together, and if I wasn't on public masses, sometimes she'd come over, and we would have Mass and pray together.*

Fr. Tim very much enjoyed Priscilla's company and experienced a depth of intimacy that he had never known before, without perceived threat to his promise of celibacy. This was also a time of healing past wounds and growth in maturity for him.

Then, after awhile, the level of closeness moved to another stage, and Fr. Tim expanded his appreciation of appropriate intimate expression. He was able to morally accommodate these personal developments in his understanding of celibacy. Such intimacy also produced a new empathy for others, a fresh love, and renewed energy to his personal life and ministry.

Thus far, but no further: Fr. Tim felt that he should limit sexual intimacy to what he referred to as *my barriers. I have always seen sexual intercourse in terms of that total commitment you make to another person in marriage, and I suppose I recognised I hadn't made that commitment to her. I told Priscilla that I have always seen my place in the priesthood, that I've made a commitment to it, and I always felt that's where God wants me to be.*

But I also recognize that you can be saying one thing with your lips and another thing with your actions. And a lot of my actions were saying something different to her, and it got to the point where she started talking about marriage. It sort of shocked me a bit because I had never really entertained that, to be honest. Yet, I must say too, that I struggled in my conscience with the fact that our relationship had become sexual, and that was something I certainly confessed in confession.

Anyhow, it got to the stage where she couldn't understand why we couldn't get married and why I couldn't continue to have a ministry. Then I went overseas and she said, "I'll be gone when you get back."

Some time later, Fr. Tim contracted a serious illness, and Priscilla nursed him towards recovery. In effect, her love for Fr. Tim was greater than her need for marriage. By prioritising his care and welfare, she changed her attitude towards their relationship. In this transformative event, Fr. Tim also renegotiated his love for Priscilla. This led him to the moral view that he could make a dual commitment to his friend and the priesthood, and sexual intercourse became a marker of that inclusion.

We really communicate at all levels, and the sexual part is really an expression of the way we communicate in everything. My physical nakedness with her says that I can bare my whole self to her. I am just completely uninhibited with her and that is something very, very precious, to be just so safe and loved. Just being naked with her has also really helped me to be a freer person. I'm sure that the love we share helps me to be more loving to other people.

For priests such as Fr. Tim, sexual intimacy is a revelation of mutual love and a welcomed venture into utter vulnerability. Such intimacy can embody the very same qualities that the papacy reifies in marriage but does not in friendship. Priests with friends, however, feel that no such moral distinction can be made because they regard their relationships as honourable and holy, and certainly worthy of priesthood.

Fr. Andrew also discovered this to be the case. Many years ago, Fr. Andrew longed for a friendship and he found such a friend in the parish secretary. *She was not too attractive, and yet I found her very pleasant and good company. I felt she was someone I could trust and felt that it was a relationship which could be kept within the proper bounds.*

What happened is that quickly I fell in love with Esther in a way that I had never expected, even though for the first year there was not even a kiss on the lips. She simply became the person with whom I wanted to share as much of my life as possible. Yet, for the first few years there was nothing in the way of any deep physical intimacy. During that time, we talked a lot about our feelings and our relationship—about how it fitted in with our faith, with the church, with God. We also admitted that we loved each other and eventually made a deep commitment to each other. I believe that if it had been possible, we would have married at that point.

Fr. Andrew and Esther have now been friends for sixteen years, and she has become his soul mate. *Esther often prays with me and certainly prays for me. She shares my religious dedication and helps me wherever possible in my apostolate. She also affirms my commitment of service to our parish, companions me in my days off, and is there for me when the going gets rough.*

God Bless Friendship

Priests with friends frequently identify the presence of God in their relationships, contributing to their belief that their friendships are moral. Fr. Tim first came to realize that God is in his friendship during an earlier disagreement.

Our relationship was really in crisis, and she said to me, "How do you know you are not turning your back on God in refusing to go on loving me in the way we have been—and bringing it to a logical conclusion in marriage?" I must say that really made me stop in my tracks, because I really believed God was in our love for each other.

In Priscilla's challenge, and upon reflection, Fr. Tim became aware that God does bless their friendship, and now he maintains that divine favour not only covers his priesthood but also extends to his relationship. Upholding this moral viewpoint has ramifications for the papacy. When Fr. Tim recognises God's presence in his relationship, he challenges the papacy's belief in the validity of celibacy. Celibacy is now an artificial barrier that makes him choose between an abundance of God's blessings and a man-made rule. Fr. Andrew is also convinced that his relationship with Esther is divinely blessed.

I have the deep conviction that it is Jesus who has invited me to follow him, and I believe that just as he has been faithful to me since I made that commitment nearly twenty-five years ago, that he will always be faithful to me. I believe that God is much bigger and compassionate than many of our church leaders, and certainly more than our church laws. I believe God has guided me through and accepted and blessed our relationship. I am prepared to let him show me one step at a time and know from past experience that he will soon let me know if what I am doing is against his will—he has done it many times in the past. The relationship for me is a great source of joy and peace. I no longer find myself half hoping that a woman may appear to seduce me. I no longer feel any need to be flirting with the women who attract me, but rather feel a security in my love for Esther which is sufficient. I know that if the opportunity ever arose to allow me to marry and continue as a priest—that decision is already made. There is no possibility or desire for me to have physical intimacy with any other person.

Both Esther and I have lived with great tension in this relationship, and several times I told her that I wanted her to feel free to follow her heart if a man came who was free to marry and whom she felt that she could love. For many years now that question is not even allowed to be raised because we have already made a lasting commitment to each other. Yet I live with the tension because I believe that it is a part of the life of every person who tries to the best of his ability to follow what is deepest in his heart. I am also conscious that if it hadn't been for my work as a priest, I would never have met Esther. I just give thanks to God that in Esther I suddenly found some of my dreams fulfilled that I believed could never be fulfilled. I have found a woman who is able to love me even with my first commitment being given to Christ as a priest.

—————

Fr. Luke similarly believes that *friendship gives you important and first-hand knowledge of God. God is love, and an experience of really authentic, tender, and powerful love has to be an experience of God. And that's* how I witness to God, the ultimate who is at the heart of everything good, and unbelievably sweet and benevolent. When you love somebody, you can see into the heart of God. It's as if suddenly you have a lens in which you can see and understand that everything is together. Fr. Aaron also recognises a divine presence in his intimate relationships.

Of primary importance are my friendships in my life, including Marianne. Those few who have given me real unconditional love have given me a glimpse of God's love. I want to live in such a way that I would never let them down. Their investment in my life I try never to take for granted—they are a reason to want to go on living.

In effect, priests with friends cast aside the celibate singleness demanded by Vatican officials and the view that their relationships are immoral, because they think, feel, and see themselves in friendships blessed by God.

Nevertheless, these priests still have to come terms with the conflict between celibacy and sexual intimacy. One such priest, aware of the irreconcilable position between the official definition of celibacy and his friendship, concludes, I don't try and work it out, because I can't. So I take it as gift. This awareness of blessing automatically confers a positive morality. Subsequently, Vatican officials are perceived as going against the divine plan for their lives because you can't live out the love you have for another person as you would want.

Moreover, Fr. Barnabas maintains that if priests are ignoring the vow or promise of celibacy, this would be the sensus fidelium at work. The sensus fidelium is that sense of faith that the People of God share, which shows universal agreement in matters of faith and morals.[28] Fr. Barnabas is convinced that if priests believe that their friendships are in accord with the corporate experience of faith and morals, church leadership should witness and proclaim what the People of God believe.

Stretching Celibate Boundaries

There are two quite distinct approaches to morality on the part of the papacy and priests with friends. The former maintains a rigid moral understanding of celibacy, which it makes abundantly clear in its canonical terminology. Indeed, its definition is so inflexible that it cannot accommodate any specific term that describes the relationship between a priest and his friend. This nondefinition is, of course, intentional. For without a formal term to describe these friendships, priests have difficulty in creating a shared language that can be collectively used to reform celibacy.

Yet priests with friends are endeavouring to remedy that situation. By using terms relatively, these priests can make room for their friendships in the broader terminology of the church. Intimate friends are therefore accommodated through inclusive characterisations, although these terms are in a sense directly opposed to the meanings given in codified law.

When priests with friends take affective descriptions conventionally associated with sexuality in marriage and then apply them to their own relationships, they affirm the normalcy of sexual intimacy in the priesthood. Such a claim, however, threatens the stability of the papacy's moral universe. By stretching the boundaries of celibacy, these priests actively promote ambiguity in the priesthood.

Ironically, this ambiguity becomes an informal but still defining characteristic of the priesthood. Friends of priests do exist and this is becoming increasingly difficult for the church to deny.

Yet those who hold an institutional view repudiate such a definition. In being responsible for the governance of the church, the papacy demands that the status quo be maintained. If ambiguity and compromise were to be considered, this could create doubt that can lead to structural disintegration. Consequently, Vatican officials are not about to listen to or take into account the creative solutions of priests with friends. Its role is specifically about the defence of orthodoxy.

It is therefore understandable that the papacy and its local representatives attempt to purge canonical contradictions from the priesthood. When a priest is found out to be not practising celibacy, he is duly penalised, as was the case for Fr. Tobias. Fr. Tobias was of the old school. He had all the answers to everyone's questions, life's problems, and even his own. But: *I was definitely uneducated and unenlightened in sexual matters, except when it came to downgrading women and girls if they were fallen (lost their virginity), or immodest in dressing. I had been trained well to despise any manifestation of nudity or near nudity.*

Eleven years after ordination, I felt the pressure of wanting to know about sex, to experience it. It became an obsession, and there was no way to express the burden of it to a confessor or to even think there might be a confidante who would understand or be accepting.

Fr. Tobias then came across Debbie, a woman of his own age who had a child. *We were both lonely and alone. We started talking to each other at first. I'd listen to her and she'd listen to me. Then we started spending a bit of time together, and she protested her love. Then one night after a meal together, and after the child had gone to sleep, Debbie stood naked before me. That was a moment of magical transformation for me. I was amazed that someone could have such willingness to trust a certain mutuality of acceptance. This was followed by a torrid few months.*

But the town gossips reported me to the bishop. He called me in, said he was concerned about my career and something about piety and good works. Then I was exiled to a small country parish. I was disappointed by my failure, my blighted career, and letting the side down. In hindsight, it was all pious piffle.

Fr. Tobias is quite aware of how ineffective the admonishments of his bishop were. Neither the *town gossips* and the bishop, nor himself at the time, grasped the idea that his having difficulties with celibacy required creative pastoral solutions. Only later did Fr. Tobias come to the realisation that celibacy is inappropriate for him: *The tensions of friendship and intimacy are still with me and worry me less, but I know that I am lacking in human development because of the celibate lifestyle.*

━━

Despite the threat of being found out, Fr. Tim continues to explore alternative meanings for the priesthood.

I know that any moment Esther and I could come up against a wall of opposition to our relationship. I believe that I have to be discreet and understand the way the system operates. I believe that this is simply accepting the realities of life and is not being hypocritical. I never hide the fact from anyone that I do not believe that I have been called by God to be celibate. All I claim is to have done my best to live out that commitment I made.

To share with authorities what I have shared here would be simply to put my head on the ecclesiastical chopping block. But I believe that the Lord is still calling me to be a priest, and I shall be prepared to fight any challenges to my ministry. Even if the system wins in the end (which no doubt it will if I am alone in my struggle) at least a new path may begin to open up for the young men who experience the same call to follow Christ in priestly ministry.

Fr. Tim uses discretion, canniness, and diplomacy to stay in the compliant boundaries of priesthood. Yet from the perspective of the papacy, Fr. Tim's friendship compromises his priesthood, and therefore he is a hypocrite. Fr. Tim, however, feels that compromise is necessary for change in the priesthood and that the changes he is proposing are both sincere and genuine. Moreover, these changes need to be practised in order to bring about a more inclusive priesthood.

I would like to conclude by saying that I have a great sense of hope and believe some of my impossible dreams may still be realised before I die. I believe that this could happen, especially if priests and others gave each other more support in this area.

∼

Some bishops are evidently beginning to take on the local language of reform. In the wake of the United States' priest sex abuse scandal, individual cardinals admitted that celibacy should be discussed but stopped short of an endorsement.[29] These papal representatives discreetly acknowledge the harm of sexual abuse and the possible connection these offences may have with compulsory celibacy. However, they have yet to recognise the positive experiences of priests with friends as a reason for reforming celibacy.

While the creative ways in which priests speak about their friendships have not yet made it to official levels at the Vatican, Catholic observers are continuing to hint at the possibilities of new configurations. Thus, one may not be optimistic about change now, but all this is a prelude to the next papacy. Bringing these ideas to Rome and putting them on the table plants seeds for the future. It puts them in the minds of those electing the next pope.[30]

∼

The papacy assumes that it alone has the exclusive right and responsibility to determine what is moral for the priest. Its moral vision is static and precise and is clearly set out in canon law.

Priests with friends reject the assumption of the papacy that it alone can determine what is moral. They believe that they have a moral licence to wrestle with the contradictions that beset their lives and ministries. In their endeavour to resolve these difficulties, these priests promote a very different vision of what is meaningful for the priesthood, a vision that has a certain degree of flexibility, latitude, and ambiguity. This further suggests that priests with friends have not abandoned morality but nuance and apply it to enhance their own and other people's lives.

What is also clear is that priests with friends do not speak or act as the papacy would prefer, but rather, they are giving much thought to sexuality and to its meaning. Moreover, it is evident that these priests can be acutely loyal and just as acutely detached at one and the same time. This suggests that the priesthood will continue, but not necessarily in the way the papacy envisages.

5

A Question of Identity

Fr. Andre was perplexed. He felt as though he was being pressured by the church to be something he didn't consider himself to be. *I have to be a priest. I am not permitted to be Andre. I am told that I have to be a priest. So what the hell is a priest?*

Fr. Andre spent time searching for an identity that spoke about his life and ministry. In due course, he arrived at a self-understanding that helps him to define who he is as a person and how his priesthood fits in with that awareness.

In my calling, I am first Andre, who happens to be a religious. And as a religious, I give expression to my commitment as a priest. So being a priest is at least third down the line. But Andre is first. Like the other day, I was wearing shorts. But one of the parishioners gave me this disapproving look. A priest never shows his knees. It's crazy. God gave them to me!

The idea about being Andre the person who is also the priest is unacceptable. Of course, the objection comes from the whole concept of cultic priesthood in which I have the power to consecrate; I have the power to dispense. As a sacral figure, I give everything to you. You can do nothing for yourself.

But in the ministerial priesthood, I need you to fulfil my priesthood; you need me to fulfil your personhood, and we need each other to fulfil our faith together. It's all about a journey together. Here in this older more established parish, people want to put me on a pedestal. People want me to be this cultic figure, a cut above everyone else. People want me to be better than the ordinary run-of-the-mill Joe Blow. But I'm not.

Fr. Andre identifies the same struggle between who he is as a person and priest and between the cultic and ministerial priesthood. The cultic model of priesthood leaves him idolised and admired to such an extent that he can only be identified as a projection of what a holy person might look like. Accordingly, such priests cover their bodies.

In contrast, the ministerial priesthood allows him to look people straight in the eye and be human rather than superhuman. In this model, his personhood is valued and integral to priesthood. In his current circumstance, Fr. Andre finds it difficult to live out his preferred understanding of priesthood. In a more conservative parish, he finds himself disembodied and revered as a cultic figure. But there is hope.

The most wonderful compliment I've ever had came from a parishioner. He said to me, "Andre, when you come around here, I don't see you as priest, I see you as Andre." That was absolutely wonderful to hear. Because most times you're not allowed to have a personhood. You're not allowed to have emotions; you're not allowed to have feelings. You're not allowed to have thoughts unless they are Godly thoughts. You're not allowed to look at a woman and think she's gorgeous, or at a man if you like guys. It's as though you have to give that up for God.

When you enter the seminary and you put on Christ, and I don't wish to make a mockery of it, but you come out as Christ after ordination. But I cannot be another Christ, I must be Andre. And in being Andre, I pray and I hope that I can allow that Christ to be radiated through this Andre enough. But I can't deny me, and that's why I can't deny my libido, my sexuality, who I am, my feelings, and all that. If I deny that, I deny the image that God gave me. And that includes my sexual responses. So I don't deny but accept it, and thank God, and come to be at peace with it.

Fr. Andre then went on to to further disclose the ground upon which he seeks to build his priesthood. *I had a relationship as a religious in formation. I was very lucky to have that. I walked in the door, and another person down at the very end of the room saw me, and I thought, there is energy here. I wasn't looking for a relationship at all, but later we happened to work and study together.*

And halfway during the year, things happened, and we realized that there was a great deal of energy between us. We could just sit together, not say a word, and then, all of a sudden, laugh. And we would tell the other person what we were laughing about, and it would be what the other person was thinking. There was a real union, a communion of spirit between us and a great deal of intimacy.

Fr. Andre seeks communion—in self, friendship, and ministry. At the core of his ideal is intimacy, revealed in appropriate degrees. First, he knows his own self, is able to express and face his feelings, thoughts, and fantasies. Secondly, to his intimate friend there is a close encounter, mediated by knowledge and respect. Fr. Andre and his friend can communicate intuitively, share thoughtfully, engage humorously, and enjoy physical closeness. Thirdly, in the outer circle of his relationships, he prefers to minister mutually and respectfully, resulting in personal and priestly growth. In these relationships, Fr. Andre attempts to figure out who and what he is, despite the pressures to be a carbon-copy priest.

Like many other priests, Fr. Andre is currently experiencing uncertainty and difficulty about his identity, and celibacy is tied up in that crisis. Officially, celibacy is one symbol and practise used to mark priests out as being separate and superior, an exclusionary tactic that protects the papacy's understanding of a total priestly identity. This identity is formalised by doctrine and canon law that define how priests are to relate to others, and any attempt to overthrow celibacy is officially resisted and rejected. Priests with friends, however, are informally renegotiating their identity within the context of their relationships and contend that sexual intimacy is meaningful for their personhood and priesthood.

The Power of Images

The papacy is able to link celibacy to the identity of a priest through the use of images. By selecting various images that correspond to its belief that God demands priests to be celibate, it is able to make celibacy an intrinsic characteristic of priesthood. Thus, for example, the papacy uses the image of Jesus as celibate to convey the idea that a priest as *alter Christus* should also be celibate.

Nevertheless, attempts to make celibacy synonymous with priesthood can, at best, be considered limited. Shifting beliefs and social change continue to shape a priest's understanding of himself. A priest might feel that there is evidence to suggest that Jesus might have married. Consequently, a priest might reasonably ask, what has celibacy got to do with being a priest?

This is in fact what has occurred. Priests who previously accepted celibacy without question are now facing new situations and relationships that affect the understanding of their priestly identity. As a result, they may no longer accept the official images used to support celibacy, whilst choosing alternative images that have relevance and meaning.

The politically powerful and central authority of the church, however, is able to limit any embarrassment caused by dissenting priests. Through access to privileged means of communication, such as, the pulpit and other church media, the papacy can continue to construct and promote images of celibacy that uphold its beliefs.

Jesus: Celibate or Married?

In order to convey a homogeneous celibate identity, Vatican officials invoke religious nostalgia. By investing their moral authority in images that have reputedly stood the test of time, celibacy is made to appear reasonable and legitimate for the priesthood.

The principal image used to secure celibacy is the representation that Jesus always lived as a celibate.[1] Even though there is no ancient source that can be used as proof, they assert that this representation is true. Yet when historical criticism is applied to the milieu in which Jesus lived, the claim is considered questionable. Jesus was a Jew, and Judaism was a religion that exalted marriage and, at times, its erotic dimensions. Conversely, celibacy was considered unnatural and detrimental to society.

In the Mediterranean world of Jesus' time, marriage symbolised the fusion of two extended families and was undertaken with a view to political and/or economic concerns. It was the father's duty to arrange the marriage contract that was endorsed by the groom and bride, who gave staunch loyalty to the family and obedience to family authorities.[2] It is important to remember at this point that the autonomy of the individual, a development of the modern West, is entirely absent from the societies and cultures reflected in the Bible.[3] Marriage was not about individual choice, but reflected a respectful merging of extended Jewish families who depended on each other.

The rabbis also imposed religious expectations on the family that included marriage. The Talmud lists five principal responsibilities of a father to his son: circumcise him, redeem him, teach him Torah, teach him a trade, and find him a wife.[4] Scripture records that Joseph carried out the four former responsibilities with no mention of the fifth, but if Jesus subordinated himself to the will of his father in these former matters, then we may surely assume that Joseph sought for Jesus a suitable bride. Jesus, like other young Jewish males, would expect to enter the married state.[5]

As a student of Jewish teachings, Jesus would have been familiar with the imposed celibacy of Jeremiah that symbolised God's disfavour, where God threatened to withdraw life and health, and grace and future from disobedient Jews (Jer 16:1-4). Vatican officials, however, do not mention any of these historical and social details in official documents that promulgate celibacy, for these facts would threaten its essentialist reading of a celibate Jesus.

Some scholars see Stoic parallels in the lifestyle of Jesus, most visible in his austere life and apostolic mission.[6] Evidence of sexual withdrawal is reflected in the Essene community, but Jesus' association with this group is unknown.[7] Yet even if such influences existed, Jesus would still have been obliged to honour kinship rules. Honour and shame were core values in the Mediterranean world, and if Jesus had not married, he would have dishonoured his parents and invited shame upon himself. Moreover, if Jesus had refused marriage, then his opponents among the Pharisees would have reproached him. His disciples would also have asked him about this omission.[8] In spite of that, the idea of a socially shamed Jesus is far removed from the official understanding of this primordial Christian figure.

Reasons are, nonetheless, put forward as to why Jesus did not marry. Richard P. McBrien lists three arguments against the suggestion that Jesus was married.

(1) The Gospels say nothing at all about a marriage; (2) the antierotic bias of the New Testament churches came very early into Christianity, and it can be supposed that if Jesus had been married, that tendency would have been checked; and, most decisively, (3) when Paul invoked his right to marry a believing woman "as do the other apostles and the brothers of the Lord and Cephas" (1 Corinthians 9:5), why did he not appeal to Jesus' own marriage to support his argument?[9]

There are historical and social responses that challenge these arguments. First, scripture says very little about sexuality, let alone marriage. There is almost total silence about the sexuality of Jesus.[10] Secondly, the anti-erotic bias occurred after the destruction of Jerusalem in 70 CE when the fledgling Christian diaspora became vulnerable to other philosophies and religions. Thirdly, Paul never met Jesus except in his vision of Christ on the road to Damascus, and since this experience became the principal focus of Paul's teachings, it clearly lessened the importance Paul gave to the historical Jesus.

Even if Jesus did remain celibate, for whatever reason, the absence of proof still renders any absolutist claim questionable. For the sexual status of Jesus would have been shaped by religious and cultural circumstances. These social conditions are vastly removed from those of the priesthood of the twenty-first century, making dubious any claims made by Vatican officials for the continuity or appropriateness of celibacy based on the life of Jesus.[11] In spite of this, they interpret slivers of history, remove them from historical and social contexts, graft them onto their own ideology, and then elevate them to eternal truths.

***

For those priests who have been raised on this truism, the realization that Jesus may not have been celibate can be quite traumatic. When I presented this evidence to Fr. Aaron, he was noticeably affected. Jesus was *the* reason for his celibacy and for sacrificing marriage and fatherhood, the loss of which he continues to grieve over.

I then presented this evidence to another priest. Fr. Peter still believes that Jesus was celibate, but is uncomfortable with the importance given to the celibacy of Jesus: *I feel awkward with the situation that is advanced, that Jesus' virginity is held up as a better way of life. For*

Fr. Peter, the ascendancy of celibacy is difficult to sustain in light of his experience of family and friends who are married. Other priests subtly reinterpret the notion of a celibate Jesus. Fr. Samuel has spent some time considering the idea of Jesus' celibacy.

For hundreds of years it has been axiomatic in the Christian church that Jesus was celibate, and that priests (who in the Catholic Tradition are seen as the representatives of Christ on earth) should therefore follow his example.

Certainly there is no direct evidence in any of the Gospels to suggest Jesus was married, but neither is there any evidence to suggest that he was not. And if we look at him not as a theological construct but as a historical character who lived in a particular social and historical context, perhaps a different point of view might emerge.

Jesus of Nazareth was never a Christian. He was a devout son of the Covenant, and claimed that he did not come to destroy the Jewish Law. Where he did break it in minor ways, he always had a convincing theological reason.

But the church through the ages has found it convenient to forget that Jesus was a loyal Jew, and has placed him formally in the Platonic/Docetist and Gnostic/Manichean syndrome, which insists that all things carnal are unspiritual, and that sex is equivalent to death.

Christianity, at least from the time when it became interested in Jesus as a human being with an identifiable biography, has always had problems with admitting that Jesus had any sexual nature at all. But in an age when emphasis is being placed on the humanity of Jesus, perhaps it is time at least to entertain the possibility that Jesus was not remote from all human passion, but deeply involved in all aspects of humanity.

Another priest took a different tack. He completely pushed the question of Jesus' celibacy aside: *Jesus chose a married man as his first pope, and we know that celibacy was not a concern for Jesus or the apostles and disciples; it is therefore not intrinsic to the priesthood.* For this priest, the notion of Jesus being celibate is irrelevant. He suggests that even if Jesus was celibate that does not mean that priests have to be.

Priests with friends no longer accept the image that connects Jesus with celibacy or, alternatively, its importance for maintaining celibacy. These priests therefore search for new images to reconstruct their identity.

Celibacy for the Sake—
or Demise—of the Kingdom

At the Second Vatican Council, two of the scripture passages put forward to justify the practice of celibacy were Matthew 19:11-12 and 1 Corinthians 7:7-9, 25-38.[12] The papacy of John Paul II continues to uphold these biblical imperatives, claiming that these preeminent counsels show that "[the] precious gift of divine grace [is] given to some by the Father in order to more easily devote themselves to God alone with an undivided heart in virginity or celibacy."[13] Nonetheless, the following exegesis brings out aspects of these passages that the pope would prefer to remain hidden.

The Gospel of Matthew was written around 85-90 for the Hellenistic Jewish Christian mission. This particular Jewish community, shaped by Greek customs, language, and a culture that valued celibacy, tolerated its practise.[14] Because of this, the author of Matthew was able to present celibacy in the name of Jesus as an ideal consequence of divorce, whilst still maintaining a Jewish model of church:

> "... whoever divorces his wife, except for unchastity, and marries another commits adultery." His disciples said to him, "If such is the case of a man with his wife, it is better not to marry." But he said to them, "Not everyone can accept this teaching but only those to whom it is given. For there are eunuchs who have been so from birth, and there are eunuchs who have been made eunuchs by others, and there are eunuchs who have made themselves eunuchs for the sake of the kingdom of heaven. Let anyone accept this who can." (Mt 19:9-12)

While the documents use verses 11-12 to endorse celibacy, an exegesis of this passage shows that such a conclusion is problematic. For instance, verse 12 is read by certain scholars as meaning that people should "devote themselves more fully to the urgent demands of the kingdom," a teaching that would have been readily upheld by the Hellenists, who believed that it was paramount to convert others before the imminent Parousia (the Second Coming of Christ).[15] Other exegetes, such as Uta Ranke-Heinemann, assert that this passage is about divorce, and the metaphorical reference to celibacy is to be read only in that context.[16] This passage deals not with any incapacity for marriage or principled rejection of it, but with renouncing adultery. Hence, it is difficult to understand how a connection can be sustained between the celibacy of the Hellenists and the celibacy of the contemporary priesthood. Priests are anxious about neither the Parousia nor divorce.

———

Some priests indicate that this scripture verse is not helpful for establishing a celibate identity, as did one priest: *I avoid that biblical text and find it distasteful.* Fr. Aaron says, *I hate that really; I'm not a eunuch!* Fr. Jerry retorts that the only image of eunuchism that can be upheld is the one inflicted upon priests: *we are eunuched only by Rome.*

Fr. Reuben offered the following reflection: *I keep thinking what Jesus said: some men are born eunuchs, some men are made eunuchs by other men, and some men are eunuchs for the sake of the kingdom, and then he said, take this in, you whose hearts are large enough. So celibacy is for those whose hearts are large enough, which is a minority; those priests have the maturity to handle it and to really love in that celibate way. But it's not everyone's cup of tea, and if I had a chance to live my life again, I'm not too sure whether I would choose celibacy at all. I probably wouldn't.*

Meanwhile, Fr. Joseph cynically suggests the Holy Spirit works at the behest of the church's bureaucracy. *To see an **individual's** celibacy as a sign and charism of the Kingdom of God is praiseworthy; to see it as the Spirit-given grace of chastity is fine. But I believe that linking that grace to the sacrament of orders in such a way as to demand it of **all** priests effectively constitutes an attempt to "force the hand" of the Holy Spirit.*

Fr. David takes a broader perspective of how this scripture verse is being officially used to support celibacy. *In giving consideration to an increasing number of communities that are experiencing eucharistic famine, it leaves open the question as to whether this ecclesial discipline is actually building or inhibiting God's kingdom.*

———

Fr. Samuel also refutes the idea that celibacy is the only way in which a priest can benefit the kingdom of God.

We are social beings, that is, each one of us is a social being. We need others. It is only through communities and relationships with others that we can be fully human. God created us that way. God made us in his image. He made each and everyone of us with a great desire, a great need to love and be loved. I believe this is what being a genuine human person is about, that is, to experience loving and to experience being loved.

We cannot make it alone. I need your love and you need mine. I need to see my worth and beauty in the reflection of your eyes, in the sound of your voice, in the touch of your hand. And you need to see your worth mirrored back to you by me in the same way. We can succeed or fail together, but separate and alone we can only fail.

What I am saying is that the general norm for human beings is to experience love. That is to love another and to be loved by another, and that when this love matures physical sexual pleasure becomes a very important part.

Even though I believe that celibacy is not normal, I am not saying that there is no place for celibacy in society. In all societies there are a number of people who will deviate from the general norms. This pattern should also be reflected in the priesthood. While I believe celibacy is a valid practice, it should be on a voluntary basis.

Therefore it should be up to the individual person to freely choose celibacy. It should not be forced on any individual. It definitely should not be one of the criteria for a vocation to the priesthood. The priesthood should be given to whomsoever the Spirit of Truth deems to give the gift of ministering to—male or female, married or single.[17]

St. Paul's Advice to the Corinthians

The second scripture passage used by the pope to construct his image of celibacy is taken from the Apostle Paul's letter to the Corinthians in which he advises them to practice celibacy (1 Cor 7:8, 32, 35). John Paul interprets these verses for his own purposes, claiming that celibacy effects "a more complete adherence to Christ, loved and served with an undivided heart (cf. 1 Cor 7:32-33) [and ensures] greater availability to serve Christ's kingdom."[18] Yet again, by restoring historical and social details relating to this letter, we can unravel the selective use of this passage.

The Christians of Corinth were a zealous people who welcomed alternative visions of Christianity and competed with one another for spiritual prestige. One ascetic faction, in opposition to the libertarianism of some Christians, rigorously followed Paul's example of celibacy and developed an inflated understanding of eschatology.[19] This group asserted that all Christians should be celibate even if they were already married.

Nonetheless, Paul insisted that love was the basis of the Christian life (1 Cor 13:2) and could not see involvement with another person as a distraction from the affairs of the Lord.[20] He therefore attempted to rectify this extreme view by restoring balance to both celibate and married life, and situated this teaching within the influence of the Parousia.

A broader inspection of this chapter demonstrates that Paul is seen to be defending both married and unmarried states. He feels that marriage is a way in which both men and women can enjoy a balanced and fulfilling sexual life where husband and wife mutually serve each other in love. For those who were unmarried, Paul is keen to protect them from the patriarchal bondage of marriage, enforced childbearing, and motivations for maintaining family inheritance. Both states, in Paul's opinion, should be directed to giving devotion to the Lord.

However, when the papacy uses this image to align celibacy with priesthood, it not only contradicts the moderating intent of the author, it also avoids the idea of marriage as a state from which a priest can give devotion to the Lord. Moreover, it has succumbed to the danger of isolating details of history and applying them in contemporary contexts that are shaped by different social concerns.

Fr. Jude also comments on 1 Corinthians 7:7-8, where the Apostle Paul states, "I wish that all were as I myself am. But each has a particular gift from God, one having one kind and another a different kind. To the unmarried and the widows I say that it is well for them to remain unmarried as I am." The second part of the first verse is minimised by the papacy in its arguments for celibacy. Fr. Jude feels that it was the Apostle Paul's counsel to be celibate, not Jesus' advice.

Fr. Mark takes a different tack and considers that *because there was no exclusive love in Paul's life, he was therefore available and free.* Yet he also points out that contemporary clergy of other denominations make themselves freely available regardless of being married. Fr. Thomas further elaborates: *We often hear the practical argument that a priest is more available to people as a celibate than as a married person. If this were true, priests would be known as more accessible than other professionals. But it is simply not the case. Nor is it true to say that most priests are busier than family men. In any one week it is possible that any number of other professional people can have far more appointments than a priest. They can also manage to integrate their different roles.*[21]

⌒

Priest respondents also contributed general arguments about the way in which scripture should and should not be used. Several priests are convinced that scriptures are formulations made by people who were trying to understand God and their relationship with God, and any rigid interpretation obviates that search for meaning. One scholarly minded priest contends: *The more we investigate hermeneutics the more we realise how much the scriptures are a product of their authors, as are the traditions of the church. This does not mean they are not inspired by God. It does mean, though, we are not dealing simply with absolute, universal propositions of revelation, but with opinions that include much more human thought and preference.*

While the papacy might assert that there are unmistakable resemblances between Jesus and Paul regarding celibacy, some priests construct different representations that take into account an appreciation of history and their own social and cultural conditions. Moreover, these priests are no longer searching for answers about celibacy from a transcendent perspective, that is, above and beyond their direct personal awareness. Instead, they appear to be looking to a more incarnate notion of God. Through an historical and social consciousness, these priests feel that God is to be found in the experiences and exigencies of their lives. From this understanding, they argue the need for a tolerance of sexual pluralism in the priesthood.

Favouring Some, Ignoring Other Texts

Biblical scholars who have given a strictly exegetical interpretation of Matthew 19 and 1 Corinthians 7 have challenged and undermined the official images of celibacy. But the pope is not unduly daunted. Convinced that God is on his side in this matter, he has looked elsewhere in the New Testament to find support.

He finds confirmation in the following texts that refer to the apostles: "they '*left everything* and followed him' (Lk 5:11; cf. Mt 4:20, 22; Mk 1:18, 20)." This is bolstered with a second selection, "Peter . . . remembered this aspect of the apostolic vocation and said to Jesus: 'We have *given up everything* and followed you' (Mt 19:27; Mk 10:28; cf. Lk 18:28)."[22] John Paul insists that the apostles renounced family life in order to follow Jesus, because the Gospels don't speak of wives or children in regard to the Twelve, although he acknowledges that Peter was a married man before Jesus called him. Accordingly, these provide reasons as to why the church legislates for celibacy.

Critical analysis, however, throws into doubt any definitive claims for the apostles' postconversion celibacy. The Jewish apostles would have felt obliged to marry, and there is no evidence to suggest they did not. Nor is there any evidence that suggests that the apostles later left their families in the permanent sense that the pope advocates. Bruce J. Malina, a theologian who uses insights taken from cultural anthropology, indicates that in Mediterranean society, both present and especially past, the focal institution has been and is kinship. The family is truly everything.[23] He goes on to say, "success in life means maintaining ties to other persons within sets of significant groups. The central group in this set is one's kinship group." In keeping these pivotal values of the first-century world in mind, Jesus and the apostles would have had to keep a honourable connection to the entire family in order to ensure the success of their mission. If they had *left everything* as the pope asserts, it would have fundamentally damaged both the ministries of Jesus and the apostles.

The papacy's strategic use of images includes downplaying alternative representations that can be found in the scriptures because they challenge the official selection. For example, it does not consider two verses in which Paul stipulates that a bishop must be married only once (1 Tm 3:2; 1 Ti 1:6). These records are reduced to "a phase in the church's process of being organised and, one could say, of testing which discipline of the states of life best corresponds to the idea and the 'counsels' taught by the Lord."[24]

The papacy also considers insignificant Paul's belief that the apostles have the right to be accompanied by a believing wife (1 Cor 9:5). Indeed, it does not even acknowledge this passage. This is because the official text used for scriptural citations is based on the fifth-century Latin Bible that was translated by Jerome (347-420).[25] As mentioned in chapter 4, during the fourth century in which Jerome lived, Christianity gave extreme importance to sexual denial. Hence, it is not surprising that Jerome translated the word "wife" as "sister-woman," thus eliminating the idea of apostles having wives. Nevertheless, most contemporary biblical scholars agree that this term is a euphemism for "wife."[26]

In effect, the papacy reduces what it considers scriptural anomalies to mere process or waives them altogether. Favoured texts, on the other hand, are highlighted and promoted.

Given that the papacy has invested heavily in select images of celibacy, it can be profoundly disturbing when seemingly loyal priests suggest otherwise.

A friend of mine had just finished a six-year term as full-time vocations director for his diocese. He's a believer in married clergy and says celibacy isn't working. His moment of glory was last year at a conference of German-speaking vocation directors in Rome. They had a meeting with the Pope who asked them what was their solution to the priest crisis in Western Europe.

By coincidence, my friend was next to Pope John Paul and said to him that one of the answers was relaxation of celibacy and the use of married priests. The Pope reacted immediately, threw his arms in the air and almost shouted, "Impossible, impossible" —and then gave them a strong defence of celibacy.

Five weeks after the conference, this priest was removed from his position because his archbishop had been pressured by Rome *to get rid of him.*

A Priest in Love

Well trained in the craft of priesthood, priests with friends are able to construct images from scripture to help clarify their identity as priests. The story of Fr. Michael is one such example.

Rhoda and I have been close friends for years. But she and I have always seen our relationship as great mates. When I needed a shoulder to cry on, it was hers and vice versa. For the last three years, Rhoda has been living in another state. She's a specialist in childcare, and her talents have helped to bring some happiness and dignity to refugee children. Just after Christmas, Rhoda rang me to say that she would be coming home because her grandmother had died unexpectedly. I arrived late to the graveside, and there she was comforting her father. I was very proud of her coming home for her family. You see, it was really the moment that this great mate of mine became something much deeper. It was the moment I really fell in love with her. I know this is sounding more like a romance story. However, it is founded on a much deeper essence.

Rhoda and I had never before this expressed such emotions for each other. In fact, we had never seen this in our relationship. Since the funeral, our lives have grown together in a wonderful, intimate relationship. But it is a relationship highly condemned by the church and the law of celibacy. So as you can imagine, confusion is reigning supreme for this priest who loves his ministry but at the same time is deeply in love. That confusion is exacerbated by what such love brings to his priesthood.

It has opened me to the enormous aspects of love, gentleness, and compassion. It has challenged my inner being to the reality of true love. For the love that Rhoda and I share, I am able, in turn, to share with those that I minister to.

Just the other day I had to celebrate the funeral mass of a youth suicide. It's one of the toughest funerals for priests. Rhoda knew how I'd be feeling and rang me and gave me her love and support while I was heading towards the cemetery. How valuable this is!

Many aspects of priestly ministry can be so draining. You can literally feel your energy levels dropping. You are constantly giving out hope, compassion, and love to the grieving. It is only natural to want a little in return. Rhoda has been that in a very special way. Nevertheless, Fr. Michael is obliged to keep his friendship secret.

For example, if we go out anywhere we are both constantly looking around to see if someone knows us, well especially me! It is only when no one is around that we are able to relax. It's a most difficult thing and sometimes it rips the heart out of me.

One aspect of all this that we have found is the great love of a number of close friends who know, understand, and accept our dilemma. It is these mostly young Catholics who can see a future vision of their church where their priests are accepted for having intimate and open relationships.

Many of them have truly surprised me and in fact have given me great joy because their faith is not static like their parents (well in some cases!) but is so very dynamic and life-giving. Their faith, though in some cases non-practising, is a faith of the people—not of someone in an "ivory tower." They understand the importance and even the gift of celibacy. They know of its all-embracing love and the availability that that loving is able to give. However, they also know the essence and value of a love that is expressed through the intimacy of two. They don't want celibacy thrown out with the "bath water," they simply see the great value of an optional promise.

However, the acceptance is not totally perfect. Some priests and others to whom I have spoken are really against our friendship. Such a friendship in their eyes is sinful. People could find out about it, and it would cause scandal. They say we've had enough trouble with sexual abuse in the church, and we don't need any more problems.

In his attempts to rationalise his sexually intimate friendship in the face of church law and the negative judgement of particular confreres and laypeople, Fr. Michael reflects on the following scripture passage:

I listen intently to the words of our Lord in the Gospel of John, "I have come that you may have life and have it to the full (John 10:10). Priesthood touches for me the very heart of these words, yet how much more enhanced are they through the love I now understand. Maybe one day these words will echo far more loudly and openly in the hearts of our priests, and so in the heart of our church.

Fr. Michael upholds the value of his love for Rhoda and is able to find a degree of resolution to his dilemma in the Johannine verse. He understands this not just for himself but proposes that if any person wants to have *life . . . to the full*, then it should be made available to everyone.

Moreover, Fr. Michael challenges the official understanding of tradition by using scripture not to exclude, as the papacy does, but to include. He suggests that this image of inclusivity should speak to the ultimate concerns of all of us.

There may also be another unspoken message in Fr. Michael's use of imagery. His selection of a fragment of a verse is situated within a scripture passage in which John the evangelist uses a monologue that concerns Jesus as the shepherd and the sheep gate (Jn 10:1-21). This discourse is an involved allegory that characterises Jesus as the gate through which persons have access to the sheep and the "good" shepherd, meaning that Jesus is the only source of salvation. Those who came before him, the Jewish teachers and the tradition to which people first appealed, are rejected as thieves (v. 8).[27] John presents Jesus as saying, "the thief comes only to steal and kill and destroy. I came that they may have life, and have it abundantly" (v. 10).

Fr. Michael could well consider the papacy as the metaphorical thief who robs priests of the chance of true love. But by not being overtly antagonistic towards church leaders, he protects his investment in the priesthood.

Saints: Past and Present

The papacy also draws upon particular images of the saints to promote a celibate identity for the priesthood. These saints have been deemed by previous and current papacies as having led particularly holy lives. Many of them have also been celibate. Richard McBrien, for example, indicates that over 70 percent of the saints in the liturgical calendar are celibate men, and that of the saints canonized in this century to the end of Paul VI's pontificate (1978) 79 percent are clergy, 21 percent lay, and a smaller percentage, women.[28] Kenneth L. Woodward also indicates that of the laypersons canonized between the year 1000 and the end of 1987 more than half never married.[29]

More recently, John Paul beatified a married couple who lived the last twenty-six years of their marriage as brother and sister, whilst none of their four children ever married. Their two sons became priests, one daughter became a nun, and the other daughter embraced a life of consecrated virginity.[30]

In the saint-making process, the Congregation for the Causes of Saints chooses heroic candidates who are celibate. In contrast, it overlooks those who are married and remain sexually intimate and others in sexually intimate nonmarital relationships. In doing so, it is able to claim a remarkably high commitment to celibacy in these selected past examples of virtue.

Priests are consequently urged to emulate the saints, with the implication that while celibacy upholds moral goodness in the priesthood, sexual intimacy destroys it.

⌒

Many priests do reflect on the lives of the saints, but that does not necessarily mean that they accept the ideal of a celibate sainthood. According to Fr. David, *when giving reflection to the lives of the saints, we find there is a whole plethora of sensitive and insightful human responses that speak to the mystery of our belief.* Fr. David sees these saints as heroic individuals who have been shaped by different contexts: theological, historical, social, and cultural. Yet, the fact that these saints are predominantly celibate is largely irrelevant to the priests I interviewed.

Additionally, Fr. Joseph challenges the idea of saints as being singular characters: *We are now well aware that other priests and those people called canonised saints, male and female, have met and have been close together—very, very close together. They didn't let us know about things like that until recent years. Only recently, did we dig these things up.*

Fr. Barnabas drew attention to such a pair and offered his thoughts about the friendship of St. Clare and St. Francis.

I have problems with using these historical examples because I don't think that relationships meant the same in the Middle Ages as they do now. Clare and Francis were pre-Freudian, and our entire world is so dominated by psychology, by Freud, Jung, etc., that it is very hard for us to think in ways that are not Freudian, that are not relational in very specific ways. And I think what is happening now is quite different from what was happening in the past.

Fr. Barnabas does not believe that the friendship of St. Clare and St. Francis, located in another time and place, is very helpful for priests in the contemporary world. Psychology has had profound and far-reaching effects on modern intellectual culture. The ramifications and influences of these psychoanalytical concepts have, at least indirectly, affected all fields of enquiry about humankind and, to an extent, empowered individual priests. According to Carl Jung, all life is individual life in which alone ultimate meaning is to be found.[31] From this perspective, stereotypical images and standardized systems, such as those found in the priesthood, are believed to leave the psyche unfulfilled.

Consequently, individuals are driven to search for fulfillment in ways that express their needs. Such a search demands that the individual care for and embrace his or her uniqueness, including sexual uniqueness.

When priests no longer find the official images relevant to their lives, they look elsewhere for meaningful images. Fr. Jacob attempted to live out the *ideal of loving everybody equally and nobody in particular.* But by the time he was given his third parish appointment, he had experienced numerous struggles with celibacy, which were recounted in chapter 4.

My third and present parish, in a miracle of coincidence, provided me with a new relationship. I met a woman who lives a great distance from this parish, is close to my age, single, and committed to her job. She was here on business.

I felt the chemistry that all the soap operas talk about—a knowing feeling that she would be important in my life. Months later when she returned to do some training, I told her how I felt and asked if she felt anything for me. She did. We made long-distance plans. I knew this euphoria was called falling in love and that that emotion would not last forever, but this set of circumstances had a lot going for it.

Loyalty to her was much more life-giving and challenging than following a discipline of the church. With a commitment to her, physical affection could be an investment in something long-term. I could be a priest, be warm and open, and still know that there was a real person in this world that loved me and wanted my love and fidelity. I felt good and yes, even holy. This felt closer to God's plan than anything else I had experienced.

She returned for a second training program and stayed for a few extra weeks so we could take holidays together. This was bliss, not just because we had sex but because we were free to express ourselves. We lived life as we wanted rather than as we were supposed to. We had talked when she came to the last program and again over the phone. We both knew that there was no way that sex would not be a part of our future relationship. We could have avoided intercourse, but that would have been a lie. To me, it put sex into perspective. Sex creates commitment. I could no longer pretend about affection. I was acutely aware that affection towards another woman would be a move towards infidelity. The commitment I felt made it easy to put the brakes on.

Several years passed but the fear of being found out undermined Fr. Jacob and Hanna's friendship: *The communication between us has practically disappeared.*

Then one night, I asked myself, "Why do I love her? What does it mean for me to love her? Would I stop loving her if she stopped loving me? Was it about me or about her?" After some tears, which flowed from the centrality of the questions, I felt the answer: I love her. I like loving her. It didn't matter what she said or did; love was in me and it was for her. It had no conditions. This, I realised as I answered my own questions, is what God feels for us. This is unconditional love. It was, I believe, the most significant spiritual experience I have ever had: to glimpse within myself the love God has for us. I thought of the song from Les Miserables: *"to love another person is to see the face of God."*

In the struggle to find new and relevant images, Fr. Jacob came to know God intimately. He now reframes his approach to pastoral care:

Ministry is now a matter of waiting for life to bring me people who have lost connection with their wholeness. Fear of misunderstanding is often the obstacle. Rules are seen as God's wishes, and breaking them, a ticket to punishment. My experience questions these naïve connections. I ask them questions about these assumptions and allow people to question themselves. I ask them to look at Christ and how he treated people and how he reacted to certain situations. I get them to look at the church: its limitations, its motivations, its intentions. Hopefully they leave me with a new direction, that they can be themselves, be loving and be loved by people as they are most certainly loved by God.

When a priest finds a meaningful image, it can have a powerful effect on how he defines his identity and consequently how he lives out his life and ministry. Fr. Jacob selects a verse from a contemporary musical and adapts it to his personhood and priesthood, producing an image that speaks to his heart. In doing so, he reconfigures his notion of celibacy, which he now understands to be about rules. In contrast, sexual intimacy is a way in which Fr. Jacob can *see the face of God*.

This particular case suggests that images drawn from experience have greater power than images that are abstract and produced at a distance. Thus, if the papacy cannot deliver relevant and meaningful images of celibacy from which a priest can draw understanding and inspiration, then he will look elsewhere.

Goodbye Father, Hello Brother

We often locate an understanding of our identity within our family, a feature that the papacy has recognised and taken advantage of to maintain the religious and social cohesion of the church. By accepting celibacy, priests sacrifice family-of-origin attachments and replace these with Catholic kin. To implement this substitute family, various customs are employed.

One of the most obvious ways in which priests are recognised as dominating the Catholic household is by the way in which both laypersons and priests address a priest as "Father." This paternal address prioritises a priest's belonging to a religious family rather than a biological family, as is well recognised by Fr. Adam. After Fr. Adam's ordination, his own mother from then on addressed him only as "Father" and treated him as such. He then went on to say how at Christmastime, his brothers and sisters would be given a variety of gifts, while he regularly receives a white shirt and handkerchiefs, gifts his mother considers befit a priest.

The Catholic Church is patriarchal in organization. In this familial and social system, priests are recognised as having sole control of the domestic church. This paternal dominance is upheld in part by the use of images that promote "spiritual fatherhood." The pattern begins with God, who is said to resemble an omnipotent male parent who is celibate—for there is no Mother God. This God is addressed as "Father," a title and form of address that is echoed in many prayers of the church, particularly the "Our Father." Next, comes the pope, from the Greek *pappas*, meaning "father." As "the Holy Father," he represents the definitive and morally perfect male celibate leader who oversees all other "Fathers." Further down in the hieararchy are the bishops who are regarded as *paterfamilias*, from the Latin, transliterated as "father: head of the family." Lower still is the priest, referred to in everyday discourse as "Father."

As well, the use of capitalisation in each of these fatherly images suggests that popes, bishops, and priests are no ordinary fathers, but *the* Fathers who should be regarded as special, superior, and set apart from biological and other fathers. Thus, from the papacy's perspective, "Father" becomes expressive of each priest's entire being. Their identity is completely prescribed by celibacy, for again, there is no "Holy Mother," *materfamilias*, or "Mother."[32]

Parishioners who address a priest as "Father" give acknowledgement to the patriarchal order of the church, for when they use this title and form of address they imply that they are willing to be childlike, submissive, and obedient to Father's authority. In creating this family attachment, a priest is symbolically excluded from having a relationship with a layperson, because in this symbolism Father cannot have a sexual relationship with a child. To do so would be symbolically incestuous.

In some cultures, particularly Western cultures, which no longer accept men as the sole authority within the family and society, this "Father" image is being increasingly challenged. First, women and children in these cultures generally have civil, property, and legal rights that veto the presumption of male dominance. Secondly, a father and mother often regard the role of parenting as a mutual and equitable responsibility. Thirdly, an increasing number of women act as both the private and public head of the household because of a father's absenteeism, effectively vetoing paternal authority.

Some lay Catholics also desire an adult relationship with priests but the "Father" image frustrates their aspirations. These men and women seek to speak and work with a priest on a basis of mutuality and equality, each pursuing their respective ministries. Meanwhile, they look on other deferential Catholics with incredulity, especially highly capable men and women who become uncharacteristically subservient in the company of Father. As a result, male celibate images for a priest are being increasingly rejected, and rightly regarded as patronising and sexist.

In the context of the priesthood, some priests also recognise the problems of the "Father" image, as indicated by Fr. David's comment: *the hierarchy breeds infantilism.* Fr. Barnabas argues, *the structures have domesticated us and keep us docile.* These priests feel locked into their "Fatherhood," sandwiched between deference to "the Holy Father" and paternal responsibility to their parishioners, who are becoming less likely to acknowledge them as "Father."

Nevertheless, Fr. Reuben, through his friendships with women, has identified a new familial image that he considers much more suited to his personal, priestly, and pastoral circumstances. Previously, Reuban held rigid ideas about being "Father."

Until I came to enjoy particular friendship[s], I was a person who was fairly self-sufficient and assured about life. It wasn't just that I didn't need women; I didn't need people, period. I wasn't unpleasant to people, in fact I was very popular. For me, a priest was the strong person, the priest was the leader, the priest had studied all these books, he knew all the answers, and he was Father and was to lead the children.

Being "Father" assured Reuben of his priestly identity and shored up self-sufficiency. His curriculum vitae added further weight to his work ethic, listing an impressive summary of educational qualifications, pastoral skills, and responsible positions on a large number of diocesan and national committees. As "Fr. Reuben," he had the means and ability to exist and minister as an independent character. In hindsight, though, he admits he was *task-orientated. Relationships complicated life. Relationships made it difficult to get the job done.*

Throughout the past ten years, Reuben has enjoyed two sexually intimate friendships with women that have fundamentally changed his attitude. He saw how these women complemented his personality and how much *he needed people, not just women, but others too. I see them as people who are on my side, so to speak, which I wouldn't have always seen that way. I just treat women as equals and appreciate their intuitive perspective, which is a wonderful perspective, because I tend to be cerebral.*

These women have helped balance out my development, and I think I am far more in touch with my feelings now than I have ever been. I also have an understanding and appreciation of my abilities better than I've ever had in my life. And that's including my weaknesses as well. In learning to feel at home with these women and having to share myself with them, I have learned to feel much more at home with myself.

I am also much more aware of the endemic discrimination against women, especially in the church, because of the attitude of superiority on the part of the male leaders of the church. I wasn't aware of my own discrimination until gradually I became aware of it through these women challenging me. So now, I've become aware of women and value them and their contribution to my own personal life. So my particular friendships have been a wonderful enrichment of myself, and in both cases have also contributed to the enrichment of my partners.

Reuben still feels that this priestly training residually affects him. *It's hard to change the spots and habits of a lifetime, but I am now very aware of what it means to relate at a head level and what it means to relate at a heart level. There's a vast difference. Now my relationships tend to be warm and spontaneous, personal rather than professional, so to speak. I'm now a "brother" in the human family. When I started out, I was a Father in the human family, now I'm a brother. You know, walking amongst equals, journeying together so to speak. Not just the journey of faith, but the journey of life itself.*

Compulsory Celibacy in Jeopardy

Vatican officials are dismissive of any alternative representation made by priests with friends. They are determined to maintain celibacy, at least on the face of it, as a permanent fixture on the landscape of the priesthood.

Nonetheless, church leaders are faced with a danger that lies within the images themselves. The images remain true only when the identity between celibacy and priesthood can be sustained. This is well recognised by priests such as Fr. Samson: *It's the images and expectations of celibacy—they don't provide celibates with a meaningful explanation for their lives. And in the larger Christian community, they don't provide reasons to appreciate why priests are celibate.*

If a priest does not recognise celibacy as adding value to his life and ministry, then celibacy as an ideal may well be abandoned.

This is the view of priests with friends who effectively locate themselves in an egalitarian community. In that nonhierarchical society, they do not recognize any importance in being set apart or made superior to others. Instead, these priests argue that the characteristic qualities of their intimate friendships herald a reformed priesthood and, more broadly, Christianity. This new model is realised through the equality and mutuality of their intimate relationships. In reimaging their identities, such priests unmask the theology and practise of compulsory celibacy as implausible and lacking in credibility.

In stark contrast to priests with friends, the pope and the curia are supplied with a vast array of resources. One of their strategies is the careful screening of orthodox and often ambitious clerics who are encouraged to develop scholarship that confirms the validity of their claims for celibacy. These scholars choose tracts from ancient and contemporary manuscripts to furnish supposedly irrefutable evidence about the celibate identity of priesthood. This exclusive material is then widely promoted, as exemplified by the Congregation for the Clergy's Web site: http://www.clerus.org/clerus/index_eng.html. Under the section "Library" and in a file titled, "Other documents," articles are devoted to promoting rationales for the practice of celibacy.[33]

Church bureaucrats also protect the images of celibacy by silencing or revoking the teaching licences of dissident priests and theologians who promote alternative views about celibacy and sexuality.[34] These licences are needed for teaching in seminaries or ecclesiastical faculties. Similarly, Vatican officials and local bishops suppress the rhetoric of individuals and groups who endeavour to have concerns about celibacy and other related issues heard.

Despite all this, the papacy's repetition of its mantra— "celibacy is a gift of God" —is proving less and less effective. Challenging and questioning images is part of the dialectical process by which humankind seeks a better understanding of the truth. Therefore, when the papacy insists that priests must completely identify with celibacy and suppress the search for intimacy, it ignores the opinions and experiences of priests and others who know perfectly well that celibacy need not be at the heart of the priesthood.

Notwithstanding the Vatican's micromanagement of the church, images are most successful when they are perceived and accepted by a particular audience as somehow natural. If priests accept celibacy as being natural, the canon will remain. However, if priests align themselves with other images that represent sexual intimacy as being part of the natural order, then the moral rejection of celibacy proceeds as a matter of course. Such a process has already been acknowledged by one bishop in his assessment of celibacy: *If we have the choice between having a sign and having priests, then let us have priests. A sign which does not in fact function specifically and psychologically as a sign seems . . . to be an ideology: a suspect sign.*[35]

In places such as Latin America, parts of Asia, and Africa, celibacy is contrary to the customs of many people. For example, the whole Andean culture is built around images of the *pareja*, the "couple." Everything goes in couples—animals, the sun and the moon. There are even two mountains, male and female. The word for a single guy is *mula*, a "mule."[36] In this culture, a man who is not married is not considered a worthwhile leader of his community.

In Western societies, celibacy is also being contested. Priests and laity are brought up in a participative democracy that promotes equal employment opportunities and stresses the importance of shared roles and responsibilities. These Catholics are not likely to value images that essentially promote an autocratic system upheld by childlike participation, sexual discrimination in vocations, and discriminatory divisions in relationships.

In effect, the tension between the idealised past of celibacy and the experienced present is building up to critical proportions under the combined efforts of priests with friends, dissidents and reformers, disenchanted Catholics, and those concerned about the shortage of priests. For these groups and individuals, celibacy is being identified as a form of religious imperialism. The papacy struggles to convince Catholics otherwise.

6

The Erosion of Patriarchy

Fr. Obadiah, an Indian priest, was encouraged by papal and episcopal pleas to help the Western world alleviate the shortage of priests. So he packed his bags and said farewell to his confreres, parishioners, and family.

Having arrived on foreign soil, he went through some training to help him get used to living and ministering in a Western culture. He underwent a language assessment, undertook some driving training to familiarise himself with the local road rules, and spent some time with the chancellor so that he might know the ins and outs of the diocese. Six weeks later, he was assigned to a quiet rural parish, far away from the bustle of city life that he had known since his childhood.

The quietness and slow pace of country life was the least of his troubles. For the first few days, he sat in the presbytery and wondered when the servant would come to make his meal and do his cleaning.

When the servant didn't appear, Fr. Obadiah tried to do some of his own cooking, washing, and ironing. But there were so many problems associated with these chores that they seemed insurmountable. For example, he didn't really know what to purchase, and when he finally did buy some groceries, it wasn't what he was used to. Cooking even the most basic of food was also a frustrating experience, especially because he had never really done it before.

Slowly his resentment built up: why should he do these things? He was after all, the parish priest. So he advertised for a servant and was promptly told by the parish chairperson that it was inappropriate to call a housekeeper a servant.

Only one applicant applied, a small energetic woman named Phoebe. At least she seemed willing to cook a curry and do his domestic bidding, but he had his reservations about her. She didn't seem to have the respect that he considered his due. She was too brash for his liking, but he had little choice. It was either do the work himself—a prospect he didn't cherish because he thought he would end up starving—or employ her.

At first, he found her bossy. One morning she came in and found the presbytery door wide-open. Phoebe was quite worried and told Fr. Obadiah that he must learn to lock up the place if he was going out anywhere. He, on the other hand, didn't appreciate being told off.

He seemed to make lots of little mistakes like that, both in his home and out in the parish. Phoebe tried to help him, but to Fr. Obadiah, she came across as critical and confrontational. To him, it was a matter of saving face. But Fr. Obadiah retained her services, and Phoebe persisted with him.

After several years, they developed an understanding and an affection for each other. Not only did Fr. Obadiah begin to realise that men and women relate differently in a Western culture, he also realised that his priesthood was out of sync. He had been raised in a patriarchal society where men and women complemented each other and were fond of each other, but women had their place. Men, and more so priests, were always above women.

But Phoebe insisted on something different. She had been raised on a farm with her brothers and had been thoroughly involved in all its workings. Women were expected to do the jobs that men do, and vice versa. Men, at minimum, were expected to help in the house. As a result, she considered herself on an equal footing with any man. Her family was also very post-Vatican II, and in a country parish, everyone was involved in the liturgy and church work, especially the women. They knew what they had to do, and that included organising the parish priest.

Phoebe was very good at that, organising Fr. Obadiah. And she learnt to respect his need to save face, even though it wasn't easy for her. She practised endless patience but was rarely rewarded with a compliment or public acknowledgement. Fr. Obadiah, on the other hand, appreciated Phoebe's help and persistence, though he found it confusing at times.

I'm fond of Phoebe, but it is very difficult knowing how to be that way when a priest is supposed to be above women. I was brought up that way; that way remains in the church, but it's not the case for people in this country.

As for celibacy, I have these desires that won't go away. I want to be close to her, but I find it hard to be comfortable when I am. Sometimes I sit very close to her, but then I feel really guilty. So I stay away.

I fear for her having a friendship with me, honestly. I hope she would know by now what she is getting herself into. I know she likes me, but this whole thing, this whole culture business, is really difficult.

Like, I am supposed to make all the decisions in the parish. But sometimes Phoebe challenges an idea I have, and she tells me so. She expects her judgement to be taken into account. But when I go ahead and exercise my priesthood, she just gets cross and calls me authoritarian.

Later when she settles down, she gets a pen and paper and writes down the pros and cons of my decision. Then she reasons with me, and I sometimes see that her point of view is right. But that just makes me more confused and uncertain. I know in my head that there is something not quite right about the way the church regards women.

During Fr. Obadiah's lifetime, his culture and the church have shaped his image of what a woman is supposed to be like. Now that he lives in a Western culture and has met Phoebe, these standardised images are being challenged. The root of Fr. Obadiah's trouble stems from the reductive character of these stereotypes. Such stereotypes that originally defined Phoebe and himself no longer seem appropriate; this leaves him in a state of confusion and anxiety.

Once an image of a person or group of people is unequivocally accepted by society, the consequent stereotypes allow for no critical judgement and, as a result, inhibit people from understanding or acting differently from what is expected. So when the papacy claims superiority in celibacy for the priesthood over other groups in the church, these stereotypes become a lived reality for Catholics.

Furthermore, these stereotypes are linked together and constitute a system of patriarchy. By organising the church in this way, people like Fr. Obadiah and Phoebe are required to live according to the expectations of their respective categories, namely, celibate priest and woman. But their experiences have led them both to question the patriarchal stereotypes that confine them.

Constructing Patriarchy

By imaging God primarily as male and Jesus as revelatory confirmation of the maleness of God, the papacy seems to confirm that maleness is divine and therefore normative for leadership in all social and familial dimensions. These standardised images consequently create unequal power between the sexes. Such inequality inevitably produces conflicts of interest, exclusion, and hostility.

The papacy, though, harnesses social conflict for its own purposes. By elevating Mary, the earthly mother of Jesus, into the Blessed Virgin Mary, Mother of God, women can symbolically identify themselves with a supernatural feminine image. Nonetheless, Mary remains subordinate to God the Father, the latter image being upheld and represented by the various priestly Fathers, whilst no women formally represent Mary in the hierarchy. Such tokenism offers the bare minimum in compensation for women's loss of authority and power. Yet this symbolic effort helps men in authority to channel the conflict and tension experienced by women in the church.

In order to control the image of an obedient and docile Mary, the pope and the curia supernaturalise the motherhood of Jesus through a selective reading of scripture. By literalising the phrase, "the virgin shall conceive and bear a son" (Mt 1:23), these clerics insist that this reading is not only historical fact but expresses God's supernatural intervention in history. Moreover, because Mary has obviously been uniquely marked by divine favour, for no other woman can be a virgin and mother at the same time, she must be honoured by supernatural rank.

This literalist reading is, however, contrary to what the Gospel writers say. These authors took the prophecy of the virgin birth from the Hebrew Testament (Is 7:14) to exalt the circumstances of Jesus' birth, not Mary's virginity. According to John Dominic Crossan, the prophecy in Isaiah says nothing whatsoever about a virginal conception. It speaks in Hebrew of an *almah*, a virgin just married but not yet pregnant with her first child.[1] He goes on to say that the virginal conception of Jesus is a confessional statement about Jesus' status and not a biological statement about Mary's body. It is a belief about Jesus as an adult mythologically thrown back onto Jesus as an infant.[2] In recognising the importance of Jesus, the Gospel writers acted as media agents in an era where they had to compete with other claims of divinity.

Church leaders continue to treat Mary's virginity and supernatural motherhood as historic events. This strategy is taken further when they reinterpret other scriptural anomalies that might contest the claim of a virgin-mother. For example, the biblical references to Mary's other children (Mk 3:33, 6:3; Mt 13:55) are interpreted as stepbrothers and stepsisters or as cousins. Mary's husband, Joseph, is also sometimes promoted as a virgin or portrayed as an old man, insurances that are intended to uphold the belief that he and Mary never had sexual intercourse. Thus an elite group of celibate males who have allegedly no experience of sexual love, women's bodies, childbirth, or fatherhood, promulgate their image of Mary.

By putting Mary on such a pedestal, the papacy not only promotes an impossible standard for women, ensuring that all women fall short of the ideal, but also directs the sexual desires of priests away from these less-than-ideal women. Indeed, John Paul frequently invokes Mary to care for her priest-sons, and specifically for their celibacy.

> Every aspect of priestly formation can be referred to Mary, the human being who has responded better than any other to God's call. Mary became both the servant and the disciple . . . [who] was called to educate the one eternal priest [Jesus], who became docile and subject to her motherly authority. With her example

and intercessions the Blessed Virgin keeps vigilant over . . . priestly life in the Church.

And so we priests are called to have an ever firmer and more tender devotion to the Virgin Mary and to show it by imitating her virtues and praying to her often.[3]

The pope encourages priests to revere the Virgin Mary with passionate prayers and romantic meditations. For she poses no threat to their celibate virtue as she is unavailable in fantasy, having been stripped of all identification with sexuality. At the same time, the pope provides an attentive supernatural mother figure to help priests tame their sexuality, protecting them from temptations and sexual sinfulness.

The papacy has specific interests in manipulating the sexuality of women. By promoting the image of Mary, the Virgin-Mother, as a model for all women, the pope is able to call all women to be mothers, either physically or spiritually. Indeed, he asserts that "virginity and motherhood [are the] two particular dimensions of the fulfillment of the female personality."[4] Only through the gendered role of motherhood in the context of religious life or marriage, both headed and disciplined by a patriarchal male, is a woman allowed to express her sexuality.

A woman cannot therefore express her sexuality in a relationship with a priest, because she cannot marry her friend. However, according to John Paul, a woman can be a "sister." Only in the sense of sisterhood can a woman licitly "light up [a priest's] human existence," but he adds this extra word of caution: "[in this] revelation they are in a certain sense set apart."[5] By idealising and promoting the image of a woman as sister, the pope makes certain that women are subordinated in the patriarchal church.

Concomitantly, John Paul confidently asserts that "if the priest, with the help of divine grace and under the special protection of Mary, virgin and mother, gradually develops [a right] attitude towards women, he will see his ministry met . . . on the part of women . . . as sisters and mothers."[6] But when that ideal is not realised, hostility results. Strong opposition is levelled by the papacy against priests with friends, discounting any advantages or value that their sexually intimate relationships may hold.

Patriarchy's Suppression of Homosexuality

By making preeminent the image of Mary as Virgin-Mother, the papacy is also able to control the sexuality of people who are homosexual. In the patriarchal order, such people are either pressured to marry or are forced to remain celibate and direct their energies towards building up the church by becoming spiritual "fathers" and "mothers."

Alternatively, they are ostracised because they refuse to fit within the parameters of patriarchy. Homosexual relationships between men, for instance, challenge the familial order in the church because they do not use their sexuality to dominate women. In the case of lesbian relationships, a patriarchal male does not govern the partnership. In effect, same-sex relationships contradict and challenge the hetero-patriarchal order.

Furthermore, because homosexual relationships do not biologically produce the next generation of Catholics, "homosexual activity" is regarded as immoral; it is incapable of transmitting new life, necessary for the maintenance of patriarchy.[7] In refusing to acknowledge any other forms of generativity, such as service to society and extended family, the papacy is able to denounce homosexual partnerships as unnatural.

Cardinal Joseph Ratzinger, the prefect of the Congregation for the Doctrine of the Faith argues, "Although the particular inclination of the homosexual person is not a sin, it is more or less a strong tendency ordered toward an intrinsic moral evil; and thus the inclination itself must be seen as an objective disorder."[8] To sustain this judgement, Vatican officials select particular scripture passages, such as, Genesis 19:1-11, Leviticus 18:22 and 20:30, and 1 Corinthians 6:9, to assert the immorality of "homosexual activity."

The first scripture passage refers to the story of Sodom in which the men of this city, both young and old, seek to sexually abuse the two guests of Lot. Yet it is generally accepted by Christian and Jewish scripture scholars that these inhabitants primarily committed sins of pride, greed, failure to welcome visitors, and fornication: a list that does not include homosexuality.[9]

Another verse used to condemn sexual intimacy between homosexual persons is Leviticus 18:22. This passage is a part of the Jewish

Holiness Code, which was used to counter idolatrous practices that included male temple prostitution, a common practice of some of Israel's neighbours at that time.[10] While Vatican officials have generally abandoned the Holiness Code, they arbitrarily use this passage to support negative pronouncements against homosexuality.

Gareth Moore adds another way of understanding this passage. Israel was a patriarchal society in which men were regarded as superior to women. For a man to take on the passive role in sexual intercourse was to take on the woman's role and thereby demean himself and all other men, and in doing so, subvert the social order.[11] This insight gives further explanation as to why homosexuality is not permitted in the social organization of the church. Patriarchy demands that men retain dominance over women.

From the New Testament, Vatican officials also select the Pauline text, 1 Corinthians 6:9, to support the teachings on homosexuality, even though contemporary exegetes cast doubt on its relevance. In this verse are listed categories of people who will be prevented from inheriting the Kingdom of God. One category, however, has been variously translated as effeminate, homosexuals, or sexual perverts. The original Greek text reads *malakoi arsenokoitai*. The first word means "soft"; the meaning of the second word is disputed. It was once used to refer to a "male temple prostitute." The early church interpreted the phrase as referring to people of "soft morals," that is, unethical. From the time of Martin Luther, it was interpreted as referring to "masturbation." More recently, it has been translated as referring to "homosexuals." Each translator seems to take whatever activity his or her society particularly disapproves of and name it in this verse.[12]

Moreover, these references bear little or no similarity to contemporary lesbian and gay relationships. Indeed, according to Elizabeth Stuart, the very word "homosexual" was not coined until the nineteenth century. The idea that some people are oriented emotionally and sexually towards members of their own sex is quite a new discovery. Up until very recent times it was believed that all people were born oriented towards the opposite sex.[13] Now many accept homosexuality as a phenomenon of the human condition.

Meanwhile, the papacy promotes its strictures against homosexuality as absolute and eternal truths. These images become socialised in stereotypes, denigrating homosexual people and their relationships. At the same time, they ensure that homosexuals who wish to maintain their faith, status, and position in the church remain closeted.

Challenging Compulsory Celibacy

The papacy ensures that patriarchy is honoured in the local church by giving each bishop the authority to establish more detailed rules about a priest's right of association. The bishops are also allowed, even encouraged, to pass judgement on a priest's observance of celibacy.[14] Effectively, a bishop is given authority to take whatever measures are deemed necessary to sever a priest's friendship, regardless of the circumstances, the culture in which he ministers, or the commitments and responsibilities he has towards his friend. A bishop can also use his position to encourage local Catholics to curb the actions of any priests who might attempt to challenge patriarchy.

But patriarchy is being eroded. During my research, I made enquiries as to whether priests ever raised the general issue of celibacy at formal gatherings of priests. Six priests responded each in different ways because each had to evaluate what one priest referred to as *the spirit of the diocese*. Each diocese or religious order has a unique character, produced by the priests who participate in that diocese or religious order. A priest becomes knowledgeable in the ways that celibacy is being characteristically maintained, information that helps him to negotiate this stereotype.

According to Fr. Peter, that *spirit* appears to mainly *revolve around the current bishop or some former bishop, so it's revolving around the power issues of the church*. Each of these priests must take into account a *spirit* that is largely manipulated by a bishop who is officially responsible for the local advocacy of stereotypes. *So much of it comes back to power and authority; it's not so much about individual priests. Effectively, the hierarchy commandeers the spirit of the diocese.*

In the diocese to which Fr. Jordan belongs (we met him in chapter 3), that *spirit* is relatively critical of celibacy: *There would be many that would talk about celibacy all right, and talk about the difficulties of it, and the loneliness of it. They wouldn't all speak, but a number would.* Fr. Jordan indicates that celibacy is being questioned and criticised, but he goes on to say that priests with friends *would be careful about the level of detail they would divulge.*

Within formal gatherings such as clergy conferences, Fr. Jordan's local bishop, who has also spoken of his struggles with celibacy, has given consent to modified discussions that have resulted in *some fairly honest stuff being said that would be appropriate for the meeting.* While *broad permissions and opportunities to speak about that issue* have been given, Fr. Jordan is still wary about how much he is willing to talk about celibacy or his friendship with Tabatha.

In another diocese, Fr. Aaron indicates that priests talk *openly enough* but that *they would talk about married priests rather than celibacy.* His bishop has also allowed particular opportunities to discuss celibacy where he and his confreres have shared with each other their lack of enthusiasm for its practise. Meanwhile, Fr. Aaron hastened to add that celibacy is a valid and a valued choice for some priests, but he desires the option of another equally valid and valued choice, that of being married.

With the adverse publicity given to clerical sexual abuse, Fr. Aaron's bishop has since reneged on his position about being open to such discussions. This bishop has issued a notice of caution to his priests that they are not to be seen compromising their celibacy in any way. *In the present climate, he doesn't want problems of that particular kind,* said Fr. Aaron. *At the moment he has a real problem of a particular court case in which a priest has been charged with the sexual abuse of a child, and he wouldn't want it out in any way that one of his priests is having a relationship. He would be very uneasy.*

Through defensive rhetoric, Fr. Aaron's bishop is endeavouring to restore the damaged image of celibacy. Yet if there is to be any chance of restoring this image, all priests must desire that restoration and there is little support for this.

Fr. Aaron went on to suggest that, although his bishop is demanding vigilance, perhaps it is time *to come to terms with his priests and understand that they have relationships like any normal human being.* However, church authorities deny the idea that a priest is a normal human being. A priest is pressured by religious and social expectations to surpass his humanity and to take on the imagined transcendence of representing Christ. But when Fr. Aaron claims his humanity, he challenges the stereotype that makes priests superior and sets them apart.

~

Fr. Cornelius commented at length on the politics that have shaped *the spirit* of his diocese. One of his confreres reported to a council his concerns *that a lot of younger chaps aren't keeping celibacy*. Fr. Cornelius supported his confrere by saying, *we should very definitely talk about it because a lot of people are concerned and it's a big problem*.

The bishop put a stop to that course of action: *We have been told by Rome that this is not to be discussed*. So Fr. Cornelius said, "OK, *but could we signal in our minutes to Rome that a number of priests are very concerned and are certain it isn't being taken very seriously by some of the younger ones and want it to be discussed but deferred to the ruling?*

The bishop agreed to the request, but no mention of this concern was recorded in the minutes of the meeting: *It was just conveniently forgotten*. Fr. Cornelius went on to share with me his disgust at the treatment given to these genuine concerns: *I knew it would be useless to talk to the bishop because he himself obviously doesn't want to get into trouble with the authorities. He wants to impress on them that he is doing a good job officially representing the Vatican in this neck of the woods, so he doesn't want to be seen breaking rank or disobeying.*

Fr. Cornelius went on to describe his bishop as *a complete servant to Rome* who is prepared to use self-promotion and ingratiating behaviours to ensure his progress up the hierarchical ladder. This behaviour, though, has come at a price. By abdicating his responsibility as a credible local leader, he leaves the problems of his diocese unattended.

Later in our conversation, Fr. Cornelius reported that his bishop *accepts celibacy because it comes with the pattern of the priesthood, but he doesn't really agree with it*.

~

Fr. Bartholomew indicated that celibacy is not discussed at formal gatherings of his religious order, except when *celibacy would be the subject of one of the talks, but that would be about reinforcing celibacy. I think the only time it would come up is if it were a cause of worry to the council. In this event, the priest would have been spoken about in a very charitable and fraternal way; not in a corrective way, because you don't always know the facts.*

Fr. Bartholomew, despite having a friendship, is of the opinion that *no matter what happens, celibacy is still going to be part of religious life, as distinct from the diocesan priesthood.*

I then asked him about his provincial's opinion of celibacy. He went on to say that he could share news of his relationship with him and his confreres *in order to ease any fears they might have about it, and to ensure them that there wasn't a problem.*

Sharing news about the sexually intimate details of his friendship, however, would not be an item for discussion. Not having *a problem* also suggests that Fr. Bartholomew is prioritising his priesthood over his relationship, and that he would do nothing to harm the reputation of his religious order.

More questions yielded comments such as, *celibacy is a fait accompli. It is not, in our lifetime, going to change. And while there is a lot of discussion, this gathering of priests is not going to make any difference. Why bother?*

While Fr. Bartholomew is in favour of celibacy for religious life, the irony is that he is committed to his friendship. Publicly he promotes his intimate friendship in quite skilled ways. This contradiction suggests that he has not fully reconciled his position on the matter of celibacy.

⌇

Fr. Tobit is quite emphatic that celibacy is not spoken about at any formal gatherings of priests in his predominantly rural diocese. *The only time that celibacy would have been mentioned would have been by priests giving retreats, but there is no real discussion about it.*

"But what about the priest who was known to be sexually promiscuous with married women," I asked. "Is that ever discussed at such a meeting?"

You hear much more about that from lay people than from priests. The priests are trying to keep that quiet. You just don't talk about that.

While Fr. Tobit feels that celibacy should not be a prerequisite for priesthood, he feels that the sexual behaviour of priests should not be discussed. Such incidents, he believes, should be handled with great sensitivity and a minimum of attention so as to preserve the reputation of the priesthood: *You've got a public image that you've got to uphold and you would never allow that to impinge on any public discussion or public thought.*

I then asked Fr. Tobit what he thought the consequences would be if he did raise the subject. *If I brought up the issue, I think some of the guys would think that I am talking about them, and some of them who aren't celibate don't want it mentioned.* For some priests it is difficult enough to negotiate their friendships without having to bear the burden of arguing against celibacy in an environment of clericalism. To do so might also blow the cover they have established to protect their relationships.

Fr. Tobit also argues that *sexuality is something personal and private; there is a lot of emotion attached to it. There are certain things I have sorted out in my own mind, but a lot of the priests have never sorted this out because a lot of them haven't faced up to their own sexuality.*

Fr. Tobit then elaborated on what he feels goes on in the minds of particular confreres. *Some are caught between the laws of celibacy, which they would see binding in conscience; and in breaking them, they would feel ashamed.* For these priests, such matters should only be spoken about in the confessional. Fr. Tobit contends that while celibacy exists in canon law, any attempts to talk about this issue should be governed by discretion and consideration.

Fr. Tobit also comments on his bishop's attitude towards celibacy: *I don't think the basic issue is celibacy alone. You get some people like our bishop, who, it has been said more than once, is basically a bachelor. And that is probably why celibacy has never been brought up at our meetings. A lot of it has to do with priests not just being celibates but being bachelors, and bachelors will choose celibacy. It is always a solitary kind of thing, then it becomes a permanent fixture or attachment, because they value their bachelorhood more than they value their friendship with somebody else.*

Effectively, celibacy allows certain priests and bishops to live life comfortably without having their choice of bachelorhood publicly scrutinised. By suppressing criticism of celibacy, their bachelorhood is secured.

Fr. Thomas further explains why it is difficult to talk about celibacy at formal gatherings of priests. When he left the priesthood to marry Lydia, a number of his confreres shared their personal secrets with him.

About eighteen months before I left, one of my ordination classmates decided to reveal to us that he was gay. I was surprised as I had never been aware of any indication. Anyway, after a long struggle he made the decision to leave the priesthood and live with his partner in what he thought would be a permanent relationship. Not long after this we had lunch together, and he told me what he had been going through. The coming out had been very hard but also a relief because friends had been far more sympathetic and supportive than he had expected. I admired him for his courage, and, in a direct way, his actions helped me to face my own problems.

But beyond his own revelation, he went on to tell me another story which further expanded my understanding of how priests around me were struggling with their own particular problems. He said that during what he called a down period of his life he was out on the streets looking for companions when he came across another member of our ordination class doing the same. They began a conversation in which personal revelations were made. Once more, this was all news to me. I had always presumed that this other fellow had the question of women and celibacy under better control than I. Now I realised that it simply was not his concern.

If this was not enough to convince me of the difference between the celibacy issue and the reality, later on that year while I was discussing my decision to resign, a third person from our class made a similar disclosure that he was gay. By now, patterns were beginning to emerge in these revelations, though each story had its own unique dimensions. But the disclosures were not over then.

After I left, another member of my ordination class rang up to say that he could well understand my situation because he himself had been in a close relationship with a woman for more than ten years. Their association had begun as an affair but had gradually developed into something much deeper, at least from his side. However, the deliberations over their future together took too long, and she eventually left him for another man. He had been the last to know and was devastated by the result. He regretted not having made a move earlier.

Bit by bit, then, I was building up a picture of my ordination class far different from the one I had presumed for many years. One from our group left in the first couple of years to get married. Two more of us since had heterosexual relationships, and three had homosexual relationships. So, out of the ten ordained, six different stories of dealing with sexuality, relationships, church and society were emerging. That left another four members of the class whose story, for me at least, remained untold. This is convenient, for it leaves room for any individual in my class who reads this to claim that he belongs to the unknown 40 percent.

What is more, I am not really interested in knowing such details. More important is the significance of what had already been volunteered, for what it reveals, and because it is not limited just to our group. The more I speak to others in this country and elsewhere about these findings, the more I learn of similar discoveries.

One effect of all these discoveries, then, was that I was not alone in my struggle. However, the most important finding was that there were different struggles, and we needed to be distinguished by much more than we had presumed. It had always puzzled me why the conversations of our group on mandatory celibacy rarely got anywhere. Now I could see why this had been so. We had not even known the fundamental issue of sexual orientation affecting each other. Not knowing this, nothing else followed. In contrast, the best conversations we had were when, after so many years of disguising ourselves, we had been open with one another. We could now talk of our individual struggles and the cost of having to cover these to maintain expectations. Thus, we were able at last to establish our true differences. Ironically, we could also establish a great similarity, which was that we all wished to be able to relate our sexualities and our need for expression with our love for the priesthood and the church.

Because the inner story was different, the rule of celibacy touched each of us differently. Those who were gay had to pretend they were heterosexual, because the Church considered their orientation aberrant. Yet it was easier for them to have casual relationships, for the expectations of men in regards to monogamy are generally less than those of women. It was also easier for them to maintain a relationship if they could find a priest partner, for then there were no borders to cross between genders and occupations. On the negative side, it could be worse for them if they were found out, for they had to face more severe reactions from church, society, and family. From the other perspective, those who were heterosexual had questions of marriage and children to deal with, but not the same level of *general opprobrium. Lastly, in both orientations, those with ongoing monogamous relationships had more reason to want to be open about them than those with liaisons of short duration. So, for once, we could compare notes that really mattered. We could also affirm each other's struggles and the quest for integrity without those struggles.*[15]

By imposing a singular, overarching stereotype of celibacy, church authorities disallow priests from acknowledging the various sexualities and relational circumstances in the priesthood within dioceses and religious orders. In doing so, they ensure that the spirit of the diocese or religious order retains the official façade of celibacy. Confreres cannot therefore be open with each other about their friends or sexual orientation or about their dreams and hopes. By maintaining a stereotype of celibacy, the clerical system maintains ongoing patriarchal control.

Challenging the Stereotype of Homosexuality

While celibacy is not commonly discussed at formal gatherings of priests, homosexuality is totally off-limits, as is recognised by Fr. Thomas and similarly acknowledged by several priests: *Homosexuality would never, ever be discussed; that would be a real taboo. There has been not one word mentioned about gay priests. It's always covered up.*

The irony is that the priesthood is being increasingly recognised as a *gay profession*, a view that is supported by United States estimates that homosexual men now make up anywhere from 23 to 58 percent of all priests.[16] Michael Kelly reports that these findings are also relevant to the Australian context. Extensive anecdotes and "guesstimates" from Australian priests tend to confirm this observation.[17] Furthermore, it is quite reasonable to suggest that these estimates are reflected in other Western cultures and perhaps in non-Western cultures as well.

Yet the increased intake of homosexual seminarians of recent decades has caused considerable alarm. During my research, I listened to priests who sounded warnings about this trend, including Fr. Jerry, a homosexual priest himself: *They have to dehomosexualize the clergy. It's obvious because the proportion of homosexuals in the clergy is far too high. Priest numbers need to reflect the demography of the society it serves.*

The Vatican is also expressing its concern but from a different perspective. Media sources suggest that the question of excluding homosexuals from the priesthood has been quietly considered for years but without finding consensus.[18] That question is apparently now receiving new and more urgent attention in the wake of clerical sexual abuse because the majority of priests who have sexually abused minors have targeted young males; in the papacy's understanding, this is synonymous with homosexuality. In consequence, Vatican officials are supposedly in the process of taking steps towards curbing the intake of homosexual seminarians.[19]

However, any cessation to this long-established source of priests is likely to aggravate problems facing the priesthood. Fr. Jerry, for example, alludes to one social consequence: *All the churches would be up the creek if they got rid of the gays and lesbians. It seems to me that many homosexual persons have special gifts for professions such as the pastorate.* Homosexual priests have been represented for centuries amongst clerics: they have effectively proclaimed the Gospel, presided over local communities, and provided pastoral care. Introducing prohibitions against homosexual seminarians may not only reduce one source of vocations, it may interrupt an unacknowledged yet significant social and cultural contribution.

One priest also predicted that such a move by the Vatican could return seminaries to an unhealthy psychological environment, one that promotes secrecy, duplicity, repression, and homophobic attitudes and behaviours intended to prove (to others and to oneself) that one is heterosexual.[20] This situation could be further aggravated if homosexual cardinals, bishops, and priests were made scapegoats. The pope's spokesperson, Joaquin Navarro-Valls, who stated that there is no room in the church for homosexual priests, has indicated this threat. He wondered whether the ordination of a homosexual priest was even valid.[21]

Such warnings could produce witch-hunts that would further destabilise the priesthood, a concern that one priest expressed: *I am nervous because of the fear that some priests have, that it will turn them into accusers to cover their own tracks. I am aware of how a friend of mine, not long dead from the effects of HIV, was kicked out of a seminary by a priest with the same predilection and mode of satisfying it. Even bishops who are friends, seem to think that it couldn't happen within their ranks that anyone was acting-out, or could get pompous and prissy in preserving their established status quo. Perhaps they think that these things happen only in the Anglican Church. That makes me very nervous. Bishops long dead have their nicknames among the gay community. That might make some others nervous.*[22]

Another key consideration is that Western societies are becoming more sensitive to discrimination against homosexuals.[23] In these cultures, civil law has been enacted to protect their human rights, and this has brought the church into potential conflict with secular society. As well, this development often includes laws to prevent vilification of homosexuals. Unfortunately, *some priests and other Catholics seem not to know this or just set out to flout it.*[24]

Meanwhile, nearly every major Christian denomination—Anglican, Presbyterian, Baptist, Methodist, and Uniting Church—is confronting this issue. Family members, friends, and work colleagues who have declared their homosexual orientation have often challenged the way they have been marginalised by the various churches. This has led many Christians to reconsider scripture and church teachings on the matter, resulting in a search for inclusivity. It would seem that the hostility and prejudice towards gays and lesbians is gradually diminishing, at least in some quarters.

Recently, after the ordination of an openly gay Anglican bishop, the Vatican indicated that there is the danger of suspending unity talks with the Anglican Communion. No doubt the inclusive policies of other denominations also jeopardise ecumenical relationships with the Catholic Church. The suspension of relations is, however, likely to be interpreted as an unwarranted exercise of force that seeks to intimidate and disregard other denominations' efforts to discuss and act upon issues of importance in the life of their communities.

Within the church itself, the maintenance of these teachings is also likely to increasingly polarise Catholics. This is made evident by secular and independent Catholic media, gay activists, and Christian reformers who increasingly accept homosexuality as part of the human condition.

The papacy is therefore being forced to either jettison "the problem" or reevaluate the presence of homosexual priests. Whatever action is taken, it is likely to incur substantial costs. Moreover, while priesthood is confined by the stereotype of celibacy, it seems unlikely that it will be unable to rid itself of the complex sexual entanglements it is now faced with.

Challenging Female Stereotypes

In the church, women are confined by stereotypes that stress the superiority of maleness over femaleness, celibacy over sexual intimacy. According to Fr. Peter, *a lot of priests are very patriarchal. They're above women. They wouldn't see women as equals but as servants.* He also added that *certain women are also very happy with the way things are in the church. They have been the ones that have learnt to accept patriarchy. They've never known any different, and that's precisely why they accept it.*

But there are some women who are beginning to think for themselves, questioning the church, and pulling out of the church. These women see the church as old-fashioned and stupid. Increasing numbers of women are realising that their position in the church is ideologically compromised. This is further evidenced by the research project undertaken for the Australian Catholic Bishops Conference in which the patriarchal system was identified as the greatest underlying barrier to women's participation.[25]

In the church, women principally attain social status by producing and socialising legitimate children with socially recognised fathers. In doing so, they maintain the man's dominant position in society. In hierarchical turn, priests act as "Fathers" of fathers, bishops as paterfamilias, the pope as "Holy Father," and God as "Almighty Father." Patriarchy then, has its foundation in a woman's fertile, constantly producing womb. Little wonder that the papacy bans artificial contraception.

Patriarchy is further reflected in doctrinal texts in which the papacy assigns human traits as stereotypes to male and female, for example, rationality, autonomy, strength, and initiative versus intuition, nurturing, receptiveness, and compassion.[26] These latter traits are distinctly associated with motherhood, a state that reduces all women to this clerical perspective.

Women who believe in the equality of the sexes regard this theology of complementarity as sexist and un-Christian. Such a theology defines men as being superior to women, and men as the ones who fully image God, whilst women image God by virtue of their relationship to men. In this relationship, the woman is helpmate, with a special, preordained, divinely decreed place in creation, whose sphere is the home and family. She is equal to, though less than, a man. Yet, as Catherine Mowry LaCugna states, this is not the preordained, intended order of creation, but the order of fallen humankind.[27] Such women reject the idea that maleness is normative for speaking about God and humankind. Similarly, they reject "sameness" for all women, because it marginalises the diversity of women's experience and limits alternative understandings of their humanity.

Meanwhile, in the local churches, conservative priests pejoratively refer to women who contest such stereotypes as *feminists*, or in the case of religious sisters, *feral nuns*. These derogatory terms ridicule and denounce the efforts of women to secure equal rights and opportunities in the church and elsewhere. Nonetheless, the continual promotion of female stereotypes is more likely to undermine the priesthood and church, rather than uphold them. Firstly, women are becoming accustomed to the idea that they should not be discriminated against.

Secondly, in the last three decades, Catholic feminist biblical scholarship and feminist theology have flourished, as have the numbers of women who have become theologically educated. These movements continue to promote awareness of the historical and social subordination of women. They also aim to correct the patriarchal biases of scripture and its interpretations so that both women and men are liberated from the idea that everything revolves around the superiority of the male sex.

Thirdly, many mothers no longer hold priesthood in esteem for a range of reasons. They don't esteem such a vocation for their sons because they are concerned about issues such as mandatory celibacy, an all-male priesthood, clerical abuse, and the loneliness of the lifestyle.[28] These women are also reluctant to promote a priesthood that excludes their gender.

Fourthly, mothers have traditionally been the primary catechists of their children. But large numbers of women have become critical of the church's sexual policies and, hence, so have their children. Thus, attempts to promote patriarchy are increasingly likely to become frustrated as calls for change by women become more compelling and egalitarian ideals more attractive to many in the church.

A Priest's Resistance

As the scandal of clerical sexual abuse has increased, the celibacy of priests has become the subject of much greater public scrutiny. This has left some conservative priests deeply preoccupied with preserving their clerical world. By highlighting stereotypes of celibacy and other sexual standards, these priests seek to maintain orthodoxy in the church. On occasion, such as, when a priests' council gathers, these priests reportedly use slurs and innuendos to attack individuals or groups perceived as a danger. Then these priests leave their meetings strengthened by assumed consensus and armed with critical comment that can be made available for public consumption.

The priests I interviewed consider such tactics uncharitable and disgraceful. Yet, clericalism can only accommodate agreement. Those who are critical of the status quo therefore often assume a policy of silence. These priests are unwilling to face the strong opposition that would result, disapproval that is backed up by a powerful church bureaucracy. One priest, however, chose to challenge this behaviour by reporting his experience to me.

In his correspondence, Fr. Philip (whom we met in chapter 1) recounts how a few of his confreres were particularly concerned about a bishop who had been accused of sexual abuse. While he shared their concern, he was also perturbed by the anger and sarcasm they levelled at people who publicly discussed this situation or raised issues of reform.

Fr. Philip considers over half the priests at clerical gatherings *very conservative, very negative, and quite emotional.* In his view, these priests are pessimistic in outlook, reluctant to accept change, and are very distressed that the status quo is not being preserved in the church.

He reports the views of his confreres who feel that the credibility of the bishop has been damaged by the allegation, and that the church's *hope for salvation—faith and loyalty to the pope and the magisterium—is now in jeopardy.*

For a conservative priest there is no salvation outside of the church, and that means dutifully submitting oneself to the directions of the papacy. Indeed, these priests would instinctively reject the idea that a bishop could commit such an offence. They subsequently lash out at those who might threaten the religious and moral credibility of the church: *Now with this false accusation and trial by media he'll never be able to effectively perform the duties he was chosen for, they lamented.*

They also target particular individuals. For instance, one high-profile Catholic female journalist was described as *a real bitch.* Particular bishops, priests, and laypersons are also considered *dangerous and disloyal to the church in suggesting that celibacy should be optional. They are going against the laws of the church.*

Fr. Philip also reports that his confreres said *a lot about paedophilia, which the priests who speak up in favour of celibacy do not understand. They are saying there is a link between paedophilia and homosexuality.* These priests confuse same-sex activities and are not interested in research that discriminates between the two states. This view broadly reflects the antihomosexual stance of the church. In contrast, Fr. Philip holds a perspective common today, that homosexuality is not pathological but a part of the human condition.

In the context of this gathering of priests, Fr. Philip and other priests were very reluctant to challenge such vehement attacks: *No priests expressed a personal view or were game to speak of their own lives. It's a power-loyalty game. Another priest and I said very briefly that celibacy is not working, but the opposition has totally closed minds and would not listen.* Fr. Philip and his confrere judged it more prudent to keep the peace and avoid conflict. In this hostile environment, with few allies that would support them, these priests remain silent.

Despite the closure of this avenue of protest, Fr. Philip still finds ways to actively resist these stereotypes, although in ways that do not threaten his priesthood: *You just go ahead and do your own thing and say bugger the others, and try and do what is right and correct. I'm not going to talk with them, because you can't change them; you just go ahead, in your own way, do what you can, and avoid doing what you can't. I wouldn't lose any sleep over it. The Lord is going to provide. The church is going to keep on going. There could be some surprising changes, some new directions in the church.*

For Fr. Philip, God has the ultimate power over what goes on in the priesthood and church, not the pope, not his bishop, not his conservative confreres. For this priest, unrealised possibilities that cannot yet be imagined lie beyond the horizon.

Humourous Defiance

When I interviewed Fr. Aaron as to whether celibacy was ever raised at formal gatherings of priests, he also indicated: *Celibacy would be more a topic for a kind of a social situation. It is the sort of thing you joke about because priests don't generally share their thoughts and feelings about sexuality—and certainly not about their own personal sexuality and what are their attitudes towards it. If they do, its very "heady," like what it would be out of moral theology books.*

Nevertheless, priests have developed a coded language in the form of joking to speak about sexuality amongst themselves. Joking is seemingly removed from the person of the priest but sometimes gets very close to the desires and distresses of those concerned. Noisy laughter is a telltale sign of just how far the joke has reached.

Fr. Aaron wanted to assure me that these jokes had a level of respectability: *They wouldn't be smutty jokes, always respectful. We don't hear jokes that are openly sexual but often there are hints and double meanings and witticisms which will raise raucous laughter—jokes that go so far but not over the limit. I would never offend anyone with a joke; at least, I would be very sorry if I did.*

But what might be considered appropriate for one priest may not be for another. According to Fr. Aaron, joking serves as a *very subtle gauge as to what others think about celibacy and sexuality. If priests do not respond with laughter, then you know you are in the company of priests who are not at ease with their own sexuality.*

━━

The following are examples of jokes that have *been around for a while, old yarns* that are familiar to a number of priests: *A lady goes to her priest one day and tells him, "Father, I have a problem. I have two female parrots, but they only know how to say one thing." "What do they say?" the priest inquired. They say, "Hi, we're hookers! Do you want to have fun?"*

"*That's obscene!*" *the priest exclaimed, then he thought for a moment.* "*You know,*" *he said,* "*I may have a solution to your problem. I have two male talking parrots that I have taught to pray and recite the Bible. Bring your two parrots over to my house, and we'll put them in the cage with Francis and Job. My parrots can teach your parrots to praise and worship, and your parrots are sure to stop in no time.*" "*Thank you,*" *the woman responded,* "*this may very well be the solution.*"

The next day, she brought her female parrots to the priest's house. As he ushered her in, she saw that his two male parrots were inside their cage holding rosary beads and praying. Impressed, she walked over and placed her parrots in with them. After a few minutes, the female parrots cried out in unison: "*Hi, we're hookers—Do you want to have some fun?*" *There was stunned silence. Then one male parrot looked over at his mate and exclaimed,* "*Put the beads away, Frank. Our prayers have been answered.*"

These colourful birds symbolise a female stereotype: wanton women who desire sexual fun, even with priests confined by the "cage" of celibacy. For a brief moment, priests enjoying the joke are able to relish the suspension of celibacy and to indulge in the fantasy of sexual pleasure. As well, they have triumphed over the prohibition that the papacy has placed on the discussion of celibacy.

━━⁓

A new monk arrives at the monastery. He is assigned to help the other monks in copying the old canons and laws of the church by hand. He notices, however, that all of the monks are copying from copies, not from the original manuscript.

So the new monk goes to the abbot to question this and points out that if someone made even a small error in the first copy, it would never be picked up. In fact, that error would be continued in all of the subsequent copies.

The abbot says, "*We've been copying from the copies for centuries, but you make a good point, my son.*" *So, the abbot goes down into the dark caves underneath the monastery where the original manuscript is held in a locked vault that hasn't been opened for hundreds of years.*

Hours go by and nobody sees the old abbot. Eventually the young monk gets worried and goes downstairs to look for him. He finds him banging his head against the wall and crying uncontrollably. The young monk asks *the old abbot, "What's wrong, Father?" In a choking voice, the old abbot replies, "The word is **celebrate**, not **celibate**!"*

The Church at the Crossroads

Despite religious and social pressures to conform, significant numbers of priests are finding ways to resist and challenge patriarchy. When I queried Fr. Tobit as to what he thought might happen if hundreds of individuals like himself were to publicly speak about celibacy and related issues, he replied: *It would start binding people together, you would find communities starting to share.* In the event of public dialogue, Catholics may come to realize that the patriarchal stereotypes currently being promoted and imposed are suspect and prejudicial. For stereotypes are essentially forms of discrimination that overlook and discard a person's skills and knowledge that could be otherwise put to good use. In effect, they maintain clericalism and minimise a wealth of goodwill and service to the church.

Nevertheless, during my research, I came to realise that even heterosexual priests with friends can be homophobic. While they may have experienced a watershed with regard to their own celibacy, they may have no time for their homosexual confreres who also have difficulties with celibacy, as well as having to grapple with the view that suggests they are "objectively disordered." Thus, in the event that compulsory celibacy was discussed, there is a danger that clerical homophobia would maintain sexual stereotyping. Fr. David elaborates the potential of this problem: *Stereotypes create antagonism. You can't have dialogue—you can't get anything done—if people don't respect each other.* Without a spirit of openness in dialogue that allows for difference, typecasting will curtail broad reform of sexual policies in the church.

Similarly, some priests hold reservations about women having any place in the leadership and decision making of the church. Nevertheless, as has been evidenced, women are increasingly challenging the minimising strategies of the patriarchal church, with consequences that will undermine the priesthood or pressure it to think otherwise. Until the time comes when individuals and groups listen to discover, rather than listen to control, it is unlikely that the Catholic community will achieve any sense of harmony.

Priests with friends are also not likely to be deterred in their pursuit of reform. As Fr. Jude comments: *I'm pretty keen on both priesthood and friendship.* Meanwhile, Fr. Tobit concludes that *the average age of priests in a lot of the dioceses would be about sixty-five and that has a lot to do with it.* Fr. Tobit holds that the older age of priests cements their conservative views on celibacy and that younger priests tend to have a completely different attitude toward celibacy and sexuality.

The irony is that Fr. Tobit is in the same age bracket as those whom he accuses of being conservative. When confronted with this he responded: *that's because I've developed an open attitude over the years, and I refuse to give it up.* Refusing to give it up is a sentiment that is echoed in many of the responses of priests. Despite the preservation of patriarchy, change is already under way as priests with friends and other groups continue to redefine themselves and their relationships in the church.

7

Moving On

Fr. Felix is a loyal servant of the church. For decades, he has gone about his ministry helping people grow closer to God. On most days, and of course on Sunday, he offers Mass. He is also a great believer in home visitation. In each parish, he visits homes in an effort to locate and meet all the Catholics residing in his parish. He has a great affinity, too, for those who are dying or suffering loss, especially loss of relationships. Fr. Felix is a diligent and empathetic priest, sensitive to the needs of others. That sensitivity has been honed by the shadows of his life.

I believed what they told me in the seminary. They told me that we were all things to all people and that there were to be no personal relationships. So for many years, he struggled with his need for closeness: *the need to be held, to be touched—that's been a big thing—to be physically touched.*

But the simplicity of his hunger for even a modicum of intimacy became mixed up with fear and desperation. In the dark of night he started to prowl the city toilets looking for illicit sex. Here he would touch the shell of what he yearned for, but his choices never let him know the love and life behind the cold and anonymous cover.

It wasn't a conscious thing but then after a while, it became a mania. I felt terribly, terribly ashamed, and then I'd go to confession before I went back to the parish. I knew I was going insane. It was pretty hard to continue his ministry after each of these times. *But I know that my parishioners love me. They didn't know about my loneliness and they thought I was sane!* Fr. Felix tried to control his problem, but it was only after a number of years that he knew he had to get out of that scene.

I suppose from the time I stood there in the toilets, I knew things had to change. My thinking had to change. I had built a wall about myself, brick by brick, and when I gave up the toilet scene, I decided the wall had to come down, brick by brick. It had to come down. I was frightened what would happen when I knocked down the first brick, because I didn't know what kind of spirit was going to blow in, as in the Holy Spirit or some other bloody spirit. I don't think I had any spirituality before this.

I did a lot of courses, I did every bloody spiritual course and psychology course. I went to counselling too, years of it. It was very painful to go through that. And I was treading a path I'd never been down before. It was bloody terrifying. During these years, Fr. Felix also met Lydia: *She was a godsend.*

Lydia was this ex-religious who was working with the homeless. I would contact her if I found someone who needed help. Sometimes I met these people near the toilets. Occasionally, she would pop into the presbytery.

One night when she visited, I was in a terrible state, almost on the edge of a nervous breakdown. Everything was building up. I just felt an overwhelming sense of loneliness, frustration, isolation. I felt like I was falling apart. Nothing made sense anymore. Lydia saw that I was a bit strained and asked if I felt well. Then I burst into the longest, deepest spell of sobbing. I really felt I would crack in two. The months went by, and she visited me several times, trying to get some idea of what to do. Anyhow, I went and did those courses, like I mentioned. They helped, but I still felt terrible, as if a train had hit me.

Lydia and I talked about it, and she said, "Look I have tried to think of what to do. It seems to me that you desperately need a personal friend. I know you are getting help, but that doesn't seem to be enough. Look, I'm willing to be that friend; I'm willing to commit myself to be there for you as a friend."

I remember sitting there in a kind of numbed misery. Then she came over to me. She said that she was about to make a gesture to reassure me that she would not abandon me. Something in me knew she meant well, that I could trust her.

She hugged me and kissed me with great feeling. Then she asked if she could touch me. I said yes. So she loosened my clothing, and fondled me intimately. Lydia's tender act was a sign of drawing his sexuality back into his humanity, unlike the fragmentation of sex from spirit that he suffered in his ventures in the city toilets. That was the beginning of some peace in his struggle.

⌒

Fr. Felix is much quieter and more content now. After nearly twenty years, Lydia and he are still close friends. He also has what he regards as *my own kind of spirituality. Ever since then, I've had some sense of value in my personal worth. I can back up my own judgement. I realize things don't have to come through books and holy people. I don't have to read them so that I could give them to other people. I realize that the most valuable things in life come from yourself.*

I also remember making the cold, hard decision whether I would be a conservative or a liberal. If I had become a conservative, I wouldn't have taken down the walls, and the only thing that made me a liberal was the example I admired in people who were. They thought and they expressed their thoughts, and their thoughts were entertaining. And I didn't see that in conservatives. They were rigid. I equated liberalism with getting better. I had a feeling that if I had taken the conservative road, I couldn't get better, and still think that. And it's an ongoing thing. Yeah it's a journey.

Later, Fr. Felix commented on how much he enjoys his priesthood. *I could never, ever see me as something else, because there's just nothing else there for me. And yeah, I get a kick out of it too. Had a funeral today. I really like funerals. It's the time when I realise that we know so little about life.*

For several decades Fr. Felix had endeavoured to maintain the lessons that he learnt in the seminary. He kept himself apart, not really getting close to anyone. But that deep need for some love and affection broke out in ways that caused him harm.

Fr. Felix then sought help in the wider world, as well as entrusting himself to broad-minded and compassionate people such as Lydia. By becoming open to a different life experience, he realised new meanings for himself and his priesthood.

Contesting Worldviews

All priests are located in broader histories and cultures that directly impact on their understanding of celibacy. These changing conditions have shaped and advantaged some priests, particularly those in the Western world.

As indicated briefly in chapter 3, during the Renaissance, European scholars and artists pressed for a reconsideration of the importance of the individual. These humanists asserted that society should exist for the benefit of human beings. Consequently, an individual should not be constrained by the intervention of political authorities or made subordinate to collective interests.

Such a view seriously challenged the authority of the papacies and monarchies of the era. During this time, René Descartes (1596-1650) rejected the philosophy of the church that asserted that things belong to different categories and are ordered in a hierarchy. Instead, Descartes felt that the construction of reality lay within the individual and, therefore, he or she has instrumental control over his or her objective experience.

From this new perspective of the self, John Locke (1632-1704) was able to argue that an individual could remake herself by methodical and disciplined action. It is here that the modern notion of freedom manifested itself. The predetermined natural order, as expressed in the classical worldview and manifested in the church in celibacy, was rejected by humanists and replaced by practical benevolence that has become one of the central beliefs of the modern worldview. In this belief, the onus is on each individual to meet the everyday needs of others. As Charles Taylor says, we should all work to improve the human condition, relieve suffering, overcome poverty, increase prosperity, and augment human welfare. We should strive to leave the world a more prosperous place than we found it.[1]

Then the Romantics of the late eighteenth century asserted the validity of subjective experience. They believed that each individual is different and original.[2] This originality, embedded in the depths of self, marks and defines the individual and determines how she ought to live. Thus, our modern identity is located in an orientation to inwardness and engaged self-remaking, a worldview that is supported by democracy.

In democracy, notions of freedom encourage self-exploration and self-awareness. This search, according to Taylor, rests on a moral foundation of authenticity. In arriving at authenticity, a person is guided by a number of signposts that include the ability to create and construct and to be open to discovery. But in this journey, a person must also take into account horizons of significance—otherwise creation loses the background and perspective that save us from insignificance. These horizons help us define our selves in dialogue with one another.[3]

From this perspective, sexuality is not just a variation within the same basic human nature, but is expressed through a person's original self. A priest is therefore morally obliged in all aspects of his life, including his sexuality, to pursue authenticity. Celibacy is fulfilling for a priest only when it expresses his authentic self. To pursue this sense of humanity, a priest therefore needs to dialogue with others to aid self-definition.

The church eventually faced the challenge that humanism presented. After a period of gestation, and at the Second Vatican Council, the papacies of John XXIII (1958-1963) and Paul VI (1963-1978) accommodated a modicum of egalitarian and democratic ideas. These papacies positively endorsed democracy for the administration of the state. Within the church, they also promoted democratic notions, including collegiality, freedom of conscience, the recognition of churches with more synodal structures, and an emphasis on human rights.[4] This change of worldview has also been reflected in the reevaluation of the status of marriage, which is now interpreted as equivalent to the celibate vocation. Nevertheless, conservative anchors weighed down these novel inroads, for the social order of the church remains hierarchical and the prominence of the priest as celibate continues to be emphasised.

The papacy of John Paul II has endeavoured to curtail the emergence of the modern worldview by promoting a classical worldview in which people are constituted by the opposing characteristics of body and spirit. This view is located in the Jewish and Greco-Roman cultural heritage of the church. As has been mentioned in chapter 2, in the Jewish religious and ethical system, those in cultic service practised celibacy on occasions because they believed that any bodily discharges, including semen, made them unclean—a state incompatible with the holiness of God.[5]

Greek philosophers, for their part, believed that the world was fundamentally a *kosmos*, an ordered world formed and guided by divine reason.[6] Plato (428 BC-348 BC) postulated that reality was situated in a divine world of eternal, nonchanging, and incorruptible Ideas. The created world was a reflection of the higher world, but its sensible and corruptible objects participated in these Ideas only in an imperfect way. This cosmological construction placed an onus on every person to strive for likeness to the divine through education, discipline, and life in a well-ordered society. Sexual desire in this classical worldview was considered a diseased aspect of the personality, distracting the well-balanced person from intellectual pursuits.

These influences made an impact upon early Christianity and were expressed in Stoicism and Gnosticism,[7] which respectively promoted austerity and pessimism about all that was material. This preference for the divine was further developed by the Church Fathers, particularly Augustine, who presented an adaptation of Plato's Ideas. According to Augustine, God was the source of Ideas, these being realised in the eternal and immutable cosmic order. Humankind, as participant in God's ideas, respected this divine order. Through attending to the inner self, a person made the step on the way "upward" to God, and implicit in this notion of hierarchy was the body-spirit dualism. Hence, many of the Church Fathers insisted upon celibacy.[8]

This dualism was structurally established in the Middle Ages when compulsory celibacy was used to bring about the centralisation of the church. This centralisation was also served by the theology of Thomas Aquinas (1225-1274). Aquinas stressed the importance of law, order, and reason, establishing a clear delineation between right and wrong, virtues and vices. He also held the view that woman is a failed man, born by chance as defective.[9] From his perspective, celibacy is about avoiding sexual sins and being separated from commerce with women. This became the official theology in the nineteenth century and remained until the Second Vatican Council.

Papacies since the fourth century have essentially upheld a classical worldview. As a result, individualism and relativism urged by the Enlightenment are officially rejected and considered immoral. Indeed, people who consider morality a personal matter are regarded as selfish at best and sinful at worst. In the classical worldview, celibacy is regarded a virtue that maintains religious and social cohesion and guarantees the continuity of the church. This leads to the view that complete sacrifice of self for the community is regarded as noble and virtuous.

The existence of these two worldviews within the church, classical and modern, has produced polarisation, confusion, and tension. According to Paul Collins, these two worldviews are "mutually exclusive, mutually corrosive, and simply incompatible: an absolute monarchy cannot be superimposed on a more democratic-synodal structure."[10]

The pope and the curia have also recognised a conflict of interest in these different official positions. Subsequently, they have promulgated teachings that reassert notions of social stratification and hierarchy over and above those of egalitarianism and democracy. So collegiality is curtailed and restricted, freedom of conscience is challenged, synods are to reflect the papal line, and human rights within the church are ignored.[11] The papacy aims to restore a classical worldview. Nonetheless, behind the façade of unity, there exists an ideological struggle over which worldview is appropriate for the priesthood and the church.

The Pursuit of Sexual Authenticity

While the Vatican perpetuates its own interests, priests with friends subtly promote a modified and more current worldview. After all, these priests participate in both hierarchical and democratic societies, and are well versed in both sets of principles. In consequence, they are able to adapt these diverse principles to their own situation in order to promote authentic sexual identity, expressed in friendship. Fr. Asher, for instance, struggled over his homosexuality and need for sexual intimacy for years: *I went through a stage—you know the legalism of it. I went through a real crisis, but then, rightly or wrongly, I've come through that moral crisis. Now I think God loves me and accepts me as I am, and understands my need to give expression to that. Now whether that's rationalising or not is not really the point. I suppose you could debate that all day long. I just feel that God is a forgiving and understanding God.* Fr. Asher has grown to accept his homosexual orientation and acknowledge the need for expression of his unique sexual identity.

Fr. Luke expressed similar efforts to overcome difficulties relating to his homosexuality and celibacy, and now tries *to cultivate "a taste for humiliations" —one of the Benedictine strategies for becoming a healthy, user-friendly human being—that is, getting out from under the power of the super-ego and becoming yourself (in modern jargon), or becoming a saint (in old-time talk). Whatever, it all comes down to the same—to keep on keeping on, being warm and open and loving and forgiving, at the same time as being straight and honest in the kindest and gentlest way possible, that is, growing up into real human maturity.*

Fr. Luke endeavours to synthesise conflicting features and he is now surer of himself, more open about his homosexual orientation, and forgiving of those who persecute him.

<hr />

Fr. James, whose story was recorded in chapter 1, also felt the need to work out his authentic sexual state, and he did so by plumbing the depths of his subjective experience. For a number of years, Fr. James had enjoyed a relationship with Sr. Evelyn: *They were the days of being "madly in love" —days of the full-blooded affair. For me, the days of "catching-up" on adolescence. For Evelyn, I filled up in her a huge need for love and acceptance and assuaged her need to be affirmed. We both operated out of our mutual need for one another.*

Later, Sr. Evelyn began to deal with her history of childhood abuse: *As Evelyn began to delve into her past, our relationship began to change. This annoyed me at the time, made me angry—for I no longer had the same access to her body. For a time we went through a rough patch and it seemed that we might have to part.*

Then about this time, I too went to therapy and began to unpack some of my agenda. I learned the necessity of relationships with women. Such relationships are vital for my growth as a man. I learned that every relationship with a woman (and with other men, for that matter), had to be a sexual relationship. We human beings are not robots; we have to communicate with one another as men and women who are sexual beings. Otherwise, our relationships will always be facile and superficial.

This therapy also gave a renewed vigour to our friendship, and we were able to communicate on a new level. We found that we had much in common—not that I had been sexually abused like Evelyn, but that we had been operating out of a repressed state and that our sexual involvement to that extent was immature.

We began to live celibately for lengthy periods of time and would only occasionally sleep together. The expression of our friendship was now different from the previous adolescent style. Nor did it concern us overly that from time to time we would cross the boundaries.

In recent years, we essentially live a celibate lifestyle with each other. We meet fairly often, enjoy one another's company, a meal and a chat, a movie. We embrace and express our love for each other "normally" and refrain from having full sexual intercourse. We are both comfortable with this level of relationship.

In Evelyn, I have found the type of relationship that now fulfils my adult masculine needs. Both of us being religious allow us to understand where we are coming from.

The official prescription of celibacy was insufficient for Fr. James and Sr. Evelyn, and both felt the need to locate their sexuality in a loving relationship. They both attended psychotherapy, a process that helped them to make autonomous decisions about their sexuality. Fr. James and Sr. Evelyn feel that it is their right before God to engage in self-determination, a view that is also expressed by a number of other priests with friends. Quite clearly, they have replaced the law of celibacy with more personal concerns.

Other priests assert their humanist position from a political perspective. Fr. Reuben contends that *any change in the discipline of celibacy will come "from below" not "from above."* He believes that the body politic, not the clerical "headship," will determine the future of the church.[12] Furthermore, *the scandal of clergy sex-abuse will effect change and is **already** impacting upon the church structures, as in the current vocations crisis. Attrition of the clergy will bring a new dawn for the church and renew the church's structures "from below"—as lay people naturally assume more responsibility for their local communities.*

According to Fr. Daniel, Catholics at the grass roots will shape the church, not the distant Vatican, and they will do so by taking responsibility for their communities. He further adds: *Since most Catholics are married or will be married and do not opt for celibacy as a way of life, a new form of "priestly ministry" will gradually take the place of the current practice.* In the pursuit of authenticity, new forms of ministry will arise. As a result, the current divide between the priest and laity will weaken and so will other characteristics of their separation such as compulsory celibacy.

Fr. Ben asserts a similar notion: *The principles of local self-determination and subsidiarity,*[13] *to which Vatican II itself pointed, must once again* be honoured. With radical decentralisation, the universal law of celibacy will disappear.

A Quest for Truth

Some priests suggest that there already exist egalitarian tendencies and democratic undertones within the priesthood. Fr. Mike, for example, enjoyed a friendship with Claudia that helped him *grow very much in his own person, in confidence and self-possession.* But the death of his brother, ill health, and the overwhelming demands of ministry, administration, and people, forced him to face questions about his life.

I knew then I had a real problem in the deepest area of my inner self. It had all to do with the basics of my relationships with God, with others, and myself. It was in the area of personal identity, the quality, direction, and purpose of my life, personal happiness, and well-being. This moment of realisation was a great grace from God!

Several months later, Fr. Mike embarked on a three-month course of personal renewal designed for people in ministry in midlife. During that time, he received one-to-one counselling and frequent spiritual direction and was required by his spiritual director to constantly focus on two basic questions:

*What did I **want** to do, as against needed to or am expected to do with the rest of my life? Who is/are the person/s, what are the situations that energise me, give me life, make me grow as a person, and let me enjoy a peaceful heart before God? I had reached the stage in the journey of faith and growth in my life, where, for the first time, I was able to listen, to own, and begin to deal with these questions, fully and confidently.*

It came to me clearly and quietly that I had to decide finally, one way or the other, either to get right back into religious life and priestly ministry, or to move right out and walk down another direction in my life.

Fr. Mike could not sacrifice his sexuality for his ministry; rather, he had to discern his own personal response to his situation. Without establishing this inner point of reference, he felt he would not survive.

Three years later, Fr. Mike left the priesthood and married Claudia. He has since adapted his ministry to the various situations in which he finds himself, including ministry within a parish, and is actively involved in a reform movement initiated and promoted by married priests and their associates.

~

Fr. Andrew, whom we first met in chapter 4, also promotes egalitarianism when he speaks of his relationship with Esther: *The basis of the intimacy of our relationship is a life-long commitment to each other, through which we both believe that we have in fact contracted a marriage that is valid in the eyes of God, even though not recognized by the laws of the church.*

What this relationship has meant for me is a whole new understanding of the complex meaning of married love and the demands and restrictions it places on one. No longer am I able to think only of what I would do or how I would spend my holidays or what I would do with my money. Everything became we and our.

Fr. Andrew also contends that his friendship significantly changed his ministry. *I found that in my ministry I could talk with couples with a new awareness and could sympathise with their struggles. I could feel with them the challenge of good communication and the hurts of mistakes and insensitivity. I found a new strength in my pastoral work and the joy of knowing that at the end of a hard day there was someone with whom I could at least spend a few moments in conversation and a cup of tea shared together, and then the moment for a hug and kiss before returning to my house.*

I believe that it was, above all, thanks to the support of Esther, that I weathered some very difficult times in my ministry, especially when I was alone for almost a year. After that, there certainly could be no turning back on my commitment to her—she was part of my life and part of my priesthood. I believe she has helped me to become a far better priest—more compassionate, more sensitive and more forgiving—and a better communicator.

Fr. Andrew feels that his relationship with Esther has had a profound effect on his priesthood. For him, rank has been replaced with equity, and cult with community; and as Fr. Andrew ministers, so too does Esther.

Esther is not secreted away in the private life of Fr. Andrew. Rather his particular circumstances allow him to publicly combine his priesthood with her ministry: *Some of the most beautiful moments of our relationship have been the moments of shared ministry: preparing events together, going out on visitation together, sharing in weddings and funerals together. One of the most beautiful moments in our relationship was the moment we began to pray together. I really felt the presence of God in our relationship, and I have been spurred on to maintain more than ever my personal prayer before God, conscious that we are walking a largely unchartered journey. No doubt, many have gone before us, but no one was allowed to share their story because it was seen as too threatening to the institution.*

By walking this priestly tightrope, Fr. Andrew and Esther have made a space in parish life that allows them both to minister. This couple, as do many others, find creative solutions to resolve questions of personal and priestly authenticity. Nonetheless, establishing these innovations in the church is neither easy nor a foregone conclusion. Each priest and each partner must determine ways in which they can incorporate their friendship into everyday life in ways that do not attract unwanted attention.

Public Presentation of Friendships

Celibacy is effectively presented in the church as an ordinary everyday practise for priests. Neither priests nor laypersons consider it remarkable that a priest is celibate. Indeed, most would consider the practise quite uninteresting and certainly not worth much comment. But this automatic acceptance maintains the papacy's idea of celibacy as the only way in which a priest should live out his life and priesthood.

Nevertheless, priests with friends can use this strategy of ordinariness to serve their own lives and ministries. By presenting their friendships as an everyday part of their lives, they can broaden the idea of what is usual or commonplace for a priest.

When a parishioner describes the local parish priest as typical, he or she implies that that particular priest conforms to the religious and social expectations of what a priest is supposed to be like. The typical priest demonstrates to his parishioners that he has mastered the rules of priesthood. Such a priest ministers constantly to his flock, but not to the point of utter exhaustion. He is charitable in his remarks and kindly in his actions, yet, *he does not suffer fools gladly.* He is generous with his material goods but not destitute. He is prayerful, generally more so than his parishioners, although not to the extent *that he is so occupied with the things of heaven that he is of no earthly good.* Such a priest strikes a balance between what is expected of him and what he regards as proper for a priest. Essentially, he masters the rules, not they him. As a result, some priests can successfully configure into their character a close friend and still be regarded as typical.

Fr. Gideon can be described as a typical priest. He is a parish priest of a large town and actively encourages his parishioners to grow in their faith and become involved in the parish. Fr. Gideon has fostered such involvement by implementing various programs in his parish, including RCIA and visitation programs. He also has a reputation for respectfully listening to his parish councilors and usually takes into account their ideas when he makes decisions for the parish. Generally, Fr. Gideon is well regarded and liked by his parishioners. As a typical priest, he has essentially mastered the rules of how to publicly communicate his priesthood. This metaphor of ordinariness suits Fr. Gideon because he has a friendship with Michelle whom he met many years ago. *I have a particular friendship that began in a previous parish; I've been in three since then (parishes not friendships) and I got to know Michelle while I was struggling desperately to wriggle out of another relationship. She helped me to resist phone calls and not to go back to this other person. It actually worked, with her support.*

When I went to another parish, we missed each other but we were able to meet often, although that involved a lot of driving. I was then appointed to a very isolated parish, but we still managed to see each other about every three weeks. The amount of petrol we used to keep our friendship on track has been amazing. And sometimes I think, why bother with this? But somehow there has always been a reason, and something good comes out of it. And it's been great, you know.

After another six years, Fr. Gideon was transferred to his present posting, but this time Michelle shifted house and was able to find employment in the same town. This new situation presented a more favourable set of conditions for Fr. Gideon and Michelle. Living in the same town enabled them to lessen the restraints imposed upon their relationship. Over time, Michelle became quite active in the parish. Then when the housekeeper resigned, she applied for the position and has been able to care for and be close to Fr. Gideon. By taking up accepted social roles in the parish, Michelle is now considered appropriate company for Fr. Gideon:

I think the parishioners have accepted our friendship, and that took a long time to get to. I have found that my ministry here has been helped enormously by her ability to make people welcome. Not that I can't, but she and I together seem to offer a friendliness and openness that I can't do by myself. With her help I have, I believe, encouraged this parish to progress.

Fr. Gideon and Michelle establish a niche for themselves in the particular circumstances that have been presented to them and, in effect, they have reconstructed their role in the church. While this is not officially acknowledged, it has become accepted in the cultural conditions of the local parish. Nonetheless, the situation of Fr. Gideon and Michelle is contingent and not free of threat:

The difficulties of maintaining our friendship revolve around the conflicts of parish and presbytery life (the goldfish bowl). There is the strain of long hours on the job. And she is a harder worker than me and is often frustrated in having to "push" me to start things or to follow them up. Often I simply say, "Look, I just don't know how to go about getting this going, can you help?" I think she likes to help but she finds her desire to help and my need to be helped a very draining experience. I suppose the upshot of all this is that we are experiencing difficulties that many couples experience and yet find it hard to get help, because we can't really acknowledge our relationship. We have no one we can really turn to for support.

Then there is another problem. Not many other people, including other priests, would really understand the relationship. Some of them have said, "you don't need her around" and that sort of thing. There has also been a real struggle about whom she belongs to. Is she just here as a parish worker, or something more? And she knows it can't be anything more and has to learn to accept it. It's so hard on the woman. If there was marriage, she would have acceptance as someone. Now as it stands, she feels like "the other woman" and the parish is the wife!

One issue we both face is what happens when I leave this parish. After all these years, I honestly don't know whether the relationship has a future, given the fact that the system ultimately makes things impossible, although we have been able to live to date in a way that other priests would find impossible.

———

Priests often encounter the problem of having to defend their relationships, and they negotiate this difficulty in different ways. Fr. Gabe indicates that he is much more circumspect about the public display of his friendship than is Fr. Gideon: *only a couple of people know how close we are.* Other priests also point to the secrecy of their friendships, including Fr. Gus who said, *when Evie and I are in public and if we see anyone we know, we just peel off.*

Fr. David also recounts a situation where he and his friend, Ruth, had been walking together late one night and encountered his bishop in the company of *a lady friend.* The bishop just looked ahead stony faced and neither priest nor bishop acknowledged each other: *we were like ships passing in the night!*

These particular priests and their friends are unwilling to challenge celibacy publicly. In effect, they reduce their relationships to what is expected. For priests are supposed to officially and publicly present themselves as single, removed from the ambiguous company of their intimate friends.

Fr. Danny, however, has been able to negotiate a degree of public exposure: *It was very, very bad the first couple of years, and I think we were sort of getting through a lot of our own tensions.* Now he and his friend are comfortable with regularly dining at a restaurant once a week. This social pattern has recurred so often that it has become accepted in his parish. In effect, Fr. Danny has negotiated a strategy of ordinariness by promoting a habit. While priests with friends might, at first, be unable to negotiate strategies in public, they may, over time, develop a range of approaches and skills they can use to promote their friendships as acceptable.

Difficult Introductions

When priests wonder if they should introduce their friendships in public, they have to take into account *the spirit of the diocese.*

Fr. Aaron finds it very hard because conservative parishioners constantly police his life and ministry. He is also aware that the scandal of sexual abuse has created difficulties. *When you have a friendship like this you want to nourish the friendship, you don't want to do or say anything that would tarnish it. Still, I suppose in those times you would want to err on the side of being careful in order to protect it. I think the present climate isn't very helpful. It's because the image of the priesthood has definitely been tarnished, and it's against this background that people would probably view a relationship with some suspicion or anxiety.*

In the current climate where the reputation of priests is being sullied by incidents of sexual abuse, Fr. Aaron is convinced that all relationships might be considered suspect. He went on to say, *you're guilty until you're proven guiltier,* which suggests that he always has at the back of his mind the knowledge that Catholics tend to think the worst.

Fr. Peter indicates that having a friendship in a small or medium-size town or a country diocese, *is different from the big cities, where there is much more liberty for the priest because he is not so well known and you could do all kinds of things.* In contrast, priests stationed in country areas, like Fr. Peter, are often well-known. *There are probably thousands of people who know who I am, for example, every time I go to the shopping centre there are always people who say, "Hello Father," and I haven't got a clue who some of them are. Or they might have kids at school and I might recognize their face but don't know their names.* In country areas, it is also more likely that both Catholics and non-Catholics know the local priest, although Fr. Peter feels that non-Catholics who knew him did not pose a problem. He found it relatively easy to confide in a select few about his relationship: *They don't put me on a pedestal like most Catholics. They don't have so many hang-ups about priests having friendships.*

In some respects, being known by a large number of Catholics does not deter Fr. Peter either; it has just made him more shrewd and careful. He has been able to negotiate his friendship with Chloe in public by taking advantage of changing circumstances within the church.

Twenty years ago, we never had parish secretaries and the priests did all the work but now it's at the stage that I've got two or three. While the shortage of priests has something to do with it, I think people realize the work of the church is expanding and becoming more demanding, and with computers and modern technology, you've got to have a secretary.

As secretaries are commonly women, and given that *there are more women keen to do the work in the church,* women have been able to take on positions in the church that were not previously available to them. In return for their services, the priest often takes these women out to lunch or to some other social event: *Some of the women in the church, secretaries, women in the Catholic Women's League, and others—I would go out with them, and occasionally I would go out with others.* The acceptance of women working with priests in parishes is becoming so commonplace that when a priest is seen in public with a female parishioner, particularly one who has a role in the local parish or diocese, it is no longer considered unusual.

The average person knows you are allowed to have friends, and people would know I have lots of friends, but I don't think anyone would see Chloe as a special kind of friend. Fr. Peter slots his friendship into an established social pattern—nothing is out of place. *The most significant thing Chloe and I would do now is that we would go out for meals together, usually to different restaurants and places. Lots of places you go to you're not recognized. It's not a parish scene, it's a public scene.* Fr. Peter has a triple insurance: not only is it commonplace that he takes out female parishioners to restaurants, he takes them to a variety of eating places, and he does so in a public venue where he has no special status.

Nevertheless, while secular society does not generally concern itself with a couple being together, even in this situation Fr. Peter maintains a degree of vigilance. *There are also certain things you don't do in public, like holding hands. The only time we might hold hands would be half past ten at night, and then we might hold hands going over to the car.* Only under the cover of darkness can they be openly affectionate.

≈

In order to promote the idea that it is acceptable for a priest to have a friend, the friend must also deal with these priestly conventions. Fr. Peter *publicly treats Chloe as I treat my other parishioners. You've got to make a special effort to make her like another parishioner. She realises it too. In public, Chloe is very careful about the way she speaks to me, so she is very, very conscious of the unspoken rules.* These unspoken rules provide guidelines for a priest's friend, but each friend, as with each priest, must discover how these unspoken rules of friendship are to be applied.

Fr. Jordan and Tabatha also negotiate the situation that presents itself after he finishes celebrating Eucharist. *Every one wants to talk to me after Eucharist, so I make sure she has the car keys, and she just goes and sits in the car. She sees my priesthood as my profession, and it's as if I were a company director, she wouldn't want to be on the board.*

Fr. Nahum and Philomena further comment on the unspoken rules. After the Eucharist, they keep their distance from each other, making themselves available to other parishioners whom they often genuinely wish to seek out. If they do need to speak to each other on these occasions, Fr. Nahum expresses appropriate friendliness while Philomena presents herself as a parishioner rather than as an intimate friend. In the case where they do need to confer about personal matters, Fr. Nahum speaks to her in priest-talk. For example, Fr. Nahum says in this public environment, *I'll keep that appointment at 10:00 AM,* which is in contrast to what he might say in a personal situation, *I'll see you around ten.* Philomena recognises the encoded difference and responds appropriately. By learning to accommodate different roles in different contexts, Philomena and Nahum are able to protect their relationship.

Priests and their friends are finding ways to promote their friendships as ordinary. By working quietly on the margins of public expectations, with the patience of the long haul, these people create intersections in the celibate route of priesthood. At these crossroads, they create pathways on which they and others can travel towards the future. But this journey is not just one for the local church. It is also a trek for the universal church. The more priests are able to promote their friendships as being ordinary and acceptable, the more likely the social balance will tip towards their preferred option.

Dangerous Situations

Sometimes strategies of ordinariness unravel. Fr. Uriah and Fr. Alec invited their respective friends to stay at their presbyteries. Each of these priests' friends had a particular reason for staying and their priest-friends considered this legitimate. Fr. Uriah's friend had business to attend in the town and stayed two days. Fr. Alec's friend was temporarily homeless and stayed longer: *The main reason for my friend coming into the presbytery was that she was going through a lot of trouble and had nowhere else to stay, so she stayed for a week.* So both priests welcomed their friends, as they would other guests.

However, parishioners, described by Fr. Alec as being *ultra-conservative*, criticised him for allowing his friend to stay in the presbytery. Fr. Alec went on to report, *They were warning me because one of our parish priests, well known for his relationships with women, had women staying here at the presbytery. And the reason they warned me about my friend was that they didn't want my friend and me being talked about like this other priest.*

Furthermore, these parishioners contrasted the idealised reputation of Fr. Alec with the demonised reputation of his friend: *it is well known that she is divorced.* In Fr. Uriah's case, he was criticised by the Sisters, who felt his friend should stay with them.

Conservative Catholics, at times, deem divorce, often regardless of the reasons why people have terminated their marriage, as somehow sinful. In the estimation of these Catholics, both women (the other priest's friend was also divorced) were unfit houseguests, so they took it upon themselves to communicate these judgements to their parish priests. While neither of these priests felt unduly pressured by these criticisms, they did rethink how to present themselves with their friends in public. Subsequently, they became cautious about meeting in the presbytery.

Priests with friends argue through their actions for a more inclusive church, but they are frustrated by the suspicion that condemns and casts out any who do not fit the patriarchal mould. Discovery is, however, only one possibility. Priests with friends continue to explore new situations in which they can present their friendships.

Practising What We Preach

While priests with friends are in a position to subtly promote change, each priest must determine how far he can go in pushing a reform agenda.

Fr. Peter is very diplomatic when it comes to dealing with controversial issues, but he still challenges the status quo in definite and conscious ways. In his diocese, there are *extremely conservative priests who are anti-pill, anti-condoms, and are quite capable of talking from the pulpit about people who break the church's rules about birth control. Some priests are very judgmental and negative; they're full of condemnation and judgment of people who don't keep the rules.* In contrast, Fr. Peter refuses to talk about matters relating to sexuality from the pulpit *because some others do. I deliberately don't mention some of those things because I think there are some much more important principles that we avoid.*

Fr. Peter *talks a lot about forgiveness and acceptance* and he does so in particular ways. *I try and stick to Gospel truths, and in the Gospel, Jesus says nothing at all about sex.* For this priest, scripture is the principal moral authority, and sexuality is not singled out for special treatment. Nonetheless, Fr. Peter has received criticism from conservative parishioners who feel that the content of his homilies is *too biblical*, and that he *should talk about the commandments of the church, rather than what the bible says.*

Fr. David, on the other hand, does speak about sexuality from the pulpit. One day, I was sitting beside his friend, Ruth, during the Eucharist. While listening to his homily about the personal cost of following Jesus, I was struck by an anomaly that subtly acknowledged the authenticity of his friendship.

According to Fr. David, Christianity makes great demands: *it's not something to be treated casually or lightly.* He then posed two questions: *Are you willing to pay the price to be a disciple? —and do you think it is really worth it?* Fr. David then went on to say that *Christ gave us certain standards, certain values, and we don't go through life without being tempted to set them aside, and human nature being what it is, we can find reasons to justify our action.* This was followed by examples of how people fail to uphold Christian values, including *the casual sexual relationship that involves no commitment.* That's when I caught my breath. In the church, the only sexual relationship that is officially permitted is in marriage. This priest, however, argues that a key element in sexual relationships is commitment, whether people are married or not.

Fr. David continued: *Nothing is free, and behaviour that dehumanises us, or spoils God's image in others or ourselves, is really not worth the price we have to pay.* In his evaluation, God's image in their friendship is un-spoilt. For Fr. David, his relationship with Ruth upholds Gospel values and he is prepared to say so publicly: *some things are worth whatever they cost. That is the really important message of this Gospel reading (Mt. 13:44-52). Some things are worth whatever it takes to get them—strong character, integrity, a clear conscience, deep, committed friendships, health—what kind of price tag would you put on that?*

Negotiating Acceptance

Fr. Jordan holds a senior position in his diocese in which he has the reputation of being hardworking and conscientious. He is also well-known for his ability to give pastoral guidance and compassionate care to those who are marginalised in society. Fr. Jordan is a typical priest, but his position in the hierarchy allows him to amplify this image to an extent that reflects his standing in the diocese. This allows Fr. Jordan to display aspects of his relationship with Tabatha.

Over the years, Fr. Jordan and Tabatha have established a network of support in which they enjoy the frequent companionship of their friends, including other priests with friends. Fr. Jordan is quite at ease when he introduces Tabatha to others and is comfortable in acknowledging the value of her presence in his life. He often says things like, *Tabatha says this or that, or I ask Tabatha what she thinks, and so on.*

When I expressed my surprise about how many people knew about their friendship, he responded, *I've always been a fairly open person.* Fr. Jordan later commented: *I'd say without blowing my trumpet that I do have the respect of people in my parish. I've got my critics of course, most of them ultra-conservative, but their criticism doesn't worry me too much.* His senior position in the diocese minimises the effects of disapproval expressed by these Catholics. This position also gives him greater freedom to negotiate his friendship in public.

Each time Fr. Jordan shares his friendship with others he tests the sexual teachings of the church, and each time he succeeds in gaining acceptance, he makes it easier for people to accept the idea that priests can have friends.

Yet Fr. Jordan's social ease with his relationship has not come easily. For over a decade he wrestled with his celibacy and with his love for Tabatha, but after numerous trials and tribulations, he has concluded that their love for each other is authentic and graced. With God's favour, he now believes he can combine both priesthood and friendship.

Moreover, having achieved moral clarity and discerned God's presence in their friendship, Fr. Jordan dares fate in skilful ways. From a place of peace within himself, Fr. Jordan feels no need to rigidly define the social parameters of his friendship: *I'm not in your face with it. It's just that she's in my life and I am a part of her life, and that's it. It comes out really naturally.*

His behaviour is not quite "normal," but it is sufficiently close to the norm to command acceptance. And he succeeds, I suggest, because his ways of acting indicate that he is unafraid of dealing with official and social expectations. In doing so he makes real changes possible within the priesthood.

Fr. Jordan is to some extent a charismatic figure, using his charm and influence to inspire confidence. Such charism is a form of authority that emerges in times of crisis and is very different from the imposed authority of a hierarchy. This is evidenced when Fr. Jordan sometimes speaks publicly about relationships in general and, on infrequent occasions, about sexuality and celibacy. At these times, he stresses the value of relationships and how important they are to people's lives because *they bring fulfillment and happiness*. This includes *relationships with God, with other people, with your family*. While Fr. Jordan does not talk about specific relationships such as that which he has with Tabatha, this relationship is uppermost in his mind.

He is also able to speak about *God's most beautiful gift of sexuality*. At the same time, he can criticise current church policy: *celibacy should be looked at as part of the overall reform that the Catholic Church is in need of, and I suggest that celibacy should be optional*. Fr. Jordan's boldness is expressed with skill and a certain flair, which he has honed over the years. He tempers his criticism with graciousness and intelligence, whilst being gently prophetic.

Fr. Jordan, in effect, reconstructs the priesthood. He invites parishioners, confreres, and others to have a say in the workings of the church. By sharing his relationship with selective groups, he gives people the opportunity to consider alternatives to celibacy. And significant numbers in his parish are saying yes to these options.

A Prophetic Call

The papacy claims for the church a classical worldview and hierarchical government in which celibacy exists as a cornerstone. Priests with friends, however, demonstrate that the priesthood must develop and change. Priests are intensely engaged in this process through a rhetoric of word and deed. They open, challenge, discard, and expand the priestly system with alternative notions. Thus, the priesthood and the church cannot be said to have fixed celibate-sexual boundaries; rather, these boundaries are in constant flux, patterned by political contest and experience.

For their part, Vatican officials fail to understand how much priests with friends are reforming and transforming the canon of celibacy. In their changing circumstances, each priest with a friend tests the limitations of compulsory celibacy. In doing so, most of them minimise the risks of social embarrassment and maximise the ambiguity of social interactions for the enhancement of their personal and priestly goals.

One incident reported to me further highlights the importance of skilled performances by both priests and their friends. Fr. Alex was aghast at his friend hanging out her washing, especially her lacy underwear, on the presbytery clothesline.

What will people think! he exclaimed. *When will they grow up?* Evette responded with exasperation. *But it's all about image.* Fr. Alex instinctively knows that he is required to keep up appearances. For the stereotype of the "typical priest" to exist, norms are presupposed. Fr. Alex endeavours to promote his friendship as being typical for a priest, but the display of Evette's lacy underwear challenges his notion of ordinariness in a direct and feminine way.

Such priests recognise the limits of their performances. When support from parishioners and confreres is not forthcoming, these priests and their friends risk being shamed and ridiculed, and the priest being removed from the parish. Yet, as some have demonstrated, a performance of calm confidence by a priest can at times protect a sexually intimate friendship and preserve his priesthood.

While the papacy defines what it means to be a priest inclusive of celibacy, it also preserves inequalities within the priesthood and church. Nevertheless, that notion of priesthood rests in particular circumstances, situations that can be transformed by priests with friends.

Thus the official rhetoric of celibacy contains the means of its own decomposition. Through ironic plays on the priestly vocabulary of ordinariness, priests with friends can negotiate the sexual rules to reconstitute typicality in different situations. A "typical priest" is rarely so very typical; more often than not, his typicality consists in actively disobeying the laws of the church. What is untypical becomes, instead, a prophetic activity.

The prophetic activity of priests with friends is clearly being heeded, as is indicated in Fr. Reuben's comment: *a married priesthood is just plain commonsense, and eventually women priests too.* Fr. Barnabas adds: *To continue demanding celibacy for all priests is flying in the face of common sense and of the development of truly human priests. Our priestly forbears have been heroic in their undertaking of celibacy and so are many priests who are faithful to it today, but one wonders at what cost to their humanity.* To these priests and others, compulsory celibacy will inevitably be revoked.

This grassroots perspective has important consequences for the papacy, for if it continues to ignore and suppress the prophecies of priests with friends, the priesthood and church will continue to experience wide dissent and the threat of dissolution. At worse, church leadership will not be able to realise its own authenticity necessary for retaining political influence, public credibility, and religious veracity. At best, church leadership will accept the profound need for change.

CONCLUSION

Beyond Secrets

Compulsory celibacy is not just simply about a priest being denied a sexually intimate friendship. Rather, celibacy is a complex practice that goes to the heart of who and what we are in the church today.

It is about the pope and the curia trying to maintain a particular way of being church that they arbitrarily consider timeless, and therefore of God. In their attempt to transcend sexuality, they communicate the priority of their version of spirituality over and above everything in the world, a world they are highly critical of. Yet these church authorities find it difficult to commend or even understand everyday dimensions of life, where ordinary people live out their faith.

Throughout the church, there are bishops who are torn between the demands of Vatican policy and the difficulties that celibacy creates for themselves and those in their dioceses. Some bishops wholeheartedly agree with the central authority; others are genuinely afraid to echo their different opinions and alternative experiences of celibacy. Priests too reflect the episcopal division. Some insist on the maintenance of compulsory celibacy; others demand reform. Of this latter group, some have chosen to have sexually intimate friendships, and in these loving relationships have created bridges between the church and the world. These priests seek to converse with everyday realities and explore the human journey that has been made available through their friendships.

As with the clergy, so too the laity. Some rally against modernity and indulge a fundamentalist reproach. These people feel that the only way forward is to recover the so-called traditional values of the church, where everyone is required to live strictly within the roles that have been prescribed: priests observing celibacy, and men and women marrying and staying married. In contrast, others, often labelled liberals, feel that the old ways do not provide solutions to the complexities they encounter in their everyday lives. In consequence, they see the church and priesthood being hindered by many "isms": centralism and legalism, clericalism and paternalism, and sexism in all its guises. Celibacy, then, can be considered a central conflict in our experience of the church.

In Sum

According to the papacy, celibacy is bound up in the total identity of the priesthood; yet, for priests with friends there are crucial contradictions between institutional expectations and their experiences of celibacy. They seek to renegotiate the terms of the priestly contract, either through a review of their promise of celibacy or through the internal forum of the confessional. This they do knowing that Vatican officials feel that only their privileged beliefs have veracity or relevance in the church.

The pope and the curia insist on hierarchical order and clerical control, so the Eucharist and its meaning is controlled by institutional exclusivity. In contrast, for priests with friends the Eucharist is a communal meal that extends an invitation to all. Such a change in attitude has not come easy for these priests. Most of them have been conditioned from birth to accept celibacy without question. But as religious and social conditions changed, these priests had to decide, often after much pain and trauma, to choose the less-travelled path, resulting in mutually committed relationships. Meanwhile, they experience a papacy that obstructs their journey and attempts to banish their friendships to the margins of the church.

The papacy asserts that morality is static and that the identity of the priesthood is uniform. Priests with friends, after having reflected on their identity and the morality of their relationships, are convinced that there should be more than one option available to themselves and their confreres. But Vatican centralising policies prohibit discussion on the practise, so there is little possibility of resolving the issue.

Church authorities use stereotypes to maintain a patriarchal church. But the various subordinated groups within the church—including those women who no longer accept patriarchal rule, homosexual men and women, and priests with friends—are not comfortable with the severe limitations that these fixed conceptions place upon their lives. As a result, each group is engaged in an ideological struggle to resolve its own difficulties.

The tide is turning against the papacy. The modern worldview is seriously undermining the classical worldview. Reform-minded Catholics derive from a modern worldview an understanding of authenticity. This gives preference to dialogue and internal knowledge of self in the context of everyday life. They recognise that much of the world and many sections of the church support their struggle. Thus, some priests with friends try to merge the idea of being an effective priest in a committed friendship, a social fusion that they express in public. Their hope is that their innovative practises will eventually result in church reform.

Hearts for Reform

Other individuals and groups in the church will surely identify with this struggle for the soul of priesthood. The one group that haunts this research makes that explicitly clear. Behind the stories of priests with friends are the many women and men who walk with priests, support them, suffer with or because of them, and love them.[1] Many friends of priests know that their relationships help those whom they love to maintain their integrity, and in fact make them better priests. Nonetheless, in the church, they remain subordinated by their gender or sexual orientation, and as a group they remain officially nonexistent and socially pressured to keep their relationships hidden. Often friends of priests endure enormous hardship, the degree of which is yet to be recognised and acknowledged.

The relationships between priests and their friends have broader ramifications for the church. Though they might not realise it, the pope and the curia are intricately connected to a diverse range of peoples in different cultures. In this connection, the church is slowly learning that it can be constituted by diverse beliefs and different practises. More importantly, the stories that have been told within these pages indicate that the will of God cannot be confined to the rhetoric of the papacy: God's desire can also be expressed through the lives and struggles of other individuals and groups. Hence, when the papacy asserts itself as the sole judge of truth whilst discounting the insights of local peoples, whether it is priests, their friends, or others, it surely contributes to both heavenly and earthly dissonance.

The engagement between the papacy and priests with friends also raises issues of social inequity and sexual inequality within the priesthood. The corollary of this abuse of power is a moral responsibility to argue against the continuation of the current clerical system, constituted by an exclusive belief system and hierarchical order. This is not to say that liberal ideas and practises should be uncritically adopted, for such logic is inherently dangerous. In the pursuit of justice and fairness, rigidity needs to be avoided, and proposals that are bounded by restrictive and narrow definitions should be resisted. That this resistance is already apparent within the priesthood and church is reassuring. Priests and laypersons generally feel that they belong to a Catholic family in which eucharistic blood runs thicker than any exclusive ideology that denies communion.

There is widespread criticism and unease about compulsory celibacy throughout the church. Yet, the rumblings of dissent over this law remain muted. Priests with friends are not the only Catholics who desire change. Some bishops and priests and many theologians and laypersons seek to express their grievances about celibacy and related issues. But these voices are severely constrained because the papacy demands uncritical support of, and passive obedience to, its rigid belief system. The policy of celibacy therefore denies the concerns of reform-minded Catholics. It also prevents creative and imaginative solutions produced by the local church from being recognised as valid and valuable contributions to the universal church. Thus, the papacy of John Paul II must bear the primary responsibility for the widening rift and malaise within the priesthood, as well as for increasing chaos within the church.

Ideas for an inclusive priesthood are already being reflected, to an extent, at priestly gatherings in which collegiality and collaboration are seen as ideals. These gatherings include diocesan councils of priests and national conferences of bishops, which recognise that authority is not just confined to the pope and the universal church, but is also manifested in the mutual relations of the individual bishops with particular churches. In this recognition, they acknowledge that their interests predominantly lie in the local church. But when these bishops and priests seek formal dialogue, they are prevented from doing so by Vatican controls. So while the official rhetoric that promotes celibacy as a gift to the church remains adamant, it is, nevertheless, unconvincing.

The papacy's actions can also be counterproductive, for such authoritarianism fosters dissension and secrecy, often resulting in the church bureaucracy becoming the butt of humour and ridicule. Fr. Aaron, for example, asked: *Why are there so many lumps in the Vatican carpet? Because that's where the papacy hides its secrets.*

Priests with friends know how much secrecy is a part of the priesthood; yet, they also realise that official representations of celibacy are unrealistic. Indeed, they generally have mixed feelings about secrecy, as does Fr. David: *Sexual activity is not the problem. The real problem is secrecy. Over the centuries this wedding of institutional inflexibility with private licence has created an entire culture of secrecy, duplicity, and fear that has ended up punishing those who tell the truth and rewarding those who defend the teachings, structures, and deceits that keep the system together.*

As a result, Fr. David and other priests feel locked into a corrupt system. Secrecy remains the principal means of communication in the priesthood, ensuring that celibacy and related issues cannot be discussed. However, church policies devoid of transparency and accountability are simply destructive, especially in a religious and social culture that idealises truth. The seeds for the demise of the official belief system are therefore planted within its own hierarchical order, nourished by its own dishonesty and the tears and blood of priests and their friends.

Thus, priests with friends search for the means to resolve the difficulties they have with celibacy, for they are not powerless. They have a faithful model and mentor in Jesus Christ, and their task is to show Christ-like courage and holy impatience in their pursuit of reform. Likewise, the pope and the curia have their duty and responsibility— to exhibit Christian charity and compassion towards their confreres, not in the form of paternalism but in ways that regard others as fellow pilgrims in the search for truth. For there is a sense in which all priests are interdependent players of the one priesthood, a priesthood whose mission is to be Good News for the world.

Personal Postscript

Many years ago, I lived in a remote rural area that could be described as the "black hole" of the diocese. In my eleven years there, our parish was consecutively assigned five priests, four of whom faced significant personal hardships. Alone on the endless highways that traverse the Australian bush, each of these priests travelled long distances to make visitations to isolated farms and to celebrate Mass in outlying parish centres. In doing so, they confronted the limits of their humanity. As parish secretary, I saw these good men crumble, one after another. During this recurring situation, I felt powerless and questioned the ability of our parish to really care for them.

The shortage of priests mercifully put an end to the hardship that these celibate men inevitably experience in such conditions. For now there is no parish priest, and nor is there likely to be, if the church continues to maintain compulsory celibacy and all that it stands for.

Some years later, I moved to another parish where I met two women who had long-term relationships with priests. One of these friendships was terminated with tragic consequences. The priest-friend of the other woman used to joke: *We're just years ahead of our time, so we're paving a way for the future!* "But why," I asked, "don't you press for change now?" He responded: *It's too risky and no one is prepared to really listen.* So after much prayer and reflection, I accepted the challenge to *really listen* in order to understand what compulsory celibacy might mean to priests and to others in our church.

In 1995, four years prior to the commencement of my PhD candidacy, equipped with some awareness of the issues relating to celibacy, I prepared myself to knock at the door of the priestly fortress. One priest-editor found the courage to advertise my request and I received correspondence from a significant number of priests with friends.

Fear was palpable in the submissions and interviews of many of them, many of whom did not disclose their identities. These priests were anxious about reprisals by powerful critics, especially those who *have an ear in Rome*. Another priest similarly said: *Sorry about the anonymity, but we are a bit spooked by this. Paranoia is OK if you really do have enemies.*

Making sure I was not an enemy as well was a concern that had to be addressed by a few priests. After I was quizzed about my intentions and about whether I practised my faith, which I do, most of the priests chose to contribute their story. But sometimes there were other layers of fear to be negotiated. One priest was concerned that his submission might not arrive at my postbox, thinking it might land in the wrong hands. He asked if I would return an enclosed stamped and self-addressed postcard worded with the message "safe arrival," which of course I did. Other priests asked me to destroy their correspondence, a request that I have also complied with.

A few warned me that various individuals and groups might try to dissuade me: *conservatives will not want their illusion shattered*, advice that ensured that I kept quiet about my research activities. I also deleted all social, geographical, and nominal information from transcripts, and organized other security measures, including destroying all records of priests' names and addresses after the interviews and correspondence had ceased.

At times, these interviews yielded information that was very difficult for me to deal with personally. News of the priest attempting to castrate himself horrified me, and I often worried about the welfare of a few priests who really needed long-term care and counselling. But there was also another side to the suffering. Some of these priests disclosed excerpts from their lives that I regard as some of the best homilies I have ever heard. For every valley of pain I entered, there were similar treks to mountains of joy, laying out for me a panorama of wonder, happiness, and love.

Another significant opportunity became available when I was employed as the diocesan director of the Pontifical Mission Societies. Although at least two of the three interviewers knew of my research, it was never mentioned during my interview, nor rarely discussed there-after. In addition to being involved in the valuable work of the missions, such employment provided favourable conditions for observing the everyday workings of church administration and organisation. Ready access to the priest population, often on a daily basis, contributed further to my immersion into the church culture, leaving me sometimes wondering who was actually under examination.

Nonetheless, a few influential priests and laypersons who knew about my research and were either privately reticent or publicly hostile to my investigations, made life difficult. Their comments and behaviour sought to denigrate me and diminish the validity of this study: *She wants to be a priest; she must be having an affair with a priest; you're one of them; you're a feminist; you're a* blacktracker (a term that insinuates that I was "chasing" after priests). Several bishops also had a go at me. One chastised me for having *entered the realm of the confessional*, inferring that my research was sacrilegious. Another bishop charged my anthropological approach as being *blasphemous*, implying that truth cannot be communicated outside of official church scholarship. The litany of put-downs continues to this day.

My employment and research also reminded me of gender discrimination in the church. The constant requirement to defer to male celibate decision making and leadership, regardless of any expertise others or I might possess, was at times frustrating and humiliating. Added to this grief was my experience of exclusive liturgical language in both daily communal prayer and in the Eucharist, leaving me feeling as though the hierarchical church had written my gender out of existence.

Initially, I coped with those difficulties by adopting a "social schizophrenic" pose. In this state, I maintained the public face of the diocesan director and uncritically promoted the works of the church. In private, I pursued my research, which nurtured and nourished a desire for reform. Maintaining this spiritually, emotionally, and intellectually divided state, however, took its toll on my health, curtailing my studies for several months. I then resigned from my job and later won a scholarship that funded, for the most part, the conclusion of my research.

Now I look back on this remarkable journey, having graduated with honours. Indeed, one friend sent me a card in which she wrote: "Your 'perspiration' has now become an inspiration for many. . . ." But any hardship I have experienced or honours received have been borne on the prayers and work of others. Many Catholics, both priest and lay, actively seek reform. Collectively, we so desire to witness the Christian message in the vehicle of the church we love that we can do no other than to be loyal dissidents and pioneers of a new way to be church.

Perhaps you too experience the same desire for our church to be healthier and happier, relevant and meaningful, open and honest, wiser and more compassionate. Yet, maybe you are like the woman I sometimes sit next to at Mass on Sunday. She is somewhat confused, sometimes angry, and certainly frustrated about what is happening to our priests and to our church: "But what can I do?" she laments.

Everyone brings to this issue their own experience, a source of wisdom that can be coupled with various talents and skills to make changes for the good of our church. The challenge for all of us is to work to the limits of those gifts that God has given us.

Many people have already recognised that invitation, and they express this in a multitude of ways. They become informed about compulsory celibacy and its consequences for their church. Having done so, they prayerfully reflect on their own faith practise; reconsider the way in which they regard priests (and their friends); and write challenging correspondence to Catholic newspapers, bishops, and the Vatican. Some people also join reform groups (see below), and in doing so they maximise the surge of hope for change. Some decide to write to the Vatican. Effectively, each person can find a way, like priests with friends, to negotiate the institutional roadblock that refuses to budge on compulsory celibacy. Now is the favourable time: the right time to listen, the day to help, and the moment to act (2 Cor 6:2).

Come, Join Us

The following are some suggestions for finding a reform group in your region, state, or country.

International Movement We Are Church (IMWAC) is a network of groups, working in different parts of the world, to create dialogue to bring about the renewal and reform of the church. The Web site indicates their presence in forty countries: http://www.we-are-church.org.

Call to Action (CTA) has published an on-line searchable database of 650 church renewal groups, small faith communities, peace and social justice groups, parish and religious order groups, retreat and formation centres, and international groups that support reform: http://www.cta-usa.org/resdir.html.

Voice of the Faithful (VOTF) is a grassroots organization that emerged because of the Catholic clergy sex scandal. This group seeks to rally Catholics to achieve a more accountable and transparent church. Their Web site provides practical ways to promote change, educational resources, and the opportunity to join groups in the U.S. and other countries: http://www.votf.org.

The International Federation of Married Catholic Priests (IFMCP) represents married priests' organizations in twenty-six countries and has contacts in six others. Its Web site is designed to explore issues surrounding compulsory celibacy. It also provides support for priests who are struggling with celibacy: http://www.marriedpriests.org/national_organizations.htm.

Good Tidings is a U.S. based support group for women in relationships with Catholic priests and those who have had children with priests: http://www.marriedpriests.org/GoodTidings.htm. Other such groups exist in England (Seven Eleven), Germany (Initiativgrüppe der vom Zölibat betroffenen Frauen), Belgium (Philotea), and France (Claire-Voie).

Women's Ordination Worldwide (WOW) promotes the theological discussion of women's ordination. It also provides links to national and state groups: http://www.womenpriests.org/links.htm.

Gay and Lesbian Reform Groups and Ministries: There are significant numbers of national Web sites that work for the respect of gay, lesbian, bisexual, and transgender persons in the church, including Rainbow Sash Movement Australia, Acceptance Sydney (Australia), HuG (Austria), Cathogay (Belgium), DignityCanada, David et Jonathon (France), Malkus (Finland), HuK (Germany), DignityNederlan (Netherlands), Quest (UK), DignityUSA.

Correspondence to the pope can be sent to the following address:

John Paul II, Archbishop of Rome
Apostolic Palace
00120 Vatican City State

Email: John_Paul_II@vatican.va
Web site: http://www.vatican.va

Notes

1. Changing Confessions

1. John Paul II, *I Will Give You Shepherds (Pastores dabo vobis): Post-Synodal Apostolic Exhortation of John Paul II* (Boston: St. Paul Books & Media, 1992), 57.

2. Ibid.

3. A. W. Richard Sipe, *Sex, Priests, and Power: Anatomy of a Crisis* (London: Cassell, 1995), 67.

4. Eugene C. Kennedy and Victor J. Heckler, *The Catholic Priest in the United States: Psychological Investigations* (United States Catholic Conference: Washington, D.C., 1972), 8.

5. Sipe, *Sex, Priests, and Power,* 18-19.

6. Ephebophiles are men attracted to minors who have attained puberty.

7. Australian Catholic Bishops Conference and the Australian Conference of Leaders of Religious Institutes, *Towards Understanding: A Study of Factors Specific to the Catholic Church Which Might Lead to Sexual Abuse by Priests and Religious* (Mordialloc, Victoria, Australia: National Committee for Professional Standards, 1999), 17.

8. Kennedy and Heckler, *The Catholic Priest in the United States,* 51-52.

9. Ibid., 10.

10. Ibid., 8.

11. Eugene Kennedy, "The Secret Cause of the Sex Abuse Scandal," *National Catholic Reporter,* June 11, 2002. Retrieved August 4, 2002, from http://www.nationalcatholicre-porter.org/dallas/newscom4.htm.

12. John McKinnon, *A Closer Look at Australian Priests* (Farrer, Australia: Catholic Institute for Ministry, 1990), 5-12.

13. Conrad Baars and Anna Terruwe (cited in ibid., 37-38) conclude from their studies of all priests in Western Europe and North America that 60-70 percent suffer from a degree of emotional immaturity.

14. Kennedy and Heckler, *The Catholic Priest in the United States,* 16.

15. Terence Collins, "Some Reasons for Expanding Horizons" (Brisbane, Australia, 1996), 4. Unpublished article.

16. Ibid., 3.

17. Ibid., 22.

18. "Chastity Critical for Priesthood," *Catholic Leader*, March 24, 2002, 2.

19. M. Francis Mannion, "Penance and Reconciliation," in *The New Dictionary of Sacramental Worship*, ed. Peter E. Fink (Collegeville: Liturgical Press, 1990), 934-936.

2. From Celibate Sacrifice to Intimate Communion

1. Harold Winstone, ed., *The Sunday Missal: A New Edition* (London: Collins Liturgical Publications, 1982), 77.

2. Robert T. Zintle, "Big Gamble on the Priesthood: Taking a Hard Line in Defence of Celibacy, the Bishops Look Instead to Strengthen the Character and Training of Candidates," *Time*, November 5, 1990, 83.

3. John Paul II, *I Will Give You Shepherds (Pastores dabo vobis): Post-Synodal Apostolic Exhortation of John Paul II* (Boston: St. Paul Books & Media, 1992), 56. John Paul II, "Church Committed to Priestly Celibacy," *L'Osservatore Romano*, July 21, 1993, 11.

4. Ibid., 55.

5. Michael M. Winter, "A New Twist to the Celibacy Debate," *Priests & People*, October 1996, 428-432.

6. John Paul II, "Church Committed to Priestly Celibacy," 11.

7. Adrian Hastings, "Catholic History from Vatican I to John Paul II," in *Modern Catholicism: Vatican II and After*, ed. Adrian Hastings (London: SPCK, 1991), 1-13.

8. Paul Collins, *Papal Power: A Proposal for Change in Catholicism's Third Millennium* (Blackburn, England: Harper Collins Religious, 1997), 192.

9. Richard A. Schoenherr and Lawrence A. Young, *Full Pews, Empty Altars: Demographics of the Priest Shortage in United States Catholic Dioceses* (Madison: University of Wisconsin Press, 1993), 266. Walter M. Abbott, ed., *The Documents of Vatican II* (Melbourne: Geoffrey Chapman, 1967), 250-258.

10. Paul J. Beaudette, "Ritual Purity in Roman Catholic Priesthood: Using the Work of Mary Douglas to Understand Clerical Celibacy" (Berkeley, Calif.: Graduate Theological Union, 1994), 362, 367.

11. Peter Hebblethwaite, *Paul VI: The First Modern Pope* (London: Fount Paperbacks/ Harper Collins, 1993), 442.

12. Abbott, ed., *The Documents of Vatican II*, 537.

13. Nancy Jay, *Throughout Your Generations Forever: Sacrifice, Religion, and Paternity* (Chicago: University of Chicago Press, 1992), 113.

14. Francis Dorff, "Killing Our Priests," *Cross Reference Newsletter* 7, 4 (2000), 7.

15. Juillenne Swinburne, "Clergy Stress and Burnout: A Lack of Person-Environment Fit" (Melbourne: La Trobe University, 1991), 46, 54.

16. Ibid., 51-56, 60.

17. "'Burnt-out' Priest Hangs Himself," *The Tablet*, June 8, 2002, 30.

18. Synod of Bishops, *Ultimis temporibus*, in Austin Flannery, ed., *Vatican Council II: More Post Conciliar Documents* (Northport: Costello Publishing Company, 1998), 689.

19. David Rice, *Shattered Vows: Exodus from the Priesthood* (Belfast: Blackstaff Press, 1991), 24. According to the *Annuarium Statisticum Ecclesiae*, the Vatican's statistical yearbook, 57,791 priests left between 1964 and 1996. It is, however, customary for this book to give only the number of departures from the ministry for which Vatican dispensation has been given. Yet, under the current papacy, the granting of dispensations has been slowed down. New policies formulated in 1980, stipulate that dispensations are to be granted only to older priests who have left the active ministry for a number of years. Furthermore, priests wishing to leave the priesthood have become less disposed to subject themselves to the degrading dispensation procedures and therefore submit no application for dispensation ("Real Number of Married Priests Worldwide," *Ministerium Novum*, 14, 25 [1999], 22).

20. Dorff, "Killing Our Priests," 7.

21. Anthony Padavano, "Urgent Questions Facing the Church," *Favourable Time*, 2000, 19.

22. David Sanders, "Three Times You Will Deny Me," *Priests & People*, July 2000, 254.

23. A.W. Richard Sipe, *A Secret World: Sexuality and the Search for Celibacy* (New York: Brunner/Mazel, 1990), 86.

24. Rice, *Shattered Vows*, 48-49.

25. Ibid., 48.

26. Sipe, *A Secret World*, 213.

27. Rice, *Shattered Vows*, 1-2.

28. Karl Hillebrand, "A Study of Their Intrinsic Relationship: The Priesthood and Celibacy," *L'Osservatore Romano*, August 4-11, 1993, 4-5.

29. Robert Mickens, "The Vatican: It's Still a Man's World," *Priests & People*, August/September 2000, 323-328.

30. Congregation for Catholic Education, "New Vocations for a New Europe," Final Document of the Congress on Vocations to the Priesthood and to Consecrated Life in Europe, May 5-10, 1997. Retrieved: May 9, 2002, from http://www.vocations.ie/IVT.html.

31. Steven Heilbronner, "Church Grapples with Clergy Shortage 'Crisis,'" *National Catholic Reporter*, February 13, 1998, 14.

32. Congregation for Catholic Education, "New Vocations for a New Europe," n. 11.

33. Eugene C. Kennedy and Victor J. Heckler, *The Catholic Priest in the United States: Psychological Investigations* (Washington, D.C.: United States Catholic Conference, 1972), 13.

34. *Catechism of the Catholic Church* (Homebush, NSW: St. Pauls, 1994), 566.

35. Schoenherr and Young, *Full Pews, Empty Altars*, 353, 355.

36. Robert McClory, "Reality Confirms Forecast of Priest Shortage," *National Catholic Reporter*, July 17, 1998, 6.

37. "British Bishop Complains About Vatican Curia's 'Oppositional Lobby' during the European Bishops Synod," *Ministerium Novum* 14, 26 (1999), 23.

38. "Costs of Clerical Celibacy are Rising," *Ministerium Novum* 14, 26 (1999), 15.

39. Peter Hebblethwaite, "Aspiring to be a bishop?" *The Swag*, June 1995, 8.

40. Hans Küng, *On Being a Christian* (New York: Doubleday, 1976), 424-25.

41. Jay, *Throughout Your Generations Forever*, 115-16.

42. John Dominic Crossan, *Jesus: A Revolutionary Biography* (New York: HarperCollins Paperback, 1995), 69.

43. Eucharist is derived from the Greek *eucharistia*, meaning "giving thanks."

3. Open to Change

1. Terence Collins, "Some Reasons for Expanding Horizons" (Brisbane, Australia, 1996), 3.

2. John Paul II, *I Will Give You Shepherds (Pastores dabo vobis): Post-Synodal Apostolic Exhortation of John Paul II* (Boston: St. Paul Books & Media, 1992), 86.

3. Ibid., 86.

4. Ibid., 87.

5. Ibid.

6. Mark Dowd, "The Place of Celibacy," *The Tablet*, July 17, 1993, 906.

7. "Church Is His, Not Ours," *The Record*, November 25, 1999, 1, 4.

8. Walter M. Abbott, ed., *The Documents of Vatican II* (Melbourne: Geoffrey Chapman, 1967), 565.

9. Philip Jenkins, *Pedophiles and Priests: Anatomy of a Contemporary Crisis* (New York: Oxford University Press, 1996), 58.

10. Ibid., 63.

11. Ibid., 63-64.

12. David Rice, *Shattered Vows: Exodus from the Priesthood* (Belfast: Blackstaff Press, 1991), 82-83.

13. For more complete lists of Reform Groups and Ministries, see http://www.married-priests.org/MinistriesAndGroups.htm.

14. David Mackay, *Red Stem* (London: Minerva Press, 1995); *Black Flowers* (London: Minerva Press, 1998); *White Root* (London: Minerva Press, 1998).

15. Jim Madden, *This Turbulent Priest: The Story of a Priest and His Church* (Sumner Park, Australia: J. Madden, 1999).

16. The earliest known of this genre is *Forbidden Fruit: The True Story of My Secret Love for Eamon Casey, The Bishop of Galway* by Annie Murphy and Peter de Rosa (London: Little, Brown, 1993). Another biographical work of note is *A Passion for Priests: Women Talk of Their Love for Roman Catholic Priests* by Clare Jenkins (London: Headline Book Publishing, 1995).

17. Rice, *Shattered Vows.*

18. A.W. Richard Sipe, *Sex, Priests, and Power: Anatomy of a Crisis* (London: Cassell, 1995). Other examples in this group include Eugene Kennedy, *The Unhealed Wound: The Church and Human Sexuality* (New York: Harper Collins Religious, 2001); Heinz-J Vogels, *Celibacy—Gift or Law? A Critical Investigation* (Tunbridge Wells, England: Burns & Oates, 1992).

19. Michael Hout and Andrew Greeley, "The Laity and Reform in the Church: A Six Nation Study," ca. 1996. Retrieved November 2, 1998, from http://www.agreeley.com/articles/laity.html.

20. Stephen J. Rossetti, "Statistical Reflections on Priestly Celibacy," *America*, June 18-25, 1994. Retrieved August 12, 1997, from http://www.epnet.com/bin/epwgargoyle/submit=text/session=533137/st=45/qu=0/ftext.

21. David Quinn, "Are Priests Really Listening?" *The Word*, November 4, 2003.

22. Collins, "Some Reasons for Expanding Horizons," 12-13.

23. Gerald A. Arbuckle, "Gossip and Scapegoating Cripple Pastoral Innovation," *Human Development* 15, 1 (1994), 11-16.

24. Thomas J. Reese, *Inside the Vatican: The Politics and Organization of the Catholic Church* (Cambridge: Harvard University Press, 1996), 5.

25. John Paul II, "Church Committed to Priestly Celibacy," *L'Osservatore Romano*, July 21, 1993, 11.

26. I related this event to a friend of mine who is an ex-religious and homosexual, and he suggested that if this priest had met with a man, any homosexual priest at the table would have reacted similarly, but that his response would have remained private.

4. *Moral Dilemmas*

1. John Paul II, "Church Committed to Priestly Celibacy," *L'Osservatore Romano*, July 21, 1993, 11.

2. "Cardinals' Statement," *CBS News*, April 24, 2002. Retrieved August 7, 2002, from http://www.cbsnews.com/stories/2002/04/24/national/main507168.shtml.

3. The cult of virginity and powerful groups such as the Encratites, Montanists, and Manichaeans believed that salvation could only be attained through sexual continence.

4. Henry C. Lea, *History of Sacerdotal Celibacy in the Christian Church* (London: Watts & Co, 1932), 30, 42.

5. Paul J. Beaudette, "Ritual Purity in Roman Catholic Priesthood: Using the Work of Mary Douglas to Understand Clerical Celibacy" (Berkeley, Calif.: Graduate Theological Union, 1994), 31. Commonly referred to as white martyrdom, white being a symbol of virginal purity implying here sexual sacrifice. This is distinct from red martyrdom, which signifies bodily sacrifice.

6. Lea, *History of Sacerdotal Celibacy in the Christian Church*, 43.

7. Beaudette, "Ritual Purity in Roman Catholic Priesthood," 195-220.

8. Beaudette refers to C. N. L. Brooke, *Medieval Church and Society: Collected Essays* (London: Sidgewick and Jackson, 1971), 72-73.

9. Anne Llewellyn Barstow, *Married Priests and the Reforming Papacy: The Eleventh Century Debates* (New York: Edwin Mellen Press, 1982), 133.

10. Lea, *History of Sacerdotal Celibacy in the Christian Church*, 178, 206-209, 268.

11. Paul Johnson, *A History of Christianity* (London: Penguin Books, 1976), 269.

12. J. N. D. Kelly, *The Oxford Dictionary of Popes* (Oxford: Oxford University Press, 1988).

13. For example, Gallicanism, a French movement against centralized papal control, pressured for legislation that no profession could debar a person from marriage. This split the French clergy; because marriage was considered a pledge of national loyalty and celibacy a silent protest against the new regime.

14. John Paul II, "Church Committed to Priestly Celibacy," 11.

15. Terence Collins, "Some Reasons for Expanding Horizons" (Brisbane, Australia, 1996), 3.

16. Jackie Robinson, "Why Celibacy Should Be Voluntary, Not Obligatory," *Irish Times*, September 26, 1996.

17. Owen O'Sullivan, "A Silent Schism in the Church," *The Swag* 2, 2 (1994), 12.

18. A.W. Richard Sipe, *A Secret World: Sexuality and the Search for Celibacy* (New York: Brunner/Mazel, 1990); David Rice, *Shattered Vows: Exodus from the Priesthood* (Belfast: Blackstaff Press, 1991).

19. Victor Kotze, "Letters," *The Tablet*, March 19, 1994, 354-355.

20. Rice, *Shattered Vows*, 111-135.

21. The Church in the World, "Half of Swiss Priests Have Affairs, Survey Shows," *The Tablet*, May 24, 2003, 28.

22. Clare Jenkins, *A Passion for Priests: Women Talk of Their Love for Roman Catholic Priests* (London: Headline Book Publishing, 1995), 231-264.

23. Maureen Fiedler and Linda Rabben, eds., *Rome Has Spoken: A Guide to Forgotten Papal Statements, and How They Have Changed Through the Centuries* (New York: Crossroad, 1998), 130-131.

24. David Mackay, *Black Flowers* (London: Minerva Press, 1998).

25. Collins, "Some Reasons for Expanding Horizons," 16.

26. Henri J.N. Nouwen, *Intimacy* (Cambridge: Harper & Row, 1969), 119.

27. Tim Unsworth, *The Last Priests in America: Conversations with Remarkable Men* (New York: Crossroad Publishing Company, 1993), 61.

28. Richard P. McBrien, *Catholicism* (North Blackburn: Collins Dove, 1994), 24.

29. "Cardinals Look to Draft Abuse Rules," *Guardian Unlimited*. Retrieved April 19, 2002, from http://www.guardian.co.uk/worldlatest/story/0,1280-1674959,00.html.

30. Jane Lampman, "Talks Test US-Vatican Culture Gap," *Christian Science Monitor*, April 23, 2002. Retrieved April 23, 2002, from http://www.csmonitor.com/2002/0423/p01s02-ussc.html.

5. A Question of Identity

1. John Paul II, "Church Committed to Priestly Celibacy," *L'Osservatore Romano*, July 21, 1993, 11; *Catechism of the Catholic Church* (Homebush, NSW: St Pauls, 1994), 404.

2. Bruce J. Malina, *The New Testament World: Insights from Cultural Anthropology* (Louisville, Ky.: Westminster/John Knox Press 1993), 126-127; John J. Pilch and Bruce J. Malina, *Biblical Social Values and Their Meaning* (Peabody, Mass.: Hendrickson Publishers, 1993), 70.

3. Pilch and Malina, *Biblical Social Values and Their Meaning*, 70.

4. William E. Phipps, *The Sexuality of Jesus* (Cleveland, Ohio: Pilgrim Press, 1996), 34.

5. Uta Ranke-Heinemann, *Eunuchs for the Kingdom of Heaven* (London: Penguin Books, 1990), 44.

6. Denis C. Duling and Norman Perrin, *The New Testament: Proclamation and Parenesis, Myth and History* (Fort Worth, Tex.: Harcourt Brace College Publishers, 1994), 68.

7. The Essenes were an ascetic Jewish group that flourished in Palestine and Syria from the second century BC to the second century AD. Its members shared property, practiced celibacy, and observed the Sabbath.

8. Ranke-Heinemann, *Eunuchs for the Kingdom of Heaven*, 45.

9. Richard P. McBrien, *Catholicism* (North Blackburn, Australia: Collins Dove, 1994), 559.

10. Scripture records a few references to sexual morality that do convey something of Jesus' attitude toward sexuality, in the context of his teachings about divorce and adultery (e.g., Mt 5:27-28; 19:1-12).

11. In the second century BC, the church assimilated Hellenistic ideas about body, mind, and soul, particularly those of Gnosticism, that asserted the body was fundamentally evil. In this milieu, Tatian (ca. 150-200), who was later declared a heretic, disseminated the first recorded idea of the celibate Jesus (Phipps, *The Sexuality of Jesus*, 159).

12. Walter M. Abbott, ed., *The Documents of Vatican II* (Melbourne: Geoffrey Chapman 1967), 565-566.

13. John Paul II, *I Will Give Your Shepherds (Pastores dabo vobis): Post-Synodal Apostolic Exhortation of John Paul II* (Boston: St. Paul Books & Media, 1992), 55.

14. Greek philosophy emphasised the superiority of being freed from the world of matter, and since sexual desire was considered a part of the world and deemed a distraction in the pursuit of truth, celibacy was promoted as an ideal.

15. In early Christianity, Christians believed that the Parousia was imminent, which tended to obviate procreation in marriage.

16. Ranke-Heinemann, *Eunuchs for the Kingdom of Heaven*, 33.

17. Part of this reflection was published in *Cross Reference Newsletter*, November, 1999, 6, 6.

18. John Paul II, "Church Committed to Priestly Celibacy," 11.

19. Jerome Murphy-O'Connor, *1 Corinthians* (Dublin: Veritas Publications, 1979), xiii.

20. Ibid., 74.

21. Terence Collins, "Some Reasons for Expanding Horizons" (Brisbane, Australia, 1996), 4

22. John Paul II, "Church Committed to Priestly Celibacy," 11.

23. Malina, *The New Testament World*, 30.

24. John Paul II, "Church Committed to Priestly Celibacy," 11.

25. John L. Allen, "Issues Loom as Bishops Take Up Revised Norms; Liturgy 'as the Life We Want to Lead'; Pontificating about Pontiffs in Milwaukee; My Wife and Her Prince of Peace," *National Catholic Reporter*, November 8, 2002. Retrieved November 15, 2002, from http://www.nationalcatholicreporter.org/word/.

26. Heinz-J. Vogels, *Celibacy—Gift or Law? A Critical Investigation* (Tunbridge Wells, England: Burns & Oates, 1992), 70-88.

27. Brown, Fitzmyer, and Murphy, *The New Jerome Biblical Commentary*, 968.

28. McBrien, *Catholicism*, 1115.

29. Kenneth L. Woodward, *Making Saints: How the Catholic Church Determines Who Becomes a Saint, Who Doesn't and Why* (New York: Simon & Schuster, 1990), 335.

30. Richard P. McBrien, 'Saints: More of the Same,' *The Tidings*, April 25, 2003. Retrieved: May 2, 2003, from http://www.the-tidings.com/2003/0425/essays.htm

31. June Singer, *Boundaries of the Soul: The Practice of Jungian Psychology* (New York: Doubleday, 1972), 137.

32. The church is often referred to as "Holy Mother Church," but "she" is subordinate to the power and authority of "the Fathers."

33. For example, Celibacy: The view of a Zen monk from Japan; *Coeli beatus:* Observations of a biologist; An Oriental Church returns to unity choosing priestly celibacy; Priestly celibacy and problems of inculturation; Priestly celibacy in the light of medicine and psychology; and Priestly celibacy in patristics and church history.

34. For example, Fr. Joseph Breen was silenced in 1992 for publicly urging the American bishops to deal with celibacy in light of the shortage of priests; moral theologian Fr. Charles Curran had his teaching licence removed in 1986 because of his dissenting views on a number of church teachings; theologian Fr. Matthew Fox was dismissed in 1996 for his views on women priests, homosexuality, and creation spirituality; feminist theology professor Sr. Carmel McEnroy was removed from her position in 1995 for signing an open letter to Pope John Paul II calling for women's ordination to priesthood.

35. Edward Schillebeeckx, *The Church with a Human Face: A New and Expanded Theology of Ministry* (London: SCM Press, 1985), 223.

36. David Rice, *Shattered Vows: Exodus from the Priesthood* (Belfast: Blackstaff Press, 1991), 163.

6. The Erosion of Patriarchy

1. John Dominic Crossan, *Jesus: A Revolutionary Biography* (New York: HarperCollins Paperback, 1995), 17.

2. Ibid., 23.

3. John Paul II, *I Will Give You Shepherds (Pastores dabo vobis): Post-Synodal Apostolic Exhortation of John Paul II* (Boston: St. Paul Books & Media, 1992), 156-157.

4. John Paul II, *"Mulieris Dignitatem"* (1988). Retrieved December 9, 2002, from http:www.vatican.va/holy_father/john_paul_ii/apost_letters/documents.

5. John Paul II, "The Importance of Women in the Life of a Priest," *Catholic International* (1995) 6, 10, 473.

6. Ibid.

7. Joseph Ratzinger, "Letter to the Bishops of the Catholic Church on the Pastoral Care of Homosexual Persons," October 1, 1986. Retrieved December 2, 2002, from http://www.vatican.va/roman_curia/congregations/cfaith/documents1986, n. 7.

8. Ibid., n. 3.

9. The Uniting Church in Australia Assembly Task Group, *Uniting Sexuality and Faith* (Melbourne: Uniting Church Press, 1997), 42.

10. John J. McNeill, *The Church and the Homosexual* (Boston: Beacon Press, 1993), 57.

11. Gareth Moore, *The Body in Context: Sex and Catholicism* (London: SCM Press, 1992), 41-42.

12. Dignity Canada, "Homosexuality and Bisexuality" (n.d.). Retrieved December 2, 2002, from http://dignitycanada.org/homosexu.html.

13. Elizabeth Stuart, *Chosen: Gay Catholic Priests Tell Their Stories* (London: Geoffrey Chapman, 1993), 2.

14. *The Code of Canon Law* (London: Collins Liturgical Publications, 1983), 47.

15. Terence Collins, "Some Reasons for Expanding Horizons" (Brisbane, Australia, 1996), 13-14.

16. Donald B. Cozzens, *The Changing Face of the Priesthood* (Collegeville, Minn.: Liturgical Press, 2000), 97-110.

17. Michael Kelly, "Father, I Am Troubled," *Sydney Morning Herald*, August 18, 2001.

18. John Thavis, "Vatican Prepares Draft Directives Against Admitting Gays as Priests," *Catholic News Service*, October 8, 2002. Retrieved October 10, 2002, from http://www.catholicnews.com/data/stories/cns/20021008.htm.

19. Robert Blair Kaiser, "Cloud Over Gay Priests," *The Tablet*, November 30 2002, 9-10.

20. Jon Fuller, "On 'Straightening Out' Catholic Seminaries," *America*, December 16, 2002, 7-9.

21. Cardinal Jorge Medina Estevez, who at the time was prefect of the Congregation for Divine Worship and the Sacraments, has also stated ordaining such candidates to the priesthood would be imprudent and "very risky" ("Signs of the Times," *America*, December 16, 2002, 4). Cardinal Anthony Bevilacqua noted that "a person who is homosexual-oriented is not a suitable candidate for the priesthood even if he had never committed any homosexual acts" (Fuller, "On 'Straightening Out' Catholic Seminaries," 8).

22. "I am One of the Nervous Ones," *The Swag* 4, 1 (1996), 11.

23. Edward Vacek, "'Acting More Humanely': Accepting Gays into the Priesthood," *America*, December 16, 2002, 10-12.

24. "I am One of the Nervous Ones," *The Swag*, 11.

25. Marie Macdonald, Peter Carpenter, Sandie Cornish, Michael Costigan, Robert Dixon, Margaret Malone, Kevin Manning, and Sonia Wagner, *Woman and Man, One in Christ Jesus: Report on the Participation of Women in the Catholic Church in Australia* (Sydney: Harper Collins Religious, 1999), 80.

26. Catherine Mowry LaCugna, "Catholic Women as Ministers and Theologians," *America* 167, 10 (1992), 243.

27. Ibid.

28. Teresa Malcom, "Study Says Parents Won't Push Vocations," *National Catholic Reporter*, September 11, 1998, 9.

7. Moving On

1. Charles Taylor, *Sources of the Self: The Making of the Modern Identity* (Cambridge: Harvard University Press, 1989), 85, 89.

2. Ibid., 375.

3. Charles Taylor, *The Ethics of Authenticity* (Cambridge: Harvard University Press), 66.

4. Paul Collins, *Papal Power: A Proposal for Change in Catholicism's Third Millennium* (Blackburn, Australia: Harper Collins Religious, 1997), 192–93.

5. Roland J. Faley, "Leviticus," in Raymond E. Brown, Joseph A. Fitzmyer, and Roland E. Murphy, *The New Jerome Biblical Commentary* (London: Geoffrey Chapman, 1989), 68-70.

6. John Victor Luce, *An Introduction to Greek Philosophy* (London: Thames and Hudson 1992), 135.

7. Stoics belonged to a Greek school of philosophy founded by Zeno ca. 308 BC, which later formed an important feature of Roman culture. Stoics believed that one should be free from passion and calmly accept all occurrences in submission to divine will or the natural order. Gnosticism was a religious sect that taught that salvation comes by learning esoteric spiritual truths that free humanity from the material world, believed in this movement to be evil.

8. The major writers of this period such as Ambrose, Jerome, Augustine, and John Chrysostom, wrote with remarkable unanimity about the higher state of celibacy.

9. Hans Küng, *Christianity* (London: SCM Press, 1995), 432.

10. Collins, *Papal Power*, 99.

11. In the case of priests who desire to marry or have married, church authorities are in contempt of the United Nations Universal Declaration of Human Rights. David Rice (*Shattered Vows: Exodus from the Priesthood* [Belfast: Blackstaff Press, 1991], 87), states: "Article 10 is violated, in that *due process* is denied to any priest in confrontation with Church

authorities. . . . Article 16, stating the *right to marry*, is violated in the treatment of priests who attempt to marry. . . . Article 21 is violated in that priests have no say whatsoever in Church *government*. . . . Article 22 is violated by depriving priests and nuns who leave of all *social security*. . . . Article 23 is violated, in that priests have no *protection against unemployment* and are allowed no unions to protect them; neither priests' senates nor priests' associations are permitted to perform such functions."

12. Theologically, the body politic can be understood as the "People of God," a phrase take from the Hebrew Testament and used in the Second Vatican Council document, "The Dogmatic Constitution of the Church." This phrase embraces both priests and laity, and emphasises the communal nature of the church rather than the hierarchical and institutional aspects.

13. Subsidiary: A principle in Catholic social doctrine which holds that nothing should be done by a higher agency which can be done as well, or better, by a lower agency.

8. Beyond Secrets

1. Margaret Johnson, "The Untold Story: Women Who Marry Catholic Priests" (Brisbane, Australia, 1996). Unpublished article.